Alaskan Maritime

Jim Gibbs

Schiffer
Publishing Ltd

ver Valley Rd. Atglen, PA 19310 USA

To my faithful wife Cherie, who got her initial introduction to a word processor, and a challenge to my faithful old Royal Typewriter that has seen me through all of my books since 1950.

Acknowledgments

Appreciation is expressed to the following who were helpful in the penning of this book. Betty and John Eicher, Captain, USNR (Ret.); Linda S. Mickle, Alaska Marine Highway system; Janis Goller, Holland America Line Westours, Inc.; Alan Stark, Totem Ocean Trailer Express; Gary L. Ritzmen, Vice President and general manager, Sea-Land Service, Alaska Division; J. M. Fritzgerald, Lt. USCG, Juneau; Bert Webber, Medford, Oregon, publisher and author; Doug Newman, Eugene newspaper feature writer; Michael Skalley, Foss Maritime Co., manager customer service; Dennis M. Myrick, vice president, World Explorer Cruises; Bob Schwemmer, researcher, marine historian, Santa Clarita, California; Royal Caribbean Cruise Line; Crystal Cruise Line; Pac Ed Moreth, USCG; and others.

Front cover: *Heavenly paradise—With Mt. Edgecumbe rising above Sitka, the trim* MS Noordam *of Holland America Line glides into focus.* Photo courtesy of Holland America Line.
Title page: *In the 1996 cruise season, World Explorer Cruises along with its* SS Enchanted Seas, *renamed* Universe Explorer, *offered unique 14 day cruises from Vancouver, B.C., to numerous Alaska ports. It marked the line's 19th year of service to many world destinations. The modernized* Universe Explorer *carries 739 passengers and 330 crew.* Photo courtesy of Dennis Myrick, V.P. World Explorer Cruises.
Back cover:

Designed by Bonnie M. Hensley

ISBN: 0-7643-0035-0
Printed in the United States of America

Published by Schiffer Publishing Ltd.
4880 Lower Valley Road
Atglen, PA 19310
Phone: (610) 593-1777; Fax: (610) 593-2002
E-mail: Schifferbk@aol.com
Please write for a free catalog.
This book may be purchased from the publisher.
Please include $3.95 for shipping.

Please try your bookstore first.

We are interested in hearing from authors
with book ideas on related subjects.

Men of the High North, the wild sky is blazing,
Islands of opal float on silver seas;
Swift splendors kindle, barbaric, amazing;
Pale ports of amber, golden argosies.
Ringed all around us the proud peaks are glowing;
Fierce chiefs in council, their wigwam the sky;
Far, far below us the big Yukon flowing,
Like threaded quicksilver, gleams to the eye.

—*Robert W. Service*

Contents

Introduction

Midnight sun, sparkling glaciers, whale breaching, tall evergreens, lofty mountains—you name it and Alaska has it. Somebody said, "Alaska! Somewhere between having a dream and having a plan." In the spring and summer season it can be akin to paradise, but during the winter, its fickle personality takes on a frown, and often a snarl. Yes indeed, Alaska is a land of contrast like no other place in all the world.

Mammoth walls of blue ice, crisp, clean air, and wildlife are spring and summer attractions for the gawking, awestruck cruise passengers.

The state flower, the forget-me-not, is somewhat symbolic, inasmuch as this mammoth piece of real estate was long neglected by Uncle Sam, but no more, for it has now come into its own.

Alaska, the great land, the last frontier, is a vast hunk of terra firma, spreading out over 586,412 square miles—twice the size of Texas. It has gone from rags to riches, most of its claim to fame dependent on its enormous coastline covering thousands of miles—intricate sea lanes sprinkled with islands and obstructions—rocky outcrops, beetling headlands, icebergs, and glaciers. Over these waterways vessels of all descriptions have traveled to supply isolated portals and bustling towns, from along the unparalleled Inside Passage, to the distant ports along the Alaska Peninsula and through the Aleutians, north to the Bering Sea and Arctic Ocean.

The maritime side of Alaska has been both a lifeline and a nemesis. Through the years millions of tons of shipping have been sacrificed to the elements and numerous souls have been lost, and none more than during the great Alaska gold rush, part of which wasn't even in Alaska but in Canada's Yukon. However, the sea route to the gold fields was for the most part via the Inside Passage, debarkation at Skagway and Dyea from which the arduous land and river route to the Yukon began. Second only to the California gold rush was the huge armada of ships assembled to carry anxious treasure seekers to the far north. Anything that could float was commandeered, and Seattle became the main port of embarkation. It was a time in American history the likeness of which had never before been seen. Almost at the same time a second gold rush started at Nome, where gold was panned from the beaches. North to Alaska! was the magic phrase in the late 1890s, and without question the rush was on. Men and women came from every state and many foreign countries seeking gold. Gold fever ran rampant.

Alaska's past and present still depend for the most part on its sea routes—the key to each of the peak periods in its history. First it was the drive for seal, sea lion, and sea otter pelts (started by the Russians in the mid 1780s), followed by a flourishing fishing industry, after which came the fabulous gold rush, and finally the discovery of extensive oil fields, the latter sources continuing to yield even as this story unfolds, in places like Prudoe Bay on the North Slope.

They called him a fool when he penned his name to the document that sealed the transaction for the purchase of Alaska from Russia in 1867—William Henry Seward. Had this man taken leave of his senses when he paid a whopping $7.2 million for this so-called worthless piece of real estate? The newspapers titled it "Seward's folly," a phrase that is still spoken today. As in many such situations, he who laughs last laughs best, and certainly Mr. Seward must be laughing from his grave site at his tormentors. That wasteland has produced a bounty thousands of times greater in value than the mere $7.2 million paid for Alaska. Russians even in our day blast their forbearers for literally giving the "Great Land" to the Americans.

Seward saw into the future and he was no fool. He was an experienced statesman—a U.S. senator from New York, 1849-61. As President Lincoln's secretary of state he sought a dominant policy, but the president's ingenuity kept him in cabinet. He proved himself during the Civil War handling adeptly such matters as the Trent Affair. He held his post under Andrew Johnson and supported Johnson's reconstruction policy. None of his achievements, however, has held a candle to the purchase of Alaska, which after years of semi-neglect as a territory was to become the 49th state on January 3, 1959. In all of its ups and downs from the Russian exploitation to the present time, its greatest population growth has been in recent decades—over a 30% increase per year. People are becoming more and more attracted to this last frontier, and tourism has become one of the top industries during the better months of the year.

Southeastern and Southwestern Alaska tend to be more wet and mild than one might think. Further north, it can be very frigid. The bitter cold during the long winter nights fade into the "land of the midnight sun," when darkness is rare. Its a land of many weather variations, contradictions, and changes. Rock-bound rookeries to the stands of spruce, cedar and hemlock are but one contrast as are the variations from tourism to industries of oil, gas, and commercial fishing. Exports include manufactured goods such as lumber, pulp, furs, ore, and fish products, as well as oil.

Alaska, long the lowest populated of the states, is now home to nearly 600,000 people, having climbed out of the cellar, leaving the lowest rung to the state of Wyoming.

Juneau (the state capital) is also a seaport, as are Ketchikan, Haines, Petersburg, Skagway, Sitka, Cordova, Kodiak, Homer, Nome, Anchorage (Whittier), Dutch Harbor, Valdez, and Wrangell, not to mention an arm's list of small cannery ports, timber, and fishing outlets spread along the lengthy coastline. Palmer, in southeast Alaska, has long hosted the state fair.

Silhouetted in an Alaskan sunset, the ill-fated SS Edith *of Alaska Steamship Company, abandoned and alone is about to slip into the depths off Cape St. Elias, in August of 1915. She was built in England in 1882.*

Little did the Danish explorer Vitus Bering, in the employment of Mother Russia, ever visualize that this cold, miserable land in 1728 could ever become something of great value. In fact, he died in 1741 on Bering Island after leading an expedition to Alaska.

And even before Bering, the doughty Russian, Semyon Dezhnev, first explored the strait between Alaska and Siberia in 1648, command-

tic regions. The early natives who were dissatisfied with the upper Alaskan latitudes moved ever southward, settling the areas we now know as British Columbia, Washington, Oregon, and northern California. All of the Alaskan natives and those who migrated southward were a swarthy people adept at living off the land, and though many of their customs were related, they also had a wide diversity of skills

USCGC (buoy tender) Sledge, *a 180 foot vessel which operates out of the Coast Guard base at Homer.* Photo courtesy of U.S. Coast Guard.

ing an inferior craft in extremely inhospitable seas flecked with ice. Courageously he pushed all the way to the northeastern extremity of Asia on the Chukchi Peninsula where a cape now bears his name. He saw nothing along the shores of what is now the coast of Alaska that he reasoned to be of any value.

The real settlers and discoverers of Alaska, however, were those who in ancient times came to the Great Land via the so-called Land Bridge, that 50 mile stretch that separates Siberia from Alaska, near the meeting place of the Bering Sea and Chukchi Sea. Some reason the two hunks of land were once connected; others say the natives came by crude water craft. Only speculation rules here, for the time frequency is also in debate.

Forbearers of American natives reputedly crossed that land bridge linking Siberia with Alaska after the last ice age, some speculating 10,000 to 15,000 years ago. Believed to be of Mongoloid nationality, both Eskimos and their Aleut neighbors populated Alaska, perhaps 9,000 years ago. It is said that Arctic Eskimos diverged from Bering Sea Eskimos about 4,000 years later. This wild land was peopled by an estimated 70,000 natives who eked out an existence in an unfriendly wasteland, frozen much of the time. Aleuts inhabited the 1,100 mile long arc of barren islands long known as the Aleutian Chain—a series of mostly barren isles resembling the rotten teeth of a sea serpent. Northwest coastal Indians settled in coves along the densely wooded panhandle, and the Athapaskans throughout interior forests. The Eskimos set up house along the coasts and rivers of the Bering and Arc-

in each respective tribe. All fished and hunted, and varied their diets with roots and berries. Depending on their exposure to diverse settings there were obvious differences among these aboriginals who, in their own right for a Pagan people, were ingenious in their ability to survive, often turning skimpy resources into a variety of tools, boats, shelter, and clothing.

Their solitary lives paralleled each other for countless generations until the Russian fur traders exploited the natives in their greed for mammal pelts, as early as 1743, later establishing a foothold. As the years rolled onward, Russian fur trading companies devastated the Aleuts. In the interim, Spain, fearing Russia but hampered by British expansion withdrew from Nootka Sound (B.C.) in 1790, after Captain James Cook's third voyage set the scene for the international fur rush. In 1799, about five years after Russian Orthodox missionaries arrived in Kodiak, the Russian American Company established a monopoly.

Meanwhile, competition heated between the British and the Yankee upstart traders who both laid claim to the flourishing Canton market, off limits to Russia. Alaskan and British Columbia natives mostly Haidas and Tlingits, were used as middlemen.

New Archangel (Sitka), Russia's capital from 1808, often went through difficult times, with sea connections poor at best and shipwrecked supply ships often the menu of the day. New Archangel was a long, treacherous land and sea route from St. Petersburg, and the survival pressures were obvious. Cruel Russian taskmasters treated the natives treacherously and only their superior fire power prevented revenge by the invaded.

Russia attempted expansion as far south as California (Fort Ross and the Farallons) in an effort to bolster their food and fur supply. They even tried a granary and a lumber mill, all of which came to a dismal end, as did their foothold in the Sandwich Islands (Hawaii).

All of Alaska's early history is in direct contrast to the Alaska of our day. Billions of gallons of crude oil have been pouring out of the 49th state. In the late 1950s, oil strikes on the Kenai Peninsula and in Cook Inlet made Anchorage the petroleum hub. When the mammoth strike on the north slope at Prudoe Bay was discovered in 1968, it reached near gold rush proportions. The following year, North Slope sales pumped nearly a billion dollars into state coffers. Cook Inlet resources sent out 36 million barrels in 1980, but the North Slope fields afforded 555 million barrels. The giant pipeline was seen as the cheapest way to get oil down to the Port of Valdez from where super-tankers could take on huge cargoes for several destinations. The trans-Alaska pipeline drew scores of workers as the project crossed hundreds of miles of Alaska's interior. It was completed in 1973 and continues at this writing to be a black gold bonanza.

Over half of Alaska's population lives around and in the Anchorage area. Yes indeed, Alaska is the last frontier, but like all other promising places, it's now seeing the greatest growth in its history.

From mighty Mt. McKinley, rising 20,320 feet, highest in North America, to the fishing, lumber, and tourist ports of the Inside Passage, Alaska is a vast wonderland of fabulous beauty, much of it set aside by the government so animal and bird life can be virtually undisturbed in an otherwise exploited U.S.A. It's a place of countless glaciers, high mountains, deep valleys, and a seemingly endless coastline dominated by maritime activity, a place where frequent aids to navigation are vital and where every year Davy Jones claims large and small vessels for his locker. Of such is the great state of Alaska.

USCGC Sweetbriar *(buoy tender), which has operated out of Coast Guard bases at Juneau and Cordova is typical of the veteran working craft that do both work on aids to navigation and patrol duty.* Photo courtesy of U.S. Coast Guard.

CHAPTER ONE
In The Beginning

She's awesome and vast and a spell is cast
by the restless and thundering sea.
She tears at the sands like a demon's hands
Like a spector she beckons to me.
—Dave Kneeshaw

One can only speculate on the difficulties faced by the first natives that came to what we know today as Alaska. If indeed they were part of the Mongol people they undoubtedly desired to part company from a savage environment in order to have a more peaceful and less demanding homeland. Though their hopes were perhaps never fully realized, they at least found a place where for decades they were undisturbed by outside influences and cruel overlords. Everything about

William Henry Seward, Secretary of State, purchased Alaska from the Russians in 1867. His notable achievement was at first labeled "Seward's Folly", but in later years became a bonanza for the United States. Photo courtesy Alaska State Library.

the features of those early people pointed to Mongol extraction. They were far less warlike, however, and were remarkable in their ability to survive.

Though we can't say for certain that they came by foot over what was once a connection between Siberia and Alaska, we do know that they must have migrated over difficult miles to reach their destination, and if indeed those two lands were not connected, the inhabitants obviously had the skill to build skin boats and travel the short distance separating the land masses. The traditional Eskimo umiaks and kayaks and coastal Indian dugout canoes of later times bear this out, for both types of craft were highly seaworthy. In addition, these early natives were not seafarers of the vagabond type as were Polynesians. Their craft were made for fishing and the hunting of whales, seal, sea lions, and otter, but seldom ever out of the sight of land. With small craft, none had greater skill, but they were not prone to far-flung navigation by sea by utilizing celestial guidance. Undoubtedly many of the earliest natives of Alaska faced miserable hardship, especially in the far northern latitudes where the bitterly cold winters made life almost unbearable. The Eskimos probably suffered much premature death from starvation, privation, and bitter cold. They learned how to exist with animal skins for clothing, and from fishing through holes in the ice when they were unable to harpoon large mammals.

As decades advanced, each of these people gained in their ways of survival. Milder climate, lush forests, abundant fish and sea mammals, along with berries and roots made life much more easy for the 12,000 Northwest coastal Indians than for the Eskimo. The Indians savored salmon and trapped them during spawning runs. Even in our present day it is hard to find a descendent of the early tribes who doesn't cherish salmon as a favorite food.

An estimated early population of 16,000 Aleuts lived in communal sod houses. Like the Eskimos, they utilized skin boats to pursue sea mammals donning seal intestine clothing and puffin skin parkas. Early Eskimo population of some 23,000 Yupik and 11,000 Inupiaq adapted to the harsh sea conditions with their walrus skin umiaks. Caribou, seal, walrus, and fish varied their diet. The land-loving Athapaskans, numbering some 13,000, mostly seminomads, existed on a variety of fish and caribou.

One of the mysteries for anthropologists is the origin of the Aleut peoples, those who for countless centuries eked out an existence in one of the most inhospitable environments the world over.

It has generally been accepted, as earlier mentioned, that most of the original natives of Alaska came by the proverbial land bridge which many feel was once a limited solid land mass connecting Siberia with what we know today as Alaska. It is also generally agreed that those ancient peoples were of Mongolian origin, both Eskimos, Tlingits, and the other Alaska clans.

But what about the Aleuts? Though they too have Asian features, they differ some from their Alaskan brothers, and it is the opinion of this writer that their origin may not be the same as those who came by the land bridge from Mongolian lands.

It might be pointed out that the great Japanese Current, which the Japanese call Kuro Shio, skims along the perimeter of the Aleutian chain. In ancient times, Japanese, Korean, and Formosan junks disabled at sea often drifted aimlessly with the current, many landing on the rocky ledges of the island chain. Most of their occupants probably died tormenting deaths by starvation, exposure, or drowning, but a handful of survivors managed somehow to survive and adjust to the seemingly uninhabitable environment.

Little is known of the early history of the Aleut but it is true that there were scores of Asian junks reported lost throughout the Pacific rim following the days of exploration in the Pacific. Centuries before recorded history, there were possibly countless unrecorded junks swept from their home waters, and many obviously landed on the Aleutian Isles. One must remember that for centuries Japan was a closed nation, and anything that left its territorial waters, including junks and their crews, would never again be permitted to return to the Land of the Rising Sun, even if per chance they could somehow make it back. If they did, death was mandatory.

Before we get further into the subject, let us first look at the geography of the Aleutians, this little known and little understood corner of the world that only came into its own because of its strategic locale for military bases during and after World War II. These strange isles are actually a chain of volcanic masses southwest from the tip of the Alaskan Peninsula approaching Russia's Komandorski Islands to the far west. Partially submerged, they are a continuation of the Aleutian Range dividing the Bering Sea from the Pacific. There are four main groups—Fox Island, nearest Alaska, includes Unimak, Unalaska (with Dutch Harbor on small Amaknak Island) and Umnak. Andreanof Islands are numerous, and they include Adak. The largest of the Rat Islands are Amchitka and Kiska. Near Islands, the farthest west and the smallest group of all, includes Attu.

All the islands are of volcanic origin, generally rugged with few good harbors and countless reefs and rocks that have always posed a navigator's nightmare. Though temperatures are much milder than the northern sectors of Alaska, thanks to the warming affects of the Japanese Current, fog is frequent and so are strong winds and contrary seas. Nearly all the islands are virtually treeless though dense vegetation is apparent on many of the larger ones.

Volcanic action is by no means dormant in that sector of Alaska. As mentioned, the isles are merely submerged parts of the Aleutian Range extending along the entire Alaskan Peninsula. In recent years much activity was noted at Katmai (Valley of the Ten Thousand Smokes), one of the world's largest volcanoes. Percentage wise, the Aleutians probably have more volcanic activity than any place in the world, and only its sparse population has kept the death toll at a low ebb. Eruptions have been numerous in recent years, and will continue to be as they have for centuries. Following are some of the more recent eruptions: Kiska, 1969; Great Sitkin, 1974; Gareloi, 1982; Korovin, Cleveland, Makushin, and Shishaldin, all in 1987; Okmok, Akutan, Pavlov, all in 1988. And in the 1990s the volcanic activity

The dramatic end of the MS Bellingham, purposely set afire for the Seattle Seafare celebration in 1950. Famous for years in Alaska sealanes, she was the first vessel of the Alaska Steamship Company beginning in the gold rush years serving under the name Willapa. After being wrecked in Alaska at the turn of the century it was salvaged by Canadian interests and eventually came back under the American flag and served as the first unit of the Black Ball Line and the initial unit of the Northland Transportation Company. Built at Astoria in 1881 as a bar tug, she was rebuilt and lengthened at Portland, Oregon in 1892, later becoming a first class passenger steamer. Photo by Joe Williamson.

continues, little heed given it by the peoples of the islands. All of these eruptions originated in peaks ranging from 4,000 to more than 9,300 feet, the latter, Shishaldin, is one of the highest in the Aleutians.

The Aleutian Islands as a whole comprise 6,821 square miles of land mass, the two largest islands being Unimak and Unalaska, 1,600 and 1,064 square miles respectively. The others are considerably smaller.

Now, after that brief geography lesson, let us go back to the Aleut people. As we earlier learned, they had survived off the land for countless centuries. They both fished the waters and hunted the terrain, living in virtual peace. Their seaworthy boats were similar to those of the Eskimo and the Indian tribes elsewhere, and they were generally content to remain in their peaceful island retreats along with the bountiful seas full of seal, sea lions, whale, etc. They were a generally mild mannered people, and were not given to warlike activities unless backed into a corner.

It is understandable that there had to be mixtures of blood among them from castaways of the hostile sea abutting their isles. It must be remembered that according to legend, Japan was founded as an empire by the Emperor Jimmu in 660 B.C., but earliest records of a unified Japan date from 1,000 years later. Chinese influence was strong in the formation of Japanese civilization. China on the other hand may date back as far as 5000 B.C.

Like early Japan, Korea was long known as the "Hermit Kingdom" and was considered a country as far back as the 1st Century B.C. It was united as a kingdom in 668 A.D. By the fringe of each of these Asian countries passed the Japanese Current and other minor current systems which formed a great circle route easterly, flowing (clockwise) for thousands of miles past the Aleutians, through the Gulf of Alaska, and down the British Columbia, Washington, Oregon, and northern California coastlines before reversing course back to Hawaii and westward in a less powerful flow. If all the areas mentioned had recorded junk wrecks it seems obvious that the Aleutians would have the lion's share.

The junk is without doubt the oldest traditional type of sailing vessel ever built. The hull has a short bow and stern with no keel, and in all probability was developed from a primitive form of a double canoe. The Pechili trading junk which generally carried a crew of 20 to 30 men is regarded as the oldest Chinese sea junk. Ironically, the foremast was stepped outboard on the port side, the two mainmasts and mizzen were stepped in line. Aft on the port side, an auxiliary mizzen was stepped just clear of the tiller and used to bring the vessel about when tacking. Sometimes a stay sail was set between the mainmasts, and occasionally a topsail was employed. A sizeable deckhouse aft sheltered the crew.

There was also the Foochow pole junk, a simple log carrying conveyance of from 200 to 400 tons with three principal battened lug sails, slow but extremely seaworthy with watertight compartments and massive hardwood frames. There were many other similar Chinese creations as well, and until the advent of modern sea transport, the Chinese junk was considered the finest and safest sailing craft. The Chinese were the first to introduce watertight compartments within the hull of their craft which gave them the capability of weathering the worst storms at sea.

Now the Japanese and Formosan junks were quite a different story. Oddly, the Japanese people, who were oriented to the sea, had only one type of junk which was far inferior to the Chinese versions. Beamy, heavily constructed, and lug sail-rigged, it had one very bad feature that often led to swamping, shipwreck, or disablement. The open well in the stern, built to allow the lowering or raising of the rudder, left it vulnerable to being swamped in heavy seas when a wave would break over the stern. The simple rigging, similar to some of the earliest Roman ships involved two, occasionally three masts, with a single lug sail per mast.

The Formosan people developed a strange craft known as a Taiwan raft, built of huge bamboos curved upward at either end forward and aft. The mast was a large stem of bamboo and the single matting sail supported by cross battens had Chinese overtones. To prevent the vessel making leeway under sail narrow boards were pushed down between the bamboo stems of the hull. A small box like structure was placed amidships where crewmen not tending the sail could sit and keep their feet dry. Unlike the much larger junks, the Taiwan raft was equipped with six oars, self-feathering, known as Yulohs. Though such craft were able to negotiate the heavy surf off the east coast of Formosa, they, like the Japanese junk, often got carried offshore when disabled.

Thus, one can see how many of these Asian craft could have wrecked in the Aleutians long before and after history was recorded, and it is not beyond the realm of possibility that the Aleuts originally came from areas other than Mongolia. The current system is the key to this theory. Sea currents, some weak, some strong, flow through the Pacific like rivers within the ocean. There are also offshore minor currents, all of which affect floating materials and carry them sometimes thousands of miles until winds deposit them ashore.

Secondly, the Aleutians are not joined to mainland Alaska where other natives reputedly came across the land bridge. They are a smattering of islands which reach westerly from the Alaska Peninsula for a thousand miles, and more than 800 miles as the gull flies from the legendary land bridge. It would have been virtually impossible in ancient times for the Aleuts to have settled the widespread Aleutian Islands except by sea, and in the beginning the only way a vessel would have reached those islands would be if they had been castaway and swept ashore by the currents and the storms making Japan, Formosa, and perhaps Korea or China the lands from which the Aleuts originated.

Wars in the Orient were often fought with war junks. History records one of the greatest, perhaps the greatest armada ever assembled, involving the Mongolian invasion fleet attacking Japan, first in 1274 and again in 1281.

Mongol emperor Kublai Khan sent out 4,400 vessels manned by 142,000 troops with orders to sail from Chinese and Korean ports and conquer the islands of Japan. Instead, they themselves were conquered, not by naval action but mostly by what the Japanese called the 'Divine Wind'—actually a typhoon of enormous proportions from which the name Kamikazi originated. The first invasion was in 1274 when the Mongol troops ravaged the coastal towns of Kyushu but failed to bring the Japanese to submission. The Mongol fleet was then hit by a storm that destroyed 200 vessels and took the lives of 13,500.

Then in 1281, the southern fleet sailed from Chingyuan, China, in late spring and rendezvoused with the northern Mongol fleet from Korea. The combined armada joined ranks near Iki and Hirado Jima. Before the assault against the major island of Kyushu could be mounted, the typhoon struck and the greater part of the 4,400 vessels were destroyed, along with the 100,000 warriors, a staggering loss of

SS Victorian, *one of the gold rush era steamers, initial unit of the Washington and Alaska Steamship Company. Later the vessel was purchased by the Pacific Coast Steamship Company. Her career was tarnished by frequent breakdowns and she was burned for her scrap value in 1910.*

life. Even to this day, armament from the Mongol's defeat is recovered from Japanese waters.

Japan was never successfully invaded and never occupied until the aftermath of World War II when U.S. atom bombs forced surrender. Had the United States been compelled to invade Japan, there could have been a ghastly death toll on both sides, as a large segment of the Nipponese people had vowed to fight to the death for their homeland.

Kublai Khan's lost fleet did even more to make Japan a closed country. Through ancient times many junks drifted away from Japanese coastal waters in the same manner as the thousands of glass fish floats have followed the clockwise current system and been swept up on beaches in Alaska, British Columbia, and the Pacific Coast like solidified bubbles from the Land of the Rising Sun.

Not until 1853 did U.S. Commodore Matthew Perry manage to get Japan open, and cancel its age-old status as a hermit nation. Perhaps it was the display of the ships of the American Navy that helped persuade Japan, but from that date they became a factor in worldwide trade.

Up until 1875, some 100 Asian junks are known to have been found adrift or castaway on Pacific shores. In that same year there were no less than 23,000 junks, ranging up to 400 tons, that were registered in that country. For the most part they were engaged in coastal trades, their most frequent cargo being fish and rice. Lost in the eons of time are the huge numbers of drifting and lost junks that were never recorded.

Already mentioned in the text was the loss of two Japanese junks in the Rat Islands in the early 1780s. Another was wrecked at Atka in 1851; one at Attu in September 1862; and another was claimed at Adak in 1869.

So again, we can well assume that before recorded history the Aleuts came by sea, perhaps from Japan, China, or Formosa, to the harsh wilderness of the Aleutian chain. They lived at peace until the Russians invaded their sanctuaries with a great lack of impunity in the mid-1700s.

The population of the original Alaskan natives increased over the centuries, but the gains were small and at times were in the negative column. Millennia of exposure continued to bring about many differences among aboriginal Alaskans, for where survival is concerned mankind will do whatever is necessary to sustain life in his respective area.

Old newspaper photo of native Tlingits in their customary garb.

the Diomedes, charted the St. Lawrence Islands, and established the fact that Asia and America were separate continents.

It was on a subsequent expedition, thirteen years later, that Bering was again dispatched to make further exploration. This time he commanded two ships, the *St. Peter* (*Petr*) on which he sailed, and his consort, the ship *St. Paul*, commanded by Aleksey Ilick Chirikof. The two ship fleet sailed on June 4, 1741, headed toward the American continent. Chirikof sighted land near Cape Addington, Cook Inlet, Kodiak Island, and the Alaska Peninsula on a difficult voyage.

The two ships had been separated from each other in foggy and often turbulent seas. Bering sighted and logged Cape St. Elias, Mt. St. Elias, skirted Kodiak Island, Chirikof Island, and the Semidi Islands. It was in November of 1741 that the *St. Peter* crashed onto the basaltic outcrops of Bering Island, the great explorer meeting his death on December 8 after being marooned on the isle that now bears his name. Facing hardship at the lonely outpost, the remainder of the crew made out the best they could until rescue came. The discovery of the charted landmarks opened the door to maritime Alaska.

The two navigators had outlined the headlands and islands from the American continent to Bering Island. Further, they had broken the mystery of the unknown, blazing across 3,000 miles of phantom seas. Bold navigators later followed the eastward passage from Kamchatka to America establishing a new and lucrative trade route. The efforts of Bering and Chirikof were invaluable, even though it cost the wreck of the *St. Peter* and its courageous Danish expedition leader, Vitus Bering.

There was no immediate rush to probe the farther reaches of Alaska, Russian seafarers concentrating mostly on the Aleutian chain of islands. There, sometimes at great cost and privation they slaughtered the mammals in droves in a wild flurry to get prized furs. By the end of the 1750s, the Aleutians had been virtually stripped of the

Despite their wide dispersal, the Eskimo is highly uniform in language, physical type, and culture. The ingenuity of their material culture is essential to their survival in the Arctic. Many a white man would have perished in the harsh northern wastes had it not been for the assistance of the Eskimo, for the most part a gentle and accommodating individual with a proportionate amount of pride.

THE RUSSIANS ARE COMING

Exploitation on a grand scale: there's no other way to explain the way the Russians charged into a harsh land, stepping on any minor opposition that blocked the way. They paid a heavy toll for their pursuit, depending mostly on navigation information afforded by none other than Captain Vitus Jonassen Bering (Behring), an adventuresome Danish sea master, descending from the ancient Vikings.

Russian skipper Simon Deschneff (Semyon Dezhnev) made a voyage to East Cape, Siberia, following along the rim of the Alaska coast in 1647, but his mission was not to land in what we know as Alaska. It was actually Peter the First who dreamed of lands that lay eastward of Siberia. In his mind were tales he'd heard from the Chukchees of a people further on who had "ivory teeth in their cheeks." He was anxious to gain more information on such a tribe and whether or not his land and theirs were separated by an unknown sea.

Such an endeavor would require an expeditionary maritime effort covering many miles into unmarked and unsurveyed waters, and he picked Bering to command the expedition. The Dane sailed from the south of the Kamchatka River, Siberia, on July 13, 1728, in the ship *San Gabriel*. He charted the Siberian coast, discovered and named

Early engraving of Icy Bay and Mount St. Elias with a Russian sailing vessel of ancient times.

Built at Philadelphia in 1878, the SS State of California *played a major role in the Alaska passenger business under the Pacific Coast Steamship Company. She set a speed record from Puget Sound to Nome and return in 1901 that held for more than a decade, under Captain H.H. Lloyd. The rakish 2,266 ton vessel was wrecked in Alaska 1913, with a loss of 35 lives.*

Then along came the British, and the cold war of exploration was instituted—several maritime nations vying for new discovery, trade routes, and prestige. Renowned navigators such as Captain James Cook, and George Vancouver along with John Meares, Dixon, Portlock, Malaspina, and others all sailed northward to chart and discover new lands along the Inside and Outside passages of Alaska. They explored Alaskan waters from Dixon Entrance to Icy Cape.

Russia's aggressiveness, as well as Spain's, seemed to have lost its gusto, and on the fringes Uncle Sam was ready to jump in the fray versus England. Yankee offense on the high seas followed the Revolutionary War as the fledgling nation sought new avenues of sea trade. What greater potential existed than the North Pacific? For decades maritime powers had unsuccessfully sought the fabled Northwest Passage, a route across the top of the globe, that would offer a short route between Europe and the Orient. Spain, however, had long before opened a transpacific trade route from Mexico, mainly Acapulco, and from the mid 1500s Spanish vessels were sailing back from Manila and other Oriental ports laden with valuable cargoes of gold, silver, silk, beeswax. and numerous other items of value.

Spanish authorities in Mexico had also sent an occasional expedition to the Pacific Northwest, establishing bases of operation at places like Nootka Sound, and at the northwest corner of what later became the state of Washington (Neah Bay). The British, however, had been a constant thorn in their side, often pillaging the galleons of their booty. Missions were active along what is now the state of (southern) California but the total effort lost steam and after a few hostile acts between England and Spain, the latter began a gradual retreat in the North Pacific.

Enthusiasm for expanded trade by the United States made Boston a busy and important port of embarkation. Many ships were con-

bounty and the hunters then aggressively searched for new haunts. S. Glotov found rich pickings on both Unmak and Unalaska Islands. Then in 1761 Bechevin sailed and landed on the Alaska Peninsula.

The news of these successes soon were in the hands of the Russian monarchs in St. Petersburg, and the excited Catherine II ordered the Board of the Admiralty to send more vessels with skillful navigators to explore and to garner further information on this mysterious land to the east, information that would enhance the further efforts of Russian traders and seafarers.

Thus a new expedition under Krenetsky visited the Pribilofs, and sailed as far eastward as coastal America. The group of four Pribilof islands off S. W. Alaska in the Bering Sea, north of the Aleutians, was also visited and named in 1786 by Russian navigator Gerasim Pribilof, and to this day is still an important seal breeding grounds. There was once a great danger of extinguishing the mammals, until the Bering Fur Seal Controversy, settled in 1911, gave the United States the right to enforce protection of the herds which had been badly depleted by Russia, the U.S., England, and Japan. The native Aleuts still make a living there by processing seal and fox furs but today the mammals are strictly controlled and the islands are a massive refuge for the creatures.

Spain, which had long dominated the Pacific tradelanes between Mexico and the Orient, moved northward in the late 1770s. Under Spanish navigator and explorer Juan Perez, Prince of Wales Island was reached in 1774, followed by Bodega de Quadra with a fleet of two ships and a schooner escort. He sighted land near Sitka the following year (1775). Two years later (1777) he discovered Prince William Sound and what is now Cook Inlet.

Death ship. Typical of the scores of Asian junks that drifted aimlessly across the Pacific from ancient times is this modern counterpart, the motorized fishing craft Ryo Yei Maru *which broke down after leaving Misaki, Japan, on December 5, 1926, and was intercepted by the SS Margaret Dollar in the North Pacific October 31, 1927. Aboard was a scene of tragedy, 12 men and one woman, all long before having succumbed to starvation. The derelict was towed to Seattle and later burned. By such means, it is believed that many of the native Aleuts were shipwreck survivors that landed in the Aleutians on broken down junks.*

structed in New England shipyards, but none as important as those skippered by the renowned Captain Robert Gray. Though his mission was furs for the Canton market, he discovered the Columbia River, Grays Harbor, Tillamook Bay, and became the first American sea captain to circumnavigate the world (1787-1790). Earlier Captain Cook told of great trade possibilities in the fur trade which was to produce dividends for those who followed, from Oregon to Alaska. Gray's probing of Northwest waters took him as far north as 55° 43' North, in 1789. Following in his wake was a vast armada of American ships which over the next quarter of a century were trading with natives for pelts in virtually every bay, cove, and doghole along the southeastern coast of Alaska. The waterway, which ran from the Strait of Juan de Fuca north through the intricate island-laced passages of British Columbia and Alaska, became known as the Inside Passage.

Still the Russian presence was very much a factor, and in 1777 provisioned to seek out new areas for garnering furs was Grigorie Ivanovich Shelekhov (Shelikof). Following discouraging Russian efforts in the Sandwich Islands, Shelikof was intent on establishing more permanent settlements in areas of the Great Land, claimed by Russia. His determination paid off by establishing the first colony at Three

Big ships don't run on land as was learned by the skipper of the SS Northwestern *of the Alaska Steamship Company after the tide ebbed at Eagle River, Alaska, in July 1933.*

Saints Bay, Kodiak Island, in 1784. Sailing onward, minor portals of trade were then found on Prince William Sound and southeastern Alaska.

On the scene came one Alexander Baranof (Aleksandr Andreyevich Baranov) who had engaged in a booming business on the Anadyr River. Shelikof chose Bananof to be manager of his company. The latter virtually claimed domination over Southeastern Alaska in 1790, although the Yankee traders paid him little heed. He established shipyards to build ships to replace the Russian vessels lost in the menacing supply route between Siberia and Alaska. The initial ship was the *Phoenix*, which slid down the ways in August 1794 at a yard on Resurrection Bay. Two others were constructed at Spruce Island, the *Delphi*, and the *Olga*.

Five years later, in 1799, Russian authorities established their official base of operations at New Archangel (Sitka) from where the Russian American Company was formed. The land was properly surveyed and the town plot laid out. Baranof is also credited with founding Kodiak as a fur trading post in 1792, moving the center from Three Saints Bay.

Crude treatment by the Russians against the natives caused skirmishes, trouble, and rebellion, and that along with other problems caused the near destruction of New Archangel. Out of the ruins of the 1802 battle, the Russian forces persisted and the 'new' New Archangel became a reality three years later. In 1804-05 it became Bananov's official headquarters and he became its governor. Then came Russian surveyor Lisianski to properly mark the area for future development, after which trade and commerce gained impetus, and a shipyard was established to build badly needed Russian sailing vessels for further trade. It became more obvious that assistance for the rugged colony was at a snail's pace as St. Petersburg was thousands of miles away and the rugged land in between difficult to traverse, yet alone the dangerous sea route. More and more the Alaskan Russians would have to depend on their own resources. In turn, their fur output was sometimes slow getting back to Mother Russia, the markets in China being pretty well controlled by England and the United States. In 1808, New Archangel was officially named Russia's Alaskan capital, and it took on a new importance.

Lieutenant Otto von Kotzebue, a Russian Naval officer in 1815, made important explorations of the Arctic in the ship *Rurik*. He discovered and explored Alaska's Kotzebue Sound in 1816, and made two voyages around the world, the last between 1823-26. Further Alaskan exploration in that time sequence was done by the Englishman Captain Beachy of the HMS *Blossom* in 1826, followed by the Russian brig *Polyphene* in 1838. In the interim, Captain A. D. Tebenkof did a yeoman job of surveying Alaskan waters. In 1845, his findings were published in a voluminous atlas titled *The Northwest Coast of America from Bering Sea to Cape Corrientes and the Aleutian Islands.*

Soon after, the Russian American Company and the Hudson's Bay Company found themselves in keen competition for trade in Southeastern Alaska, along the river systems and well into the Arctic. The business of trade and barter also brought a growing number of ships into the partially charted Alaskan waters. Some paid a heavy toll when shipwreck occurred and no assistance was available. Nobody knows how many vessels were wrecked in those historical times, but a partial list of some of the better known vessels from the mid 1700s to the early 1800s follows:

1745	Russian ship *Eudokia*, on Kanaga Island
1750	Russian shitik *Petr* (plank construction), Attu or Agattu Island
1753	Russian (S. V.) *Leremiia*, Adak Island
1758	Russian ship *Kapiton*, Kiska Island (17 died on the island)
1762	Russian (S. V.) *Petr I. Pavel*, Shemya Island
1764	Russian ship *Trinity*, Umnak Island
1779	Russian (S. V.) *Andrie Pervozvannyi*, off Amchitka Island
1785	Russian (S. V.) *Evpl*, Pankov Harbor, Amlia Island
1791	Russian ship *John the Forerunner*, St. Paul Island
1799	*St. Alexander*, Russian S. V. between Alaska and Siberia, all lost
1799	*Northern Eagle*, Russian ship, Montague Island
1801	*Avoss*, Russian tender, lost at sea
1801	*Sitka*, Russian brig, lost at sea
1801	*Otkrietie (Otkrytie)*, Russian brig, wrecked at sea
1809	*Chirikof*, Russian schooner, wrecked at sea
1813	*Neva*, Russian ship, wrecked off Cape Edgecomb
1831	*Sivutch*, Russian ship, near Wall Bay, Atka Island

Not included in the above list were numerous Asian junks, mostly Japanese, that became disabled and were carried with Kuro Shio (Japanese Current) across the Pacific, several of which were wrecked in the Aleutian chain, mostly unrecorded. Japan ridded itself of any craft that drifted from its territorial waters, forbidden to foreigners and to its own people once out of Japanese jurisdiction. Two are known to have been wrecked on Rat Island, one in 1780 and another in 1782. The latter ended its days on the then uncharted island, the wreck yielding a pack of rats that took up residence after fleeing the wreck. That's how the island got its name and is still known as such today.

The other junk stranded in a storm. Survivors were picked up by a Russian vessel and taken to Okhotsk, Siberia. Numerous other wrecks followed in subsequent years. The Russian sailing ship *Kapiton* was driven on a rocky reef, an outcrop of Kiska Island. The crew made it to shore, but 17 died while struggling for survival on the barren outpost. The others made it to Shemya Island, where gaunt and starving they were finally rescued by the Russian sailing vessel *Petr I. Pavel*, three years later. When the *Pavel* was wrecked in 1762 on Shemya Island most survived, some of whom eventually made their way to Attu in a baidara.

Research by former Commandant of the 13th Coast Guard District, Rear Admiral Frederick A. Zeusler, found that some 1,661 vessels were lost in the waters around Alaska between 1740 and 1953 (with numerous others since the latter date). All causes; stranding, foundering, fire, explosion, crushings by ice, striking icebergs, and collision were taken into consideration. At first glance this does not appear to be a great total, but when one considers that Alaska was among the last in the world established as a major field of commerce, the totals are substantial. Of that total, the ships involved over 100 tons are broken down in the following table.

1740-1953 WRECKS

In addition to the major losses, there have been countless numbers of small craft not recorded in Admiral Zeusler's list, and of course there have been an arm's lengths list of all types of vessels claimed in Alaskan waters since 1953.

	Ships	Barks	Schooners	Steamers	O.S.	G.S.	Barges
Arctic Ocean	28	70	18	17	4	19	6
Bering Sea	71	58	86	53	12	76	75
North Pacific	15	22	102	51	57	203	67
Inland Waters	3	11	44	52	55	332	54

O.S. = Oil Screw
G.S. = Gas Screw

Panning for gold in the retrieved wreck of the SS Islander *which was pulled to the beach in 1933 in a major salvage project to recover the reputed treasure aboard. The ship went down in 1901 after reputedly striking an iceberg in southeast Alaska. Inset shows a section of the engine room (see story in text).*

Preparing to depart for Alaska from her Seattle pier, the SS Oregon, a formidable passenger liner finished her days off Cape Hinchinbrook in September of 1906, in command of Captain Horace Soule. The skipper was not blamed for the wreck as the waters off the island were for the most part poorly charted and no navigation aids were in the area. The Oregon, dating from 1878, had an iron hull, but some called her "old stone bottom" as tons of cement had been poured in her bilge to keep her more free of leakage.

Artist's sketch of a large Tlingit canoe, the type used by the Tlingits when the renowned French navigator and explorer LaPerouse discovered Lituya Bay, Alaska, in the late 1700s. At that time the natives roamed the area in large numbers, but today the bay is seldom visited. LaPerouse named the place Port Des Francais, but likened the natives as fierce savages.

Early sketch of a Japanese junk, many of which became disabled at sea and were wrecked on the shores of Alaska in ancient times. Several Japanese sailors and fishermen were castaway in isolation. Many perished, though others survived enduring severe hardship.

Types of Asian junks. Many of this type vessel was wrecked along the isles and mainland beaches of Alaska from the earliest times. Though numerous lives were lost, the few survivors often eked out an existence in some of the most isolated spots. Chinese junks, represented in the upper drawing, were far superior to the Japanese variety, shown in the lower sketch; far more Japanese junks were lost, their survivors being castaway and forbidden from returning to Japan under the edict of the Nipponese law as a hermit nation.

Forgotten in a port of no return on the bleak shores of Alaska rests an unidentified wreck, its glory days long ended.

Below: *Latter day descendants of natives which in ancient times probably crossed the reputed land-bridge between Siberia and Alaska and worked their way down the southeastern Alaska coast. British Columbia and the Pacific Northwest, settling in areas along the way.* Courtesy of the Joe Williamson collection.

The Yukon River Sternwheeler Reliance, *pictured here in the early part of the century packed with hopeful miners ready to seek their fortunes in the gold fields.*

CHAPTER TWO
The Russian Connection

The will of our hunters, the spirit of trade,
On these far shores, a new Muscovy made.
In bleakness and hardship finding new wealth
for fatherland and czardom.
—Baranov's anthem

New Archangel (Sitka), located in a beautiful little harbor with pleasant surroundings of the natural variety, had something to be desired as far as the town was concerned. It had a castle of sorts where the governor held forth, surrounded by a fortress and a spread-out arrangement of buildings and dwellings which would have won no prizes for architectural design. There was a Russian Orthodox house of worship and a shipyard.

When Russian or foreign dignitaries visited, they were royally treated at the castle, as Baranov was always the proper host despite the

An early sketch of New Archangel (Sitka) when under control of the Russians. It was Russia's Alaskan capital and headquarters for the building often referred to as Baranof's Castle. At the right is the St. Michaels Russian Orthodox church. A ship is seen under construction on the waterfront. Sketch by Wm. Wymper, 1837.

isolated location. He ruled with an iron fist and the opposition by the local natives gradually faded: they no longer had the will to fight a losing battle against overwhelming odds. The Russian military establishment was well entrenched.

Despite the location of Russia's Alaskan Capital there was no small amount of activity, and many a fancy ball and celebration were held at the castle, much as they would have been in St. Petersburg, except on a much smaller scale. Many foreign flag merchant vessels and an occasional naval vessel would visit the port.

Barnanov was without equal in his control, the chief factor of Russian Alaska from 1799 until 1817. In fact, he was governor of all Russian activities in North America until 1817. He passed away two years later, but his name has ever remained as one of Russia's premier statesmen, regardless of his shortcomings. He gained the moniker of "Lord of Alaska", and he lived it to the hilt, at times acting like the Czar of Russia himself.

From his original governorship that old Russian rule for outposts was adopted—"God is high above and the Czar far away." In other words, his authority was law and woe be to any who defied it. His demanding and ruthless treatment of the native Thlingits and Aleuts after they nearly wiped out the Russian fortress and garrison in 1802 brought terrible reprisal and many of the natives who reasoned their land had been purloined from them were often annihilated or mistreated on a regular basis, few questions asked. His autonomous authority broke down nearly all resistance from the natives, as the Russian American Company grew more powerful, backed up by the military.

The so-called "castle" was multiple. The first was built by Baranov, the second by Kuskov, the third by Murayev in 1823, and the final one by Kupreanov in 1837. The latter was the largest and most commodious. It appeared that each respective governor built his own "castle", all of which were of frame construction. The 1837 edition has long been called Baranov's Castle but was in actuality the Government House and administration building constructed nearly two decades after Baranov's death. Somehow, after Uncle Sam's purchase of Alaska, the name Baranof's Castle was applied to the structure and the label held. The box-like building with its cupola stood on the highest land within the city limits surrounded by a fortress that afforded an overall vista of the area in every direction.

Unusual was the fact that each of the four "castles" were alleged to have been frequented by a ghost, especially the 1837 structure. A story circulated many years ago, told of a Russian princess who haunted the "castle", a story related through the years in many different versions. Perhaps it began at Baranov's original government administration building (or castle) where he asserted authority and power.

One of the more circulated stories told of the ghost of the princess that returned at six month intervals to haunt the northwest corner of the structure. Reputedly the daughter of one of the high branches of royalty, she was forced to marry into nobility against her will. As the ceremony began and the groom awaited her appearance, the congregation became restless and annoyed when the princess failed to show. A quick search was made of the "castle" when it was discovered the fair maiden had taken her own life inside her chamber. The announcement of the tragedy left the wedding party in deep sorrow. Why should she do such a dastardly thing on her wedding day? The

Russian-American Company ship Nickolai (Nikolai) *from a painting by an unknown artist.*

the attractive bride in her wedding gown which swished ominously as she walked the corridor wringing her jeweled hands. Always accompanying her appearance was the sweet scent of wild briar roses. All who witnessed the frightening phenomena agreed that she appeared to be crying as if seeking her lost lover.

A further, and perhaps more accurate account of the supernatural came from an American chaplain assigned to Sitka in 1867, after the United States took possession of Alaska. After a banquet, the chaplain returned to his room in the "castle" and saw the ghost of a beautiful woman suddenly appear. At daylight he hurried to the home of the local priest, in charge of the Cathedral St. Michael, whom he had befriended the night before. As they were sipping tea together the priest was quite aware of the paleness of the chaplain and asked if he had seen a ghost. The chaplain was amazed at the intuitiveness of the Russian priest.

"What kind of ghost did you see?" he asked, "was it a lady in blue?"

"How did you know?" asked the chaplain.

"Well," said the priest, "pale blue is the color which brides of Russia wear. How was her appearance, was it in the style and fashion of today?"

"No, that is what bothers me" said the chaplain. "I would have taken an oath on the Bible that the beautiful woman who stood before me was a living breathing creature, a masterpiece in flesh and blood, was it not for her style of dress and the hair with cork screw curls down the side of her face."

"Had she a rose in her hair?" interrupted the priest.

truth will out, and it was soon learned that she had been madly in love with a common seafarer whom Baranov had banished from his domain after finding out about the romantic ties of the couple. A common marriage with no royal overtones was unacceptable to the governor. Rather than marry one she did not love, and pining deeply for her lover who was by now far at sea with orders never to return, the princess with a broken heart elected to take her life.

Above and left: *Two vintage sketches of New Archangel during the years of Russian occupation. The center building in both sketches is the government house where four different "castles" were built, the last in 1837. The sketches are believed to depict the earlier castles.*

"Yes, I believe she had red roses fastened in the curls at each side of her head. She also had a silver band resting on her head."

"The silver crown of a Russian bride. Yes, yes, that is likely so," granted the priest.

"But what I intended to say," countered the chaplain, "was that the style of her dress and the way of dressing her hair reminded me of a painting of my mother when she was a young girl."

"How long ago was that picture of your mother painted?"

"Oh," said the chaplain, "I'm now 24 years old so it must have been about 27 years ago."

With an understanding glance, the priest commented, "Yes, that figures, that was the style several years ago."

After a reminiscent pause, the priest asked the chaplain if he ever heard of Father Veniaminoff.

"No," said the chaplain.

After the tragic episode, the haunting of the government mansion became legendary. Those who lived there or were guests of the governor often complained of strange happenings during the deep hours of night. The ghostly appearance of the lady always resembled

St. Michaels Cathedral in New Archangel, early 1800s.

"Well, he was the greatest bishop in the Russian Orthodox church in my estimation," replied the priest. "He left here on Christmas Day 1844 to take up duties in the Moscow Church. Large of stature, he was 6½ feet tall, broad shouldered and muscular. He towered over the governor. Further, he was the first bishop of Sitka, popular with the people and the one who ordained me as deacon of the Holy Mother Church."

"Yes," interrupted the chaplain, "but what did he have to do with the ghost, if indeed it was a ghost?"

"He had everything to do with it," insisted the priest, "It was his influence that conquered when the brute force of the great governor failed. It was he who married the lady in blue to the prince."

The priest continued, "Did the ghost you witnessed hold a candle?"

"Why yes!" said the astonished chaplain.

"Did she shield the candle with her hand and protect it with her hand from the draft? And did she leave your quarters and ascend the steps of the cupola where the beacon light glowed for ships in the harbor?"

The chaplain gazed off in space pondering the facts set before him when the priest continued his dialogue.

"She dropped the candle did she not, then shrieked and suddenly vanished."

"Indeed yes!" exclaimed the chaplain, "But how can you know?"

"Oh," said the priest, "others have seen the lady in blue too. You saw a real ghost last night."

"How can you prove that?" said the frustrated chaplain.

"Let me tell you the sad story of Princess Olga Feodorovna; you occupied her bed chamber last night."

The chaplain listened intently as the priest unveiled the story:

It was in 1840 that the 'White Czar' sent the lieutenant commander in the Russian Navy, Count Adolphus Paulovitch Etholin, to become governor of all Alaska residing at New Archangel (Sitka). The count had been here before as a midshipman and as a young lieutenant, but that was long ago.

Now his hair had grayed and his face had wrinkled in the service of the Czar, but he was still handsome enough to win the heart of an attractive Finnish countess who had the reputation of being the most beautiful and best hearted of all the maids of honor at the St. Petersburg court.

When Etholin came to Sitka as the manager and director of the Russian American Company, he brought with him his young and beautiful countess, and also the Princess Olga Feodorovna, an olive complexioned orphaned niece, very wealthy and attractive. She was courted by many, and it was said that noblemen in St. Petersburg would have killed for her hand. The Czar thought it wise to exile her elsewhere.

Needless to say, the Russian officers at Sitka were captivated by her beauty even though she encouraged none of them. Some even dueled for her attention. She stood out at the dances and at the race track. She however, distributed her favors impartially.

Her dark eyes were captivating but no pursuers won her over until the blue eyes of Victor Gregorovitch Schupkin, a young nobleman of fine bearing and appearance and a midshipman in the Czar's Navy aroused her attention and favor at a reception at the officer's club. Olga confessed to her aging and faithful mistress, who had accompanied her across the ocean, that she had at last found the only man she could ever love. That mutual love was reciprocated by the midshipman. As the romance developed, the other naval personnel were jealous and envious of the one who had captured the heart of the most beautiful lady in the governor's court.

A person of tender heart and merciful in her royal calling, Princess Olga was willing to give it all up for the light of her life. It didn't at first appear that the governor objected to the romance, but then came along Prince Ivan Sergovitch to Sitka. The aggressive roue had wasted his fortunes in riotous living and gambling. He had depleted much of his parent's fortune as well as that of his wife. It was said he'd driven his spouse to despair, insanity, and finally death.

This despot had unfortunately fastened his attention on Princess Olga earlier when she was in St. Petersburg, and was quick to learn of her presence in Sitka. The Prince boasted of his and the Alaska

Old (Baranof) castle, or governor's administration building, the way it appeared in its last year before burning. One source says the fire occurred in 1894, but the above W.H. Case photo is marked 1899. It gradually fell to disuse after the U.S. Army contingent was pulled out in the late 1870s.

This photo probably taken in the 1920s shows a new building where the four Russian "castles" once stood. Sitka Harbor with its historic waterfront city is nestled in a highly picturesque setting.

governor's boyhood friendship back in Mother Russia. It was that friendship which led him to Alaska after the death of his wife. The aging tyrant's attention to the Princess Olga became very assiduous but she wanted no part of him. He probably was most interested in her considerable wealth.

Somehow, he worked his devious ways in a continuing dialogue with Governor Etholin. It was then learned that the governor and the prince in their youth had been members of the "Society of the North", a secret revolutionary assembly of the 1820s, among its members, a number of young officers and students belonging to nobility.

It was generally believed that the governor of St. Petersburg, the redoubtable Miloradovitch, hero of 52 battles, was assassinated while addressing a mob engaged in rioting during the first days of the reign of Czar Nicholas. He was supposedly killed by a bullet from the gun of a member of that revolutionary society.

The account was revived at Sitka through rumor, and it was reasoned at the Officer's Club that the governor had been the designated tool by the "Society of the North" in the assassination of the general, and that his friend the prince was aware of the fact and had threatened to reveal the secret to the "Third Section", feared by all political offenders of the country. In other words it was imagined that this piece of information, call it a type of blackmail, gave the wicked prince some control over the governor.

Thus it was that the governor demanded his niece accept the prince's hand in marriage.

Princess Olga was adamant; no way would she marry this individual who totally revolted her. In fact, she declared she would die first. In turn, she revealed to the governor that she was passionately in love with the young midshipman, a man with no ties to royalty.

Her retort angered the governor and he took out his revenge on the young naval officer. First he barred him from the "castle", insulted, and belittled him at every opportunity. It was his plan to drive Victor into a desperate act whereby he could legally imprison the man.

The young couple secretly pledged each other a vow according to Russian custom. By the princess giving her lover a lock of her hair, and by his presenting her with a consecrated silver engagement ring, some bread and salt plus an almond cake, they agreed to meet each other in secret rendezvous.

Lover's lane was near Indian River, a place of natural beauty. In a small town, word of any happening was quickly spread, and when the governor learned of the situation, he plotted a way to break it up.

It was in September of that year that the Russian sloop of war *Ouropa*, skippered by Captain Tebenkoff, was given secret sailing orders to depart immediately on a cruise along the west coast of Alaska for the purpose of bringing the Eskimos, north of the Yukon, under strict submission to the Czar.

Guess who was ordered aboard the ship? Young midshipman Gregorovitch came aboard with orders to report to the captain. Totally unsuspecting of the nefarious plot he was imprisoned below, after which the vessel cast off in the night shadows. The victim found himself at sea having been given no opportunity to communicate with the princess nor any of his young friends.

The crafty governor now figured that with the handsome midshipman long gone he could get Feodorovna to submit, and marry the wicked prince. Little did Etholen know the strong will of the princess. Her heart was broken when she learned of the devious plot, and made no secret of the fact that she hated the prince and would gladly face death rather than ever marry the man. Four months elapsed with never a day that Princess Olga didn't pine for her lover. It was then that the governor forcefully enlisted Father Veniaminoff's services, demanding that he unite the prince and princess in holy matrimony. Told to persuade the beautiful girl to sacrifice her love and happiness in order to save the threatened honor of her uncle, the reluctant priest began his unholy crusade. The bishop told the princess that she had a royal obligation to her deceased foster-mother. Against every resistance, the priest persisted until the teary-eyed girl was virtually forced to relent. Made to appear less painful, she was told that if nothing more was heard from her lover that she would marry the prince on the governor's birthday, March 18, 1844.

Of course, the fatal day arrived without word from the midshipman, and the princess was made to believe that her lover had perished at sea under some mysterious circumstance. The truth had purposely been kept secret from Olga. Even with the terse rumors, she still refused to believe her man had perished. The servants in the government house claimed that often at night she would go to the "castle" cupola accompanied by Nataschenska her faithful mistress. There in the "lighthouse" where the oil lamp gleamed, with a commanding view seaward, she would hold out hope that the running lights of the *Ouropa* would come into view, bringing her lover. Alas, the day of the wedding arrived. Trembling and pale the troubled bride was dressed in the customary pale blue with a silver crown on her raven locks. Her dark eyes appeared dazed as she bravely faced what she had been told was her royal duty. Before the ornate bronze doors in St. Michael's Cathedral she stood staring in space. The cathedral doors enclosed the holy of Bibles, where under church law women were forbidden to enter.

Came the ceremony during which the earthen vessel was broken symbolizing the submission of the wife to her husband, even to the point of dying for him. When the prince tapped her bare shoulder with a whip she was reminded of the punishment in married life should her charms be focused on another. It was then that her lips revealed a slight snarl like that of a cornered canine. There was a savage glint in her eyes. She was obviously broken hearted, but submissive.

As midnight approached and the bridal banquet was in full progress, the insidious aging prince boastfully strutted about overly indulging in wine. The princess on the other hand put on a pretense, but inside all was infelicity. Without eating or drinking she sat rigidly next to the prince trying to force a smile which just wouldn't come.

Came a sudden thunderclap. No, it was not thunder at all but the booming sound of a ship's cannon. The resonant blast brought the revelry of the wedding banquet to a halt. It was immediately learned that a ship had entered the harbor guided by the navigation beacon in the cupola. As always, there was great excitement when a ship came in from the often turbulent waters outside Sitka's harbor. Bonfires were lit on Signal Island. The long absent ship had come home at last.

As the Russian priest closed down his sad tale he looked at the American chaplain. "I imagine you can guess the rest of the story," he repined.

"I reckon I can," said the chaplain.

"Yes," continued the priest, "her broken heart could take no more. She went to her chamber, the very place where you were quartered, and it was there that she took her life."

The chaplain whose ear had been glued to the story of the lady in blue confessed. "I never before believed in ghosts, but I surely do now."

As the two men of the cloth parted company, both left in a state of melancholia, for no jubilation was to be found in such a chronicle.

Perhaps one of the better descriptions of old Sitka (New Archangel) is in the narrative of the British naval officer Sir Edward Belcher R.N., who made a diplomatic visit to the Russian Alaska capital in September of 1837, in command of the H.M.S. *Sulphur*. He was royally entertained at the governor's mansion (castle) which had just received its final touches, having been re-erected over the former edifice. Belcher explained it as being a log structure some 140 feet in length and 70 feet wide. Some of the logs in the building were up to 80 feet in length, dovetailed over each other at angles and treenailed together vertically. The building was rugged, but extremely sound, and fit in well with the rough nature of the frontier town. It was built, as earlier mentioned, by Kupreanov (Kupreianov) and was aptly protected by a fortress containing 40 cannon, mostly ship type cannon, 12 and 24 pounders.

Belcher also wrote that the fortress was well stocked and could come to immediate action in case of provocation. He did wonder how well the building would stand up if in a battle with an enemy warship. Fortunately, the stronghold was never tested. It had a vulnerable pitched roof covered with sheet iron.

It was at that governor's mansion and administration building (erroneously referred to an Baranof's castle) that all of the important political and ceremonial programs took place.

Belcher noted that the town was a place of many activities, and was impressed by the sawmill where fine-grained yellow cypress and other softwoods were cut for export to the Sandwich Islands and for use at the local shipyard.

Further, he visited the lighthouse, a cupola atop the "castle" where burned the only marine beacon or lighted aid to navigation in the whole of Alaska. A whale oil lamp had previously existed at the site but with the completion of the new building it was somewhat refined. It was a beacon of hope to Russian seafarers after the long and arduous voyage from Siberia. It was also the place where the ghost of the late princess would often appear, a wraith that frightened those who maintained the copper lamp. They often complained of strong drafts and a flickering flame when the lady in blue appeared.

Belcher was the guest of governor Kupreianov (Kupreanov), while his ship swung at anchor just off the waterfront. The crew had been given orders to conduct themselves in a proper manner inasmuch as the ship was on a diplomatic mission.

The governor told Belcher to consider himself at home and to feel free to visit any of the interesting facets or sites in the town. Belcher, who befriended his host, wrote:

"He speaks English well, and with true English feeling acted up to all he professed; indeed his civilities were overpowering."

The *Sulphur* was only a cable's length from the arsenal opposite an observatory on an island in the harbor. Belcher observed that, "We had the good fortune to obtain complete sights and secure our meridian before midnight."

The natives were allowed to visit the *Sulphur*, bringing with them salmon and furs. The governor, however, had already provided the ship with more fish than the crew could consume, and the captain forbade any traffic in pelts by his crew since the practice was forbidden by the laws of the colony. The governor further discouraged further contacts with the Tlingits, claiming that two years earlier their fortress had been threatened. He cautioned that even though there were only 700 natives in and around the colony, 7,000 could arrive in a matter of hours. The attack by Tlingits three decades earlier was constantly on the minds of the Russians. Belcher wrote that the establishment was out of all contact with the Tlingits, "except through a portcullis door, admitting into a railed yard for those bringing goods to market. This door is closely watched by two or three guards who upon the least noise or dispute in the market, drop the portcullis, and proceed summarily with the delinquents."

Trade according to Belcher was generally conducted by native women and children. The Russians even employed women spies in the native village, who warned the Muscovites of any hostility. Further, Kodiak Islanders conducted the greater share of the business with the Tlingits who caught and cured fish for general consumption.

The British ship commander noted the absence of able-bodied men in his stroll through town. The majority were out on Russian American Company vessels in a constant search for more furs for export and for local supply. On their return the ships would be laid up until the following spring, and repaired and supplied for future voyages.

Belcher noted that the standards of cleanliness in Sitka were much less than those of a man-of-war, but did concede, "comparative cleanliness and comfort, are found much to admire, particularly in the school and hospital."

On attending a church service, he found the interior of the house of worship, "splendid, quite beyond conception in such a place as this."

The padre, Father Veniaminov (Veniaminoff), who revealed the earlier tale of Princess Olga, was officiating when Belcher visited the capital. In his splendid robes the bishop was described as a powerful athletic specimen of a man, about 45 years of age, Herculean in stature. He took a liking to the visitor and made him feel most comfortable as he showed off his workshop, barrel organ, a barometer, and numerous other articles of his own creation. He was obviously a clever and articulate individual, and despite the fact that he spoke no English the two men got along famously.

On Sundays, both civil and military officers dined at the governor's house. Said Belcher, "They reassemble at 5, take tea, and remain until supper, at 10 or 11, during which interval cards and billiards occupy their time." He went on to say, "The native chiefs pestered the governor for permission to visit the *Sulphur*."

The commander, who kept his man-of-war shipshape and Bristol fashion at all times, consented to a party of 37 of the more desirable natives. Great ceremony was observed on behalf of the Tlingits who were dressed in the most colorful, almost bizarre creations, being generally painted with vermilion. Some wore helmets of wood with carved images of fish, birds, seal, and frogs. It was a parade to behold. Others of the chiefs wore plain conical hats without a rim, which warded off sun and rain. Further, they carried their native shawls, which had been laboriously fashioned of animal fur. A few had cloaks of American sable, superior to those of the Siberians. Most of the natives wore ermine skins loosely about their person. The event was a real treat for the ship's crew, a sight most had never before seen.

Even more impressive than their garb were their canoes which transported them to the ship's side. Excellent examples of water craft, all were carved with grotesque artful figures. After the canoes had circled the *Sulphur*, occupants singing and gesticulating, they were permitted aboard and were presented by the governor.

By now, the native party had swelled to about 100, including wives and hangers on. Seated at tables on the main deck the natives were treated to a feast of rice and molasses followed by diluted grog. All had seconds and again thirds until the excited visitors were feeling quite relaxed. The natives then launched into song and dance, clapping and yelling using musical instruments composed of three hoops with a cross in the center, the circumference closely strung with beaks of the alca arctica.

Come time for the departure of the *Sulphur*. On the night before sailing Belcher recalled, "the governor gave an evening party and dance to show us the female society of Sitka. The evening passed most delightfully; and although the ladies were almost self taught they acquitted themselves with all the ease, and I may add elegance, communicated by European instruction. Although few could converse with their partners, they still contrived to get through the dance without the slightest difficulty. Quadrilles and waltzing were kept up with great spirit, and I was not a little surprised to learn from our good friend and host, that many of the ladies then moving before us with easy and graceful air, had not an idea of dancing 12 months previous. I believe that the society is indebted principally to the governor's elegant and accomplished lady for much of this polish," reasoned Belcher.

It was on May 1, 1840, that governor Kupreianov was replaced by another government official who would take over Russia's affairs in Alaska. He was Captain Second Rank Etholen, who arrived aboard the Russian ship *Nikolai*. In order that he could be instructed in his new duties in the colonies, Kupreianov remained at the post until September 30, affording full instruction to the newcomer. Then, boarding the *Nikolai*, the ex-governor and his wife embarked on a lengthy voyage to the old country by way of San Francisco, Cape Horn, and Rio de Janeiro. The ship finally arrived back at Kronshtadt June 13, 1841, after a stormy trek across thousands of miles of ocean.

Shortly after, Kupreianov was pressed into naval service commanding frigates on the Baltic. In 1852, the gold on his tunic was increased, he being promoted to the coveted rank of vice admiral in the Russian Navy. Death came to him five years later on April 30, 1857. He was survived by his widow.

Kuprieanov's name is prominent in Alaska's geographic features. Kupreanof Harbor, an anchorage between Paul and Jacob Islands in the Aleutians and by Kupreanof Peninsula; by Kupreanof Island, a strait and a mountain, the latter on the north coast of Kodiak Island.

Why Russia elected to give up the Great Land to the United States for a modest sum has always been somewhat of a mystery, but apparently the Czar's administration in St. Petersburg was too absorbed in political and social problems to be concerned about the future of Alaska. Their loss was America's gain.

A slightly different picture angle of Sitka Harbor showing the Booth Fisheries (cannery) building, the hotel, and St. Michaels Church, probably in the 1920s.

CHAPTER THREE
The American Occupation

In thrilling region of thick-ribbed ice;
To be imprisoned in the viewless winds,
and blown with restless violence round
about the pendent world.
—Shakespeare

Uncle Sam's interest in Alaska while under Russian authority was never seriously challenged. America managed to share in the seal hunting bounty by the mid-1800s, and even earlier in 1835 the American whaling vessel *Ganges*, out of Nantucket, took the first whale off Kodiak Island, which was the beginning of the whaling industry in the North Pacific. Between that year and 1869, whaling operations extended well up into the Arctic, but the absence of proper charts, the ice, and enemy action took a toll on American flag vessels. In fact, over two decades, 1846 and 1865, an average of two ships a year were lost.

To protect against foreign fur poachers, Czar Alexander declared a hundred mile offshore limit north of the 51st parallel in 1821. Conventions in 1824 and 1825 with the United States and England legitimized their fur trades, established less extensive Russian boundaries to the south and east, and increased Russian dependence on American supplies.

The vast stretches and little known Alaska waters made it difficult for Russia's Pacific naval fleet to patrol its claimed boundaries. In 1839, the Hudson's Bay Company was granted a pact by the Russian government whereby territory was leased in exchange for supplies from HBC's Oregon territorial farms and London headquarters. That freed the Russians from dependence on Boston merchants and enabled them to sell their meagre California holdings.

A bonus for the United States with the purchase of Alaska from Russia was the acquisition of the sidewheel steamer *Politkofsky* which had been built at Sitka, and was to have been used for both utilitarian and patrol duties. In later years, the tough old vessel was acquired by the Port Blakely Mill Company as a tug.

The Civil War reached Alaskan waters on June 26, 1865, when the confederate privateer *Shenandoah* cruised into the Bering Sea prey-

ing on American whaling vessels. She captured and burned five ships and barks, all unarmed whaling vessels that were taken by complete surprise.

It was easy pickings for the heavily-armed *Shenandoah*. On June 27, the ship *Brunswick* was caught in the ice and the other whalers went to her assistance, as was common practice. In that incident, however, the raider swooped in on the helpless vessels like a tiger shark and destroyed them all. Some 34 whaling vessels were burned in the Bering Sea and Arctic Ocean, exacting a grievous loss to the industry. Four other vessels were captured and bonded, the survivors taken aboard. The multimillion dollar loss from the warfare activities put many New Bedford and Nantucket shipowners into bankruptcy, and gradually San Francisco became the center of the whaling industry in the Pacific. The *Shenandoah*, one of the top confederate raiders, took 38 prizes, and along with the *Florida* and *Alabama* caused a disastrous depletion of the U.S. Merchant Marine.

After the North's victory in the destructive Civil War an epic event occurred in Alaska in Mother Russia's willingness to sell the Great Land to the United States for an agreed $7.2 million, which as has already been mentioned, was fabled as "Seward's Folly". Troubled Russia appeared glad to rid itself of the vast piece of real estate. The average American reasoned that the purchase was only a new government headache.

On that day of transfer after a series of rain storms and overcast skies the sun made a welcome appearance, bathing the town of New Archangel in sparkling hues. Russian craft were abundant in the harbor, ordered there by Prince Dimitrii Petrovich Maksutov. A short distance away were anchored a trio of U.S. Naval vessels. The personnel aboard were ordered to remain on deck until the arrival of a fourth vessel flying the Stars and

Vintage photo taken by Winter and Pond in 1897. It is titled "Str. George W. Elder discharging freight on the rocks near Dyea, Alaska." *Dyea is just north of Skagway, and it is believed that supplies landed for the men on the beach were for their trek to the gold fields. The* Elder *is far in the background near the opposite shore, while the smaller craft are pictured in the foreground including a steamer and two sailing schooners.*

Stripes which carried two commissioners, one representing Russia and the other the American government.

The awaited vessel arrived on that October 18, 1867, occasion and the ceremony took place at 3 P.M. that afternoon—a monumental signing of a document that would transfer away a Russian possession and increase the land area of the United States by more than 20 per cent.

Sister tugs Stacey Foss *and* Sandra Foss *plow proudly through the brine, northbound from Puget Sound for a special project in Alaska. The twin tugs and two Foss barges are on a 20 year ore lightering project in Alaska for Cominco in the Chukchi Sea, north of Kotzebue. The vessels will run a shuttle service from the shallow water loading dock near Kivalina to a position about three miles offshore where the deep-draft bulk carriers anchor to receive the lead and zinc ore. The Foss barges are self-unloading directly into the holds of the mammoth bulkers.*

As the time officially arrived for Uncle Sam to take over, there was an obvious sadness on the faces of the Russians. Further, there was no jubilation on the part of the Tlingits and Aleuts who reasoned that "one master would sail away and another would come." The natives were pensive wondering what the newcomers would bring. Unfortunately, as had happened with many Indian tribes in other parts of the United States, disease, whiskey, and a minor reign of terror persisted. With the indifference of the average American citizen over Seward's folly, the new territory became an obvious undesired white elephant.

American general and statesman Jefferson Davis renamed New Archangel, Sitka, and within a decade of the purchase virtually turned the place into a ghost town. Schools and hospitals lost their staffs. Sanitation was disregarded and looting and debauchery brought about mayhem. Many felt Uncle Sam had destroyed one of the cultural centers of the west and reduced the population to a mere 20 families of which five were Russian, the latter having remained following the purchase. Federal mismanagement and a lackluster military presence turned Sitka into an unacceptable destination. Maksutov had supervised the sale of the properties formerly owned by the Russian American Company and businessmen, mostly from San Francisco, made low bids on materials and sold them for handsome profits in the southern states.

Such excitement had never before been seen in New Archangel, a colony of 2,500 citizens. At that time in history the colony had become culturally mature for a frontier capital. There were some beautiful public gardens, and a theatre in the government administration building where both French and Russian plays were performed to the delight of the social circle. There was also a public library, two scientific institutions, and a cultural center.

The arts were not uncommon in the colony. Several of the upper class citizenry owned a piano or a musical instrument. Further, there were four hospitals to care for the sick and the educational system was sufficient to enroll several students for higher learning in Mother Russia.

As the transfer ceremonies turning Russian Alaska over to the United States continued, there was no small amount of merriment, but it was mixed with a modicum of nostalgia on the part of the Muscovites. Occupied with the packing of their furniture and other personal belongings it was kind of a difficult transition, many of them having adapted well to the Alaskan environment. To have protested the transfer would have been futile, for the Czar's law was final—a deal had been consummated. All of the effort that had gone into the building of the community, the good and the unfortunate, was now water under the bridge. To Baranov (Baranof) went much of the credit for originally getting the colony established, but when he was sent back to Russia in 1819, it was with a small amount of disgrace for some of his cruel practices. He passed away en route to his homeland.

The tug Stacey Foss *mothering one of the specialized* Foss *self-unloading barges being used in a long term operation hauling lead and zinc ore at a dock near Kivalina, Alaska, out to deeper water where large bulk ships will receive the cargo from the barge.* Photo courtesy Foss Maritime Company, with thanks to Michael Skalley.

Three-masted codfishing schooner Azalea, *one of several such vessels that fished the waters of the Bering Sea in bygone years. Built on Humboldt Bay, California, in 1890 as a coastal lumber schooner, she, like many of her breed, ended her days in the cod fishery. Photo by Joe Williamson.*

The onion dome on the St. Michael Russian Orthodox Church was one of the few bright spots in a dismal appearing town that had been reduced to rags. Due credit must go to the Russian administrators who had created a colony of merit out of a pristine wilderness, despite often cruel tactics. That curtain was now closed and the new era began on a very low note. New Archangel had been a flourishing trade center when San Francisco was but a mere village. Other U.S. Pacific Coast ports had never been established or were in their infancy in the early 1800s.

As the Russian flag came down at Sitka and the Stars and Stripes were raised on October 18, 1867, to the beat of drums, nearly 300 Russian sailors and soldiers marched across the parade field. Many reviewed in their minds the years of Russian occupation—the hardships and victories. The local graveyard bore the bodies of many who had given their lives in the Russian crusade in the colony, some back to the time when the Tlingits almost succeeded in driving out the invaders.

A contingent of 250 Americans had marched onto the parade grounds facing the Russian militia as the imperial Russian flag was exchanged for the American banner. Ironically, all did not go according to protocol. While the former flag was being lowered, a brisk wind wound it around the pole, and in spite of tugging and twisting it refused to come down, almost as if in a reluctance to end the imperial rule. As it turned out, a bos'n's chair had to be rigged and a U.S. sailor hoisted up to get it down. Matsutov's attractive young wife then fainted as the Russian flag landed on the bayonets of the soldiers beneath.

More fortunate was the raising of the American flag which snapped to the wind as it climbed the tall pole. Secretary of State William Seward had earlier personally presented the flag to Brigadier General Lovell Rousseau, acting commissioner representing the United States at the ceremony. The general attempted to hold down the cheers of the Americans in deference to the Russians, but his efforts were somewhat in vain. There was however, not the great revelry at the ceremony that Seward had anticipated. In fact, following the celebration most of the Russians prepared for their departure as if in a death march. Only a few of them remained to test out the new regime. Many of the departed had been born in Alaska and had never before seen the Mother Country, nor did they know they'd be losing some of their freedoms enjoyed in Alaska, when under authoritarian rule of tsardom. It was indeed a scene of lamentation as the Russian ships weighed anchor and passed out over the western horizon, most of the passengers and crew glancing back for the final time at a place that had long been their home.

The acquisition of Alaska proved a blessing to American cod fishermen. The Russians didn't necessarily welcome American fishing vessels. Only three schooners composed the Yankee fleet in 1867, but a year later, 14 were engaged. Casualties to the fleet claimed about 30 vessels between 1877 and 1927 with the loss of more than 100 lives.

Captain Mathew Tiernan was first to engage in the codfishing business in 1864 in the brig *Timandra*. He later fished in Siberian waters and then in the Bering Sea with the schooner *Alert*. The Shumagin Banks were discovered in 1867 by the schooner *Minnie G. Atkin*'s skipper.

Within four years of the acquisition of Alaska one of the worst peace time tragedies occurred. It was perhaps the greatest whaling disaster of all time. It happened during the whaling season in the Arctic in the year 1871.

Captain and Mrs. Gus Peterson on the poop deck of the schooner C.A. Thayer *in 1905. Originally a lumber schooner, she later entered the salmon and codfish industry in Alaska. Today, the old vessel is enshrined in San Francisco as an historic and tourist attraction. Another former lumber and later codfish three-masted schooner, the* Wawona, *is on display at Seattle's Northwest Seaport. She too played an important role in the Alaska fishing industry. Both vessels operated only under sail. Photo from collection of the National Maritime Museum Golden Gate Recreational Area.*

Proud full-rigged ship A.J. Fuller *of Northwestern Fisheries Company, operated in the canned salmon industry in Alaska for several years. She came to an unfortunate end in 1918, having just returned from Alaska with a full load of canned salmon. While at anchor in Elliott Bay, Seattle, she was rammed and sunk by the Japanese freighter* Mexico Maru. *Down she went in 40 fathoms with 48,000 cases of canned salmon and 4,000 barrels of salt fish. A large number of passengers on the ship (cannery workers) from Uyak, near Kodiak, had debarked shortly before the accident. The photo is vintage 1915.*

Annually, the fleet sailed for the abundant far north whaling waters, frozen from the Arctic to the Bering Sea in the winter, but open in the spring when the vast field of ice retreats and breaks up. By May and June of 1871 the whaling fleet, under sail, had pushed into that lonely corner of the world.

The whale—sperm, humpback, right, bowhead, and sometimes blues—entered the waters and often the whaleships would follow in their path off the coast of Japan to the Bering Sea. The chase terminated when solid ice appeared. There the ships would spread out off the ice flows for many miles. On this occasion as they arrived at their destination in May of 1871, plowing through the ice floes south of Cape Thaddeus on the Siberian shore to the southwest of Bering Strait.

During the first week of June the seas remained calm but fog predominated. By the middle of the month the ice had broken up more and the fleet pushed farther northward harpooning the great leviathans as they went. By the time the ships reached Plover Bay, a small indentation on the Siberian coast, the whale had all passed into the Arctic waters

Those who manned the whaleships were rough and rugged seafarers used to the hardships of a life on the oceans of the world where ships could sometimes be more than three years away from their homeports. The natural enemies of the whaling fleet were icebergs, ice packs, treacherous seas and currents, not to mention the contrary winds and diminishing food supplies. Whaleship captains were not only prime navigators but diplomats in keeping their crews in subjection on such lengthy voyages.

As far as the Arctic and Bering regions were concerned the skippers of such craft were never too proud to ask the Eskimos for information on the ice and wind conditions, a source that sometimes was the difference between life and death for the ships. During the 1871 season the word was that the whaleships hugging the American shore too closely

would be jammed in—icebound. Unfortunately the advice was not heeded, as the biggest bonanza lay farther north. However, seven of the whaleship skippers finally heeded the warning and returned to the more southerly haunts.

The first disaster occurred on June 14, when the 280 ton bark *Oriole*, out of New Bedford, was stove in by the ice. Her crew was rescued by one of the other whaleships. Often in such cases the fleet captains had wives and families aboard and it wasn't unusual for the rescued to become part of the crew of the rescue ship.

By June 30, all of the fleet had passed Bering Strait and entered the Arctic Ocean. The previous whaling season had claimed the whaleship *Japan*, the crew forced to live among the natives through the long winter season near East Cape. Their ship had become a pawn of the ice, crushed, forcing the 31 survivors to the Siberian shores. Eight of their number perished while eking out an existence among the Eskimos who could only afford them rotten walrus blubber for their diet. Those weary, emaciated survivors were finally rescued and distributed among the whaling fleet, but little did they know what awaited them.

As the leviathans were hunted with impunity, their great carcasses were hauled aboard the respective ships, cut up and rendered, casks filled with their oil. During that season there was an abundance of fog, but it didn't curtail the frequent "Nantucket sleigh rides", when a whale was harpooned in the chase by the whaleboats. Late in July, strong winds set in from the northeast and veered around to the southeast. That cleared the American shore of ice and the fleet sailed for Icy Cape. Considerable ice had grounded along the shore but the fleet, most of the vessels shallow-drafted, crept in behind it. When on August 6 the wind moderated, the ice shifted from the shoals and the ships found a bonanza of whale, off Wainwright.

Less than a week later, the wind hauled to westward and the heavy ice was driven back, encasing some of the whalers. Other units of the fleet under yellowed canvas worked their way among the floes. Unfortunately some of the whaleboats had drifted far away from the mother ships and were frozen in. Their hunters were forced to manually drag their craft up on top of the ice and pull them over the hummocks back to their respective ships.

The wood hulled steamer Humboldt, *a regular on the Alaska run, hard aground on Pender Island in British Columbia on September 29, 1908. She was eventually freed by the salvage steamer* Santa Cruz *and returned to service after an overhaul.*

The sidewheel steamer Politkofsky, *built at New Archangel by the Russians, and left behind as part of the deal when the United States purchased Alaska in 1867. Obviously, the Americans were not overly impressed with the acquisition as was described in the* Victoria Colonist, *evidently from a Yankee's opinion, in 1868. It read: "The steamer POLITKOFSKY is one of the most magnificent specimens of home-made marine architecture we have yet beheld. She looks as if she had been thrown together after dark by an Indian ship carpenter, with stone tools. Her engines are good and were formerly in a Russian fur company's steamer, which was wrecked near Sitka several years ago. Her boiler is of copper and is alone worth the price Captain (Wm.) Kohl paid for the whole concern. We hear she is to be rebuilt; she needs it."*
After reconstruction the vessel held up well after passing to the Port Blakely Mill Company as a tug on Puget Sound.

In the interim the ice solidified, and with no power but sail, the situation smacked of trouble with a capital T. The ships were gradually backed up until iced in and grounded. Refusing to submit, the swarthy whalermen continued to hunt the whale in their open boats even with their ships hemmed in behind the ice jams.

"The wind will change and sweep the ice to sea," they reasoned, "and the whale among the flows will be easy kills," they claimed. In fact, initially they were right, for on August 25, a northeast gale did break up the ice temporarily and drove it offshore. Fair weather and calm seas prevailed for two more days and whale were being harpooned and hauled aboard in large numbers.

After two more days the wind worked around to the southwest, driving the ice back to the Alaskan shores, pinning the fleet between the ice and the land. After some of the ships anchored on the shoals, in less than five fathoms, squalls of snow erupted and the temperature dropped dramatically.

Eskimo advice still went unheeded and now it was too late. On September 2, the 361 ton bark *Comet*, out of San Francisco, was crushed in the ice, followed five days later by the ship *Roman*. The 376 ton New Bedford whaleship *Awashonka* met her demise on the following day, and within the week the remaining ships had to be abandoned. There were 1,219 persons aboard the trapped vessels. Under the capable leadership of Captain D. E. Frazier, of the *Florida*, all were instructed that they must make their way over the ice to shore and then southward to Blossom Shoal. That area was still free of ice and seven whaleships, the remnants of the fleet whose masters had heeded the warning of the Eskimos, would be the means of survival for the displaced.

Before the escape, Captain Frazier held a conference with the survivors pointing out all the problems they would face over the 70 mile obstacle course. First, a boat crew of volunteers was sent out to set the course and alert the seven whaleships of the disaster.

It was on September 14, that the marooned party officially abandoned the 29 ships crushed in the packed ice, lowered and provisioned the whaleboats which had to be dragged over solid ice and rowed through open waters. The first night they camped on the beach. Next day, a fierce wind came up creating more hazards for the over-

loaded boats. Curses filled the air along with prayers for heavenly guidance, but there were no tears nor hysteria. All were people of the sea and courageous in every respect, resigned to their chosen way of life.

After reaching Icy Cape and relative safety, they rendezvoused with the awaiting whaleships which took them to Plover Bay. From there the ships sailed for Honolulu where most of the whaling fleet traditionally wintered over. All 1,219, including some wives and children, had survived safely with a dramatic account to tell of their escape. The ship losses caused a major setback to the whaling industry. American whaling in Alaska during the sail ship era is estimated to have taken nearly 54,000 whale with a fleet numbering 744 vessels. Seventy ship losses were recorded—nearly ten per cent of the total whaling fleet, plus their catches.

The loss of 31 whaling vessels in the 1871 catastrophe was a tragic event in the history of the American merchant fleet, but the fact that no humans perished in the aftermath was somewhat of a miracle. The vessels lost in that disaster in addition to the *Comet*, *Roman*, and *Awashonka*, were the ship *Julian*; brig *Kohola*; bark *Carlotta*; bark *Fanny*; bark *Monticello*; ship *Champion*; bark *Concordia*; bark *Contest*; bark *Elizabeth Swift*; bark *Emily Morgan*; bark *Eugenia*; ship *Florida*; ship *Gay Head*; bark *George*; bark *George Howland*; bark *Henry Tabor*; bark *James D. Thompson*; bark *John Wells*; ship *Mary*; bark *Navy*; bark *Oliver Crocker*; bark *Paiea*; ship *Reindeer*; bark *Seneca*; bark *Thomas Dickason*; brig *Victoria II*; and ship *William Rotch*.

All those staunch vessels were gradually reduced to little more than ice cubes by the powerful unrelenting forces of packed ice.

The New Bedford bark *Eliza* of 296 tons was the next victim of the icy wastes in the 1874 season, followed by the San Francisco-based whaling bark *Clara Bell* two years later. And the toll on the fleet continued in 1897 and 98 when four whaling vessels and a schooner were crushed in the Arctic ice, their crews rescued by the U.S. Revenue Cutter *Bear*.

After the valuable oil-rich bowhead whales were discovered in the western Arctic in 1848 by the whale ship *Superior*, American whalers converged on the area in growing numbers. By 1850, 200 ships were involved in the hunt retrieving oil and bone. Most of the fleet were from New England ports. The earlier mentioned catastrophe off Point Belcher that claimed so many whaleships in a single season put a crimp in the industry due not only to the loss of the ships but also for the huge number of captured whale whose oil and bone were totally lost in the confines of the wrecks. Ice was also the culprit in the sinking of 15 additional whaleships off Point Barrow between 1870 and 1877.

As the last century waned, so did the whaling industry. New sources of fuel and other material extracted from the leviathans were found elsewhere. Some foreign countries have continued the hunt, even in our day. Alaskan natives are allowed to take limited numbers of mammals for their necessities.

The dramatic and adventuresome era of hunting the whale had a parallel in the slaughter of the seal, the sea lion, and the otter. Alaska also played a major role in that industry.

When the Muscovites gave up the foothold in California there was a lull in fur hunting, except in Alaska and Siberia, where the Russians held a monopoly. High prices were paid for the yield, especially in St. Petersburg.

It was an enterprising Scotsman, Captain William Spring, born in Russia, who was the grandfather of the later commercial sealing industry. He and Captain Hugh McKay began trading along the northwest coast in the early 1850s and established posts where they often enlisted the assistance of native hunters. The Indians would bring in seal and sea otter skins to the posts to barter. In fact, it was the natives that had long been catching the mammals from their canoes, most of the skins and oil used for their own subsistence.

Another who entered the business in that time frequency was Captain J. D. Warren. He, along with the other pioneers, developed a good relationship with the Indians and encouraged them to catch more seal and otter. By 1868, the redmen were playing a big role, many becoming crew members on sealing schooners such as the *Surprise*, *Alert*, and *Kate* which carried crews up to 30 men each.

Captain Spring had the schooner *Favorite* built at Sooke, B.C., for trading, but she proved too small as a freight carrier between British Columbia and Hawaii. She was converted to a sealer in 1874, and as her name indicated became a favorite in the business.

Americans earlier became interested in the sealing opportunities in Russian Alaska waters but were restricted. After the purchase of the Great Land things were different. The rich breeding grounds were reputedly the only place where handsome profits could be made. Within a year of the Alaska purchase the schooner *Pioneer* made a successful haul in the Pribilof Islands. Later that same year Hutchinson, Kohl, and Company secured exclusive rights to capture seal on both St. George and St. Paul Islands. Because of those rights the grant began a series of problems in the Bering Sea. Protection of the monopoly by Uncle Sam brought about an expenditure of millions of dollars. In order to compete, many of the sealers sought the protection of the British flag.

Nobody realized the magnitude of the business at first, but monopolies such as were granted the Alaska Commercial Company forced many of the sealing fleet to hunt in British Columbia, Washington, and Oregon. The prices of skins remained high and catches were profitable even in the lower latitudes. Hauls such as made by the schooner *Ariel*, which in a single day took 131 seals, while the *Juanita* captured 500 in two and a half days, were common. One schooner, the *Mary Parker*, in the 1878-79 season had more than 40 Makah Indians as the compliment of the schooner. Later Indians in some cases became the sole owners of their own schooners and sloops.

The year 1883, was the basic beginning of the full scale thrust of American sealing vessels into the Bering Sea. The initial vessel was the *City of San Diego*, out of San Francisco, in charge of Captains Cathcart and McLean. With some trepidation they entered the disputed territory arriving back in Victoria with 900 skins plus a few from polar bears.

The Alaska Commercial Company, successors to Hutchinson, Kohl and Company received furs from the brig *Salina*, Captain Miller, from far away as Petropaulovski in 1884, and then promptly secured the right to slaughter 100,000 seals annually on St. Paul and St. George Islands with equal privileges on Copper Island. The largest take in the 1884 season was by Captain Alex McLean in the *Favorite*, some 1,754 skins. Such huge takes would over the years begin the depletion of the mammals unless some kind of control was started. However, the rich rewards from the catches left control in the disputed phase with no real effort for conservation.

As the schooners increased in number, the prices for skins decreased and who was crying "Uncle" but the Alaska Commercial Company that had held a 20 year lease on the breeding islands. It was then that the USRC *Corwin* was dispatched to the Bering Sea with orders to seize all vessels engaged in hunting seal. Three vessels, the

Two old prints depict whaling in the Arctic in the early days. Upper print shows a typical whaling vessel surrounded by whaleboats pursuing the leviathans. Lower photo shows a portion of the whaling fleet in 1871, the disastrous season that claimed several of the ships in the unrelenting ice floes. The scene probably depicts the barkentine Roman *being crushed like an eggshell among the ice floes.* Mystic Seaport print.

Thornton, Onward, and *Caroline* were the first captured by the government cutter.

A cry of foul play echoed across the country as that most regrettable practice was carried out. Sealing vessels were seized on the high seas, a territory recognized under international law as free maritime waters open to all countries. Some of the captured crews of the schooners were set adrift in dories without food or water while others were imprisoned and fined. Still others were marooned in the northland to fend for themselves. Uncle Sam had succumbed to an Alaska Commercial Company monopoly. It was a blatant disgraceful act to say the least, in fact one seal schooner skipper, Captain James Ogilvie, mysteriously vanished after his schooner *Caroline* was seized, and the blood was on the hands of the federal government. All of the schooners seized in 1886 were at least 60 miles offshore, in international waters. Despite the increasing takes of seal the rookeries continued to be populated. The main reason for the seizures was that the government, at the insistence of the Alaska Commercial Company, claimed the seals were in danger of extinction. The situation continued to be hotly contested. It was, however, true that some of the maverick sealers were greedy of overkill.

At the trial of the captured schooner *Thornton*, Captain Gullormansen, Judge Dawson announced that, "By the treaty of March 30, 1867, between Russia and the United States, the western boundary line of Alaska passes through a point in Bering Strait on the parallel of 65° 30' north, at its intersection by the meridian which passes midway between the islands of Krusenstern and Ignalook and proceeds north without limitation into the same frozen ocean. The same western limit, beginning at the same initial point proceeds thence in a course nearly southwest through Bering Strait and the Bering Sea, so as to pass midway between the northwest point of the island of St. Lawrence and the southwest point of Cape Chaukotski to the meridian of 172° west, from the intersection of that meridian in a southwesterly direction so as to pass midway between the island of Attou and the Copper Island of the Kounavdoski couplet or group in the North Pacific Ocean to the meridian of 193° west so as to include the territory conveyed to the western end of the Aleutian Archipelago and the chain of islands are to be considered as comprised within the waters of Alaska, and all penalties prescribed by law against the killing of fur bearing animals must therefore attack against any violation of law within the limits before described."

The three schooners meanwhile lay in abandonment on Alaska beaches, and though Judge Dawson's ruling was right in a sense, the government was afterward called to a point of contradiction that was overlooked in the trial, that of the period when Russia secured her rights to the disputed waters. Reference was made to a Bering Sea seizure of an American whaler, the *Bounty*, by Russia in 1821. In that incident, the U.S. government protested that Russia had no jurisdiction beyond the three-mile limit. The *Bounty* was in turn released and an indemnity paid its owners.

A red-faced Uncle Sam was in turn forced to release the three schooners, but indignantly refused to recompense the owners for their losses. The prisoners were set free but not given so much as an apology.

Seizures continued in 1887 for violations; six American and six British (Canadian) sealers were captured. One of their number, the *Champion*, Captain Dwyer, was ordered to Sitka. Her crew mutinied and demanded her skipper set a course back to Victoria to avoid imprisonment of the crew. Another schooner defied orders to sail for Sitka by the USRC *Rush* and made a run for San Francisco. Still the

The regrettable whaling season in 1871, which destroyed the majority of the fleet in the Arctic Seas, in an artist's rendition of the trapped ships awaiting their fate. Photo courtesy of Mystic Seaport.

hunt went on and crafty skippers found more ways of escape when the black smoke plumes of the cutters were spotted on the distant horizon. Some of the schooners were now returning with up to 2,500 skins. In one year the Victoria fleet took 12,084 skins along the coast and 12,716 in the Bering Sea.

Not only were Revenue Cutters patrolling American waters, but the Russians, out of Siberian ports, were patrolling their territorial waters and capturing units of the sealing fleet.

Continued protection of the seals by the American Government brought worldwide mocking as the cagey Canadian shipmasters often gave the patrol craft the slip.

Though some of the seized vessels were sold at auction, the illegal hunt went on as usual. One schooner was actually taken while in for repairs at Unalaska in 1890, but later released, and another, the *Pathfinder*, was seized for the second time in 1890, in port at Neah Bay, by the USRC *Corwin*. Her captain was accused of running away with a prize crew. The vessel, however, was soon released.

The United States and British diplomats endeavored to solve the continued differences by setting up several rules and regulations over the next few years. There was even an international parley at Paris over the dispute, but even though the business declined in the 1890s it wasn't solved until four nations—the United States, England, Japan, and Russia—convened in an effort to save the seal from extinction in 1911. The Bering Sea Fur Seal Controversy gave the U.S. the right to enforce provisions.

Japan withdrew in 1941. Under the protection, the seal herds, especially in the Pribilofs, have greatly increased. Proper control is strictly exercised, and much to the consternation of several present day commercial salmon fishermen, the seal are protected not only in Alaska but all along the Pacific Coast.

The era of the sealing schooners was a rough and rugged occupation for crew and hunters. In fact, there were no acceptable accommodations on any of those vessels. Food was barely palatable at times although they seldom ran out of fish to catch between the killing of seals.

One might ask what was the worst occupation, whaling or sealing? Though the whaleships were considerably larger, the long tedious voyages and endless months away from home made it a trying profession, not to mention the odiferous decks smeared with blood, guts, and oil. On the sealers the quar-

Named for Navy Lieutenant William P. McArthur, the auxiliary schooner pictured here was constructed at the Mare Island Navy Yard in 1870 to survey the waters of Alaska and the Pacific Coast. A second ship of the same name was built at Seattle in 1966. Lieutenant McArthur, pictured below, was 34 years old when he received orders in 1848 to command the hydrographic party sent to make the initial major survey of the west coast for the U.S. Coast Survey in the topsail schooner Ewing. After departing New York for San Francisco he found it next to impossible to keep his crew together, with many jumping ship to join the gold rush in California. Most of the deserters were captured, four of whom were hung for mutiny. Photo courtesy of Naval History Magazine photo.

ters were overcrowded, sometimes 30 to 40 men on a 70 or 80 foot vessel where, if one had to relieve himself, he either balanced on the tip of a boom or squatted half way over the gunwales. Unlike the whalers, the seal hunts were seasonal but always subject to ice-filled seas or capture and imprisonment for poaching in restricted waters.

Indeed, the loss of sealing schooners and those who manned them was somewhat legion as indicated by the following disasters in 1895 alone:

Schooner *C. G. White* wrecked in a driving snowstorm at Kodiak Island, April 14, 1895, with a loss of 11 men.

Schooner *Walter A. Earle* capsized in a storm off Cape St. Elias with the loss of her entire compliment, six white men and 26 Indians.

Schooner *Rosie Olsen* struck a reef and was wrecked entering Hakodate Harbor, June 1895, but crew was saved along with 627 seal skins.

Canadian schooner *Brenda* lost July 2, 1895, on Shumshu Islands off the Kuriles.

Schooner *Dart* wrecked April 1895, off Carmanah Point, B.C., etc.

The following year in the summer, the Schooner *May Belle* was lost with all hands, sealing on the Asiatic side.

Other regretful tragedies among the sealing fleet were vessels like the *Felix* lost with all hands in 1885 in a gale off Robben Island. The *Cygnet* was lost with all hands in the North Pacific in 1876 in the Bering Sea. *Carolina II* was lost with all hands in the Pacific, 1880s, and the *Lottie* capsized off Tillamook Bay in 1892 with 28 contraband Chinese aboard. All hands lost. The *Maggie Mac* vanished in North Pacific in 1892 with a crew of 22. *Mary Brown* was lost October 1893, off Banks Island, B.C., with the loss of all hands. *Mascot* capsized off the Japan coast in 1894, all hands lost. Likewise the *Matthew Turner*

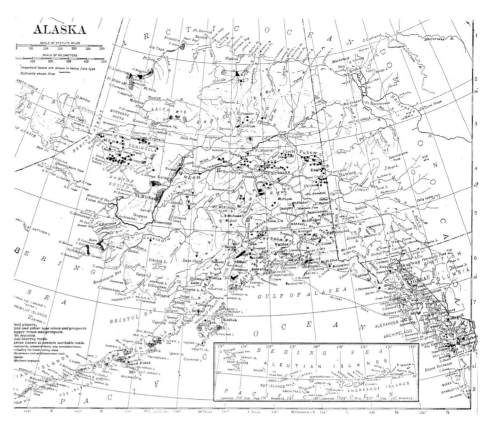

Map of the vast Territory of Alaska as it appeared in the 1921 edition of the P.F. Collier and Son's New World Atlas and Gazetteer. *The territory did not become a state until 1959, the 49th star in the American flag.*

was lost off the Japan coast in 1894 with the loss of her entire crew and 857 skins. *R. Eacrett* was wrecked on St. Lawrence Island in a snowstorm, November 1899, all hands except one survivor died of starvation. *Sarah Louise* was lost in the 1880s in the North Pacific with all hands.

The above are a few of the many ship losses in the sealing fleet. At best it was a daring and demanding challenge.

A typical sealer for instance was the *Mary Ellen*. She was a Canadian schooner of 77 tons, built at San Francisco in 1863, 75 feet long with a beam of 23 feet. She sealed continuously from 1881, after coming from other trades. Owned by Captain William Spring of Victoria, B.C., she was skippered by the well known Captain Daniel McLean. As a Canadian schooner she was first to carry all white men as hunters (usually natives) and the first pelagic sealer to enter the Bering Sea. In 1884, her catch was 1,954 skins for which $7.50 a piece was paid. The following year the vessel took 2,309 skins, a record up to that time. Then in 1886, McLean broke his own record, in fact, the all-time record for pelagic sealing, some 4,268 skins for the season.

McLean's brother, Captain Alex, then took command of the *Mary Ellen* and was likewise successful the next two years with catches of 3,525 and 2,319 respectfully.

In 1890, the vessel was wrecked near Sand Point, Alaska, after taking 1,066 skins. The wreck was sold for a mere $150. Enterprising Captain William Jacobson then managed to salvage the sealer and refurbish her. For the next two seasons, he was her master, but the take of seal was somewhat minimal. Then Captain William Hughes skippered the schooner with some success off the coast of Japan.

In 1898, only 276 skins were taken, and the *Mary Ellen*'s role in the sealing industry came to an end. In that same year, numerous other sealing vessels threw in the sponge and gradually, with more restrictions, and governmental controls, the free-wheeling pelagic sealing industry began fading into oblivion.

Left: *Gold fever reigned when this photo was taken at Seattle following news of the Alaska gold strike in the Klondike, just before the turn of the century. Despite a sprinkling of snow, people swarmed on the dock and aboard the famous SS* Victoria. *Courtesy of the Joe Williamson collection.*

CHAPTER FOUR
Lighthouses and Other Aids to Navigation

And or'e them the lighthouse looked
lovely as hope. That star of
life's tremulous ocean.
—Paul M. James

Alaska has always been declared as America's last frontier. And, Alaska was the last part of America that was given consideration for primary aids to navigation. For more than a quarter century after this huge land was purchased from the Russians, it was almost entirely disregarded when it came to safeguarding its waterways. Still the coastline covered multi-thousands of miles. It took a gold rush to finally awaken Uncle Sam to the urgent need for increased buoys and major lighthouses, but most of the latter were not established until the stampede began to slow. The great armada of ships that traveled the Inside and Outside passages often fell victim to the rocks, reefs, and shoals which for the most part were unmarked.

It was on July 27, 1868, that the "customs, commerce and navigation" laws of the United States were applied to Alaska. Then why was the government so slow in taking action, the reader might ask? There was a certain amount of apathy and indifference as authorities considered the coastline of Alaska. It was greater than that of the entire contiguous states. The task was formidable to say the least, but inaction appeared the immediate response, with a wait and see attitude. True, Alaska was later included in the 13th Lighthouse District with Oregon and Washington, but it was treated like a long, lost cousin.

Alaska's initial navigation beacon was shown from the cupola atop the Russian administration building (erroneously called Baranof's Castle) from 1837 until the time of the American purchase of Alaska in 1867. Prior to the 1837 installation it is said that a small lamp of sorts was mounted above the fortress walls surrounding the government building. The U.S. Army afforded an attendant for the light after the take-over in 1867. When the contingent left a decade later, little care was given to the lamp and the only lighted navigation light in the whole of Alaska no longer shined. The official Light List of 1895 published by the Government Printing Office did list a light, Alaska's only one, as a fixed white Tubular Lantern 108 feet above sea level on Castle Rock, the site of Russia's old castle. It was a lantern on a white gallows frame as a guide for the channels leading to Sitka Harbor. It was established in the year 1895. The sketch shows the "castle" as it appeared under the Russians.

After the purchase of Alaska, President Andrew Johnson submitted a report prepared by the eminent George Davidson, of the U.S. Coast Survey, who was in charge of an expedition to Alaska in 1867, at Secretary of State William Seward's request.

In the aftermath of that report, the Lighthouse Board requested the Coast Survey to appoint a qualified individual to locate logical locations for lighthouses in Alaskan waters. That job logically fell to Davidson who submitted his findings in 1869. He suggested two lighthouses be placed in Sitka Sound, one at Edgecumbe and Biorka Islands; one at Long Island and Near Island, close to Kodiak, and two lighthouses near Dutch Harbor, Unalaska Island.

Further, Davidson suggested logical places for buoys and unlighted beacons. Oddly enough, no suggestions in the early reports were made for aids to navigation in Southeastern Alaska, where existed the intricate Inside Passage. The latter section of Alaska was still extremely virgin in those early years and most settlements nothing more than native villages. It was indeed ironic that the Inside Passage would eventually become the prime trade route of Alaska with its capital located in Juneau. It must be remembered, however, that those early reports involved the utilized sealanes of Alaska which had been developed by the Russians, Sitka being the main port of call.

To Davidson's credit was the fact that all of his recommendations eventually received aids to navigation, but none a lighthouse. Congress, however, took no action to reserve lands in Alaska for lighthouse purposes. Almost like rubbing Seward's face in the mud after his so-called folly, the solons in Washington D.C. considered the far north more a liability than an asset. Commerce to the far north was limited at that period in history, and with distressing indifference Davidson's recommendations were dropped into file 13.

Instead, the Lighthouse Board burdened with the installation and expenses of building lighthouses in contiguous maritime states decided to take the easy road out. "Use whatever the Russians left behind," was their final decision. The only lighthouse in all of Alaska under Russian rule was at the top of the Administration Building or Governors House, referred to as Baranof's Castle. Other minor aids to navigation left by the Muscovites were red and blue buoys that marked a submerged rock near Long Island (called Williams Bank) where the Russian American Company ship *Kodiak* met with disaster in April 1860. Those buoys in question tended to move out of position, dragging their moorings in time of howling winds and contrary seas. In all probability they were ignored when the Yankees took over, and probably not maintained.

So, the only usable beacon inherited by the United States in the exchange was in the cupola, a lantern house at the top of the castle, 110 feet above sea level, a place where the Russians maintained it from the completion of the building in 1837. Prior to that time, it is believed a lantern was maintained at the fortress near the earlier government buildings, especially when a company vessel was expected to arrive.

Following instructions from the Lighthouse Board, an agreement was made with the customs official at Sitka whereby the U.S. Army contingent stationed there would be responsible for the maintenance of the light. It was upgraded from the beacon the Russians had used consisting of oil lamps fueled by either whale or seal oil, made up of four copper cans placed in front of a large reflector.

The U.S. Army keeper of the light was paid by the Lighthouse Board a sum of forty cents a day. He, acting ordinance Sergeant George Golkell, performed his duties faithfully until his unit was moved out of Sitka in 1877. What happened in the maintenance of the beacon

century. Between 1895 and 1900 the number of aids actually decreased by one iron buoy. The lighthouse tender *Columbine* would travel from Puget Sound to maintain the buoys.

The most northerly of the buoys was placed on Indian Rock, 20 miles south of Skagway. It was actually removed from another location because of increased ship traffic in the wake of the Klondike gold discovery, which made Skagway the terminus for the northerly overland trek by thousands of gold hungry individuals heading for the Yukon via Whitehorse.

When a Seattle newspaper reporter came out with the dramatic story of the SS *Portland* arriving from Alaska with a ton of gold, the news spread across the nation and around the world like wild fire. Suddenly the quiet city of Seattle became a beehive of activity, and ships of every kind and description came to Puget Sound ports to meet the demands of the scores of passengers willing to pay inflated prices to get to Skagway. A popular song in recent years pretty much told the story, "North to Alaska, goin' north the rush is on."

SS Princess May high and dry on reef off Sentinel Island, Alaska. She stranded August 5, 1910, embarrassingly near the Sentinel Island Lighthouse. All passengers were safely evacuated and a major salvage effort begun, which resulted in the eventual removal of the ship. She was ushered off to drydock for extensive repairs. The passengers were temporarily cared for by the keepers at the lighthouse. Photo courtesy of Winter & Pond.

after that date is somewhat sketchy in historical annals, but whatever the case, it appeared the light was mostly neglected as the importance of Sitka as a seaport declined. In addition, no other lighthouses were established in Alaska for the next two decades, a travesty of sorts.

Before the old "castle" building burned in 1894, it had slowly gone into disrepair, appearing for all the world like a genuine haunted house. The exterior was badly weathered, most of the windows broken, doors smashed in, and roof leaking. The cupola where the beacon had once glowed was a shambles, with most of the lantern panes broken and paint peeling. Even the fortress that had once surrounded the building was almost nonexistent, vegetation having shadowed the remains.

Cries of outrage were now coming from other parts of Alaska where increasing maritime traffic demanded the government do something about protecting shipping from the peril of shipwreck. On the rise were industries like salmon-canning, mining, and tourism in the late 1870s, and in the following decade commerce by sea showed a substantial growth in Southeastern Alaska. So great was the need that the Pacific Steamship Company even offered free transport of buoys, while pointing out the perils in both Tongass and Wrangell Narrows to theirs and vessels of other lines. Pacific Steamship had already suffered the loss of the SS *Eureka* in Peril Strait. Owners of sailing vessels, steamships, and fishing craft, including the whalers, were joined by chambers of commerce and newspapers in lighting a match under the seat of those on the Lighthouse Board to get immediate action.

In 1884, with stingy funds, the agency managed to send 14 iron buoys to Southeast Alaska. Navy workers placed them at strategic locations. Naval Commander L. A. Bearslee insisted on an aid to navigation at Vitskari Island, near Sitka, close to where Davidson had earlier suggested a lighted beacon and a fog signal in the form of a cannon (such as the one used at Point Bonita, near San Francisco).

Preoccupied by growing pressure for more lights and buoyage in Oregon and Washington, the Lighthouse Board continued to give Alaska the cold shoulder.

Finally in 1895, a year after the old "castle" burned, Uncle Sam placed a lens-lantern on Castle Hill with William Marrett appointed as its keeper. There would not be another until after the turn of the

To say the least, the waterways to Alaska from Puget Sound and British Columbia were totally unprepared for what was to follow. Further pleas to the Lighthouse Board still fell on deaf ears because financially the funds were not available. In fact, the lighthouse agency had requested funds for a lighthouse on Mary Island at the important entrance to Revillagigedo Channel as early as 1890. Two years later a customs house was established on the island and the Lighthouse Board recommended that the inhabitants, for a fee, might maintain a minor light there. The suggestion fell flat.

Despite the fact that the gold rush did focus attention on safeguarding waterways, there was still a lot of red tape in the nation's capital. Meanwhile, shipwreck and minor strandings became weekly occurrences.

Not only did the gold rush spur activity, it was also the opening of Alaska as a territory of importance. Every facet of business followed the gold seekers, and the ports of Southeast Alaska took on a golden glow. Once the Russian center of Alaska's maritime commerce, Sitka's importance greatly diminished.

Alaska territorial governor John G. Brady got on the bandwagon with the backing of steamship companies and allied industries with his following remarks:

"Commerce has grown so rapidly and there are now so many millions of dollars invested in steamships plying in these waters that the time has come to separate Alaska into a Lighthouse District. There is work enough to keep an inspector and tender busy. British Columbia is far surpassing us in this particular. Soon they will have completed four new lights at important points upon the Inside Passage. We should have as many now between Tongass and Skagway."

In its annual report of 1893 the Lighthouse Board pointed out the many requests for navigation lights in Alaska and urged the implementation of a separate lighthouse district. A request by that agency for $300,000 for lighthouses at eight strategic locations in both southeastern and western Alaska were made, but Congressional foot dragging continued.

Finally on June 6, 1900, Congress, shaken up by the powers to be, coughed up an appropriation of $100,000 for light stations in Alaska. Immediately the board ordered the 13th Lighthouse District to dispatch the district inspector and an engineer to survey the suggested sites. Their findings not only confirmed prior recommendations but added five more of their own. Priority was given to Southeast Five Finger Island and Sentinel Island, important locales on the Inside Passage.

Without further delay details and plans were approved, and Alaska's first American lighthouses were under construction in July

1901. First to be lighted was Five Finger, followed by Sentinel Island, both on March 1, 1902. At last, a new era had dawned and by now the world was very aware that Alaska was of commercial value.

The Lighthouse Board recommendations were henceforth handled with rapidity, and appropriations of $500,000 were allocated for other lighthouses in the 1901-03 period. It was in the latter year that the Lighthouse Board was transferred from the Treasury Department to the Department of Commerce and Labor. By then, five lighthouses manned by capable civilian keepers were displaying their beacons nightly. By 1904, the number of navigation lights had doubled, some only minor lights, displaying what the agency labled lens-lanterns, fixed lights with reservoirs attached, for lamp oil. All of the new installations were in Southeast Alaska except those at remote Unimak Island-Scotch Cap and Cape Sarichef, the most lonely locations for aids to navigation in the Pacific.

As the lighthouses gained prominence as navigation aids on Alaska waterways, little attention was given to minor aids such as buoys and daymarks. Of the 15 lighted aids in 1905, 11 were lighthouses, a poor balance.

A major problem in Alaska sea transit were the frequent pea soup fogs and the long winter darkness. The 15 lighted aids were only the tip of the iceberg, and the urgent necessity for more and better signals were continually in demand. Those demands would lead to the badly needed Alaska Lighthouse District. A lighthouse tender, to be Alaska's own, was necessary to supply the increased number of installations with oil, food, mail, and other necessities. Additionally, and just as important, was the placing and maintenance of buoys.

The stranding of the famous SS *Portland* in this time frame was due to the inability of the lookouts to spot the Spire Island buoy which had been carried away from its assigned anchorage. Reefs, rocks, and uncharted menaces to navigation were taking an increasing toll in ships and human life.

The Lighthouse Board felt it now had a tiger by the tail with the demands in the northland. Only Nome and Nunivak Island in the further northern latitudes received minor navigation lights, but the Bering Sea, icelocked for part of the year, was given little heed. Post lights were, however, placed on the Yukon River near its mouth.

Other places given priority were at remote outside locations— Cape Spencer, Cape Decision, and Resurrection Bay, and with the new Alaska Railroad at Seward, an increase in marine traffic from Juneau via Cross Sound would demand other lights and fog signals in the sector.

Eldred Island Lighthouse in southeastern Alaska overlooking Lynn Canal has been active since 1905. In the foreground is the tramway leading up to the island plateau. Beautifully situated, it is frequently photographed by tourists on the many cruise ships that pass the island. Inset shows the lighthouse on a flat water day before the station was automated. Photo courtesy of U.S. Coast Guard.

Aerial view of Eldred Island Light Station showing the rocky terrain on which it stands. Photo courtesy of U.S. Coast Guard.

excess of $31 million. It further pointed out 46 total ship losses in a ten year period. There were seven ship losses in 1910 alone, valued at $625,000, plus several additional strandings where salvage efforts proved successful. Between 1878 and 1911 some 79 large vessels were lost, not counting smaller craft for which no records were documented.

It was pointed out that a large share of the ship disasters might have been prevented had aids to navigation been on station. Increasing protestors noted that if Canada could supply 105 navigation aids along 600 miles of coastline, the Lighthouse Service should be able to do considerably better along 3,000 miles of coastline.

In the interim, successful tests on navigation lights burning acetylene gas brought about changes. Where kerosene lamps needed constant supervision, the acetylene lamps could sometimes go for six months unattended, and only cost $1,800 to maintain annually. For the most part, the major lighthouses were equipped with fourth order prismatic lenses, some fitted with incandescent vapor oil lamps, attended daily by keepers.

Congress approved the building of Cape St. Elias Lighthouse in 1911, plus additional minor lights, but public demands for more and better installations continued unabated.

In 1914, Congress, in conjunction with the Alaska Engineering Commission, provided funds for a federally-owned railroad for Alaska. That rail line would increase

At that juncture, shipping interests again were accusing the board of falling behind the Canadians in providing lights and buoys. Costs, however, ran high and distances were a problem in supplying oil and other necessities. After 1905, funding still dragged somewhat, in fact, the following year when Congress authorized construction of a lighthouse at Cape Hinchenbrook, sufficient monies were not available for nearly four years. In the interim, some of the minor installations were made more substantial with concrete bases provided. Post lamps were placed at remote locations in the 1909-10 period at western Alaska points—Cape Stephens, Canal Point, Point Romanoff, and Cape Espenberg. Also lights were placed on Prince William Sound and at Resurrection Bay in southeastern Alaska.

The U.S. Lighthouse Board was replaced by the new Bureau of Lighthouses in 1910, and another round of requests, debate, and inspections were made. The steamer *Lindsay* brought buoys to open the Kuskokwin River to navigation.

Attention was next focused on south central Alaska where four steamships were wrecked in 1910. Elsewhere, the SS *Ohio* struck a reef off Steep Point near Ketchikan on August 27, 1909, with the loss of several souls. Her remains can still be seen there at this writing. The SS *Olympia* struck an uncharted reef off Bligh Island on December 2, 1910, and the venerable old *Portland* was wrecked near the mouth of the Katalla River, and this time she became a total loss. The Canadian Pacific passenger steamer *Princess May* ground up on a reef off Sentinel Island within full view of the lighthouse, April 15, 1910. As the tide ebbed she was held fast, her snout pointing skyward. It was at first feared she'd be a total loss, but after the evacuation of passengers and discharge of cargo she was salved, floated free on a later high tide and ushered off to dry dock in British Columbia.

Of importance in 1910 was the creation of the long awaited Lighthouse District for Alaska and the erection of a sizeable supply depot at Ketchikan. On the negative side, however, the Lighthouse Service authorized only $60,000 for Alaskan navigation aids for the fiscal year ending June 30, 1910, only five per cent of the $5 million expended. That paltry sum brought a blistering criticism from the Cordova newspaper, citing that it was ridiculous to believe that small sum was supposed to meet Alaska's needs on 3,000 miles of coastline used annually by 1,000 ships, carrying 50,000 passengers, and cargoes valued in

Eldred Island Lighthouse as it appeared under the U.S. Lighthouse Establishment before takeover by the U.S. Coast Guard in 1939. The durable structure has a concrete base and a frame upper structure and tower.

Anchor Point Light, a minor installation installed 12 miles south of Petersburg, August 2, 1915. The light was eliminated many years ago.

Minor lights on Alaskan waterways were popping up everywhere. Dewey Rocks, at the southern tip of Prince of Wales Island on the sea-road to Cordova was lighted June 19, 1916. Another light was the badly needed at the North Ledge structure in Wrangel Narrows, 12 miles south of Petersburg in 1918, and another at Anchor Point, south of Petersburg.

Though the Ketchikan Lighthouse Depot was not fully completed until 1920, other installations included small lights on the Yukon River, and the eventual funding for Cape Spencer Lighthouse, marking the entrance to Cross Sound. From 1912 until 1923 aids to navigation increased from 230 to 634, followed by the good news in 1916 of no major shipwrecks which the press claimed was due solely to the increased and improved navigation lights and fog signals.

Though many shipwrecks followed in later years, including Alaska's most terrible disaster, that of the Canadian Pacific passenger steamer *Princess Sophia* on Vanderbilt Reef in 1918, the waterways of the territory had been made considerably safer. On some occasions wrecks were from negligence on the part of navigators rather than from the elements.

The Lighthouse Service was frequently aided by the U.S. Coast and Geodetic Survey vessels with their dragging efforts throughout the various sectors of Alaska.

export by sea. And that would demand more navigation aids. Secretary of Commerce, William C. Redfield, pushed for the rail project but warned of the greater need for protection of waterways to assure shipping safety. His continued talks produced results when he told a Seattle audience that he expected a half million dollars from Congress for three new Coast Survey vessels and the largest lighthouse tender in the Lighthouse Service fleet.

His efforts were fortified by the 1913 wreck of the Pacific Coast Steamship Company's SS *State of California*, torn up on an uncharted reef in Gambier Bay, where 31 persons perished. In the same year the SS *Curacao* was wrecked in Warm Chuck Inlet and written off as a total loss, though months later in an uncanny recovery operation she was salvaged and rebuilt. The two above wrecks alone amounted to a half million dollar loss.

To make things even more frightening was the fact that on May 20, 1912, the Lighthouse tender *Armeria*, the only such vessel servicing the lighthouses and buoys in the whole of Alaska, struck an uncharted reef off the precipitous basaltic cliffs near Cape Hinchinbrook and became a total loss. She had been bound for the Hinchinbrook lighthouse with coal and supplies when the tragic accident occurred.

The venerable tender *Columbine* thereafter had to be pulled from her duties in Washington and Oregon to the pressing needs of Alaska.

Redfield was backed by growing public opinion which earlier resulted in a special expedition to the Great Land by Commissioner of Lighthouses, E. R. Putnam. Redfield's pleas for Alaska eventually produced results. Funding for Cape St. Elias Lighthouse came in 1914; and wire dragging operations were carried out by the chartered tug *Chehalis*.

During the period from 1915 to 1923 with the construction of the Alaska Railroad, the Bureau of Lighthouses was smiled on by Congress, and a large portion of available monies went to Alaska's navigational needs.

In 1916, the tender *Rose* was constructed in Seattle for use mainly on the Inside Passage, followed by the largest lighthouse tender yet built for the Lighthouse Service, the trim-lined *Cedar*. In later years, the *Rose* was replaced by the *Fern*, and still later by the tender *Hemlock*. Other improvements involved the wide use of gas buoys starting in 1917. The following year, as earlier mentioned, Congress released $90,000 for added construction of a lighthouse depot, exclusively for Alaska, located at Ketchikan.

Low Point Light, Taiya Inlet, Lynn Canal, October 8, 1915. This minor navigation aid is being checked by an employee of the former U.S. Lighthouse Service.

mand of her right from the builder's yard in 1917. To know him was to like him. This writer was privileged to make his acquaintance. One could sit for hours listening to his experiences in the service, including the major role he and his ship played in the aftermath of the *Princess Sophia* disaster. That friendly billy goat-whiskered individual had friends in most all parts of Alaska.

A whole new era dawned in Alaska with the advent of World War II. The Coast Guard and Navy were given a huge role in protecting American military transports, cargo vessels, and allied craft, always with the threat of a Japanese invasion. New navigation aids were hastily installed after a blackout was lifted at places like Spruce Island and Smith Island while other signals were upgraded to meet the demands. Despite every precaution, shipwreck continued at a heavy pace with the greatest armada of ships descending on Alaska since the gold rush days.

Last to receive the proper attention for aids to navigation in early times, Alaska was also among the very first to enter the age of automation. Due to the long coastline and isolated facilities, the territory got priority as part of the Coast Guard's "Operation Lamp," to automate the service's manned lighthouses nationwide.

Upper photo, Fairway Island Light Station as of 1944 after takeover by the Coast Guard. Right, the keeper's dwelling as it appeared in 1915.

By the era of the 1930s radio beacon facilities were installed at several lighthouse stations and at remote locations such as St. Paul Island and Soapstone Point, to pinpoint the position of ships with radio receiving equipment.

Many of the original frame type lighthouses were later replaced by reinforced concrete structures, far more durable in the harsh, changing climates of Alaska. More powerful beacons with higher intensity were also installed.

It was on January 3, 1959, that Alaska was accorded statehood status after being a territory from the time of its purchase from Russia in 1867. That placed an entirely new stamp on Alaska, the 49th state of the union, all of which increased the economy and industry of the northland.

Under the "Lamp" program all of the lighthouses in Alaska were automated by 1984, the last being Five Finger Light Station which was also the first established in Alaska. It was the greatest innovation since the Coast Guard introduced the Loran program (long range aids to navigation) in 1945. Loran stations were located at Tok, Kodiak, St. Paul, Attu, Port Clarence, and Shoal Cove. Perhaps the most isolated was the Attu facility on the most westerly of the Aleutians, commissioned in 1960. Radio beacons had also played a major role in Alaska's latter day navigational operations. Most of the lighthouses were so equipped.

Just before the U.S. Coast Guard took over control of the U.S. Lighthouse Service in 1939, several other accomplishments had occurred, including the establishment of Cape Decision Lighthouse at the southern entrance to Chatham Strait in 1932. Also, the lighthouse tender *Alder* joined the *Cedar* and *Hemlock* with the increasing work load. With the end of the Bureau of Lighthouses, the transition to the Coast Guard had both good and bad aspects.

With the clouds of war forming over a troubled world there was not enough thought given to the fact that many of the experienced civil lighthouse employees would retire and their duties taken over by inexperienced young Coast Guard personnel, unfamiliar with the situation, namely proper care of Fresnel lenses and fog signal equipment. True, the former lighthouse employees were offered a chance to continue working with a Coast Guard rating if they could pass the physical. Some stayed on but most decided to retire on a pension. To say the least, it took a long time for the young replacements to learn the rudiments performed so well under the Bureau of Lighthouses. Nor in many cases were they able to endure the lengthy stretches of isolation at many of the facilities. Eventually the Coast Guard cut the length of duty periods and offered long vacations, especially at the most isolated locales, of which Alaska had more than its share. Transfers of personnel were more frequent by necessity. Reclusion is a thing that the majority of men do not prefer.

Perhaps one of the most personable and qualified individuals in the former Lighthouse Service was Captain John W. Leadbetter, long time skipper of the 200 foot Lighthouse tender *Cedar*. He took com-

If one is able to visit any of the 12 remaining Alaska lighthouses at the time of this writing, they would probably feel the loneliness—structures standing solitary, void of humans, undergrowth covering pathways, birds nesting in peculiar crevices around the towers that still stand. Coast Guard civil engineers survey the buildings every two years. Some have already been eradicated or boarded up.

Buoy tender crews or Coast Guard land-based personnel coming by helicopter or plane maintain the navigational facilities periodically, but no keepers are any longer in attendance, and with such new innovations as the Global Positioning System (GPS) the lights and fog signals have lost much of their importance.

FIVE FINGER ISLANDS LIGHTHOUSE

At a contracted cost of $22,500, Five Fingers Light Station was under construction in July of 1901, and completed in January of 1902. It stood proudly on a rocky, tree-lined island, 37 miles northwest of Petersburg at the north part of Frederick Sound. The two-story frame structure had its tower rising from the roof. The light was first displayed on March 1, 1902. A debate continues as to which was the first to be lighted, Five Finger, or its sister light on Sentinel Island. Both lit up the same day, but the former got the nod because more of its station facilities had been completed.

The lantern house was fitted with a fourth order "fixed" Fresnel lens, 49 feet above the ground, and 69 feet above sea level. There was also a Daboll fog signal, an oil house and a workship, plus a landing platform, hoisting derrick, and an engine house. Comfortable quarters were afforded for the keepers. The island was both pristine and picturesque, a perfect setting for a lighthouse on the Inside Passage.

In 1931, the reservation was fitted with a third class radio beacon. Two years later, tragedy hit the station. It happened on a cold December 3, 1933, when the tower and fog signal building caught

Point Sherman Light Station as of June 1929, one of the minor installations on the Inside Passage.

fire. Despite every effort the keepers could exert the fire consumed the structures. Fortunately, the *Cedar* was landing supplies at the time and her crew joined the keepers in fighting the flames, managing to save the carpenter shop and boathouse.

Three years later, at a cost of $92,267, a new reinforced concrete tower was established on one of the nearby Five Fingers. It stood on a concrete pier, a two-story building surmounted by a tall, square tower. The light was 81 feet above the water and the building housed all equipment and quarters for three keepers, including a kitchen, four bedrooms, bath, boiler room, radio room, engine room, battery room, and storage area. The basement included machinery for alternate operation in case of emergency.

In other words, the facility was self-sufficient and virtually fire proof. The radio beacon was synchronized with the compressed air diaphone fog signal. There was a hoisting machine at the landing and adequate cisterns to catch water.

It was somewhat a nostalgic event when on August 14, 1984, the lighthouse was the last in Alaska to be automated, and the four Coast Guard attendants transferred to other duty. There is still a light and radio beacon at Five Finger.

SENTINEL ISLAND LIGHTHOUSE

At the northerly end of Favorite Channel, leading into Lynn Canal, 23 miles northwest of Juneau, stands Sentinel Island Lighthouse. As earlier mentioned, its light was first shown over the dark acres of the Inside Passage on March 1, 1902. Constructed at a cost of

$21,267 by builder George James, the station included, in addition to the tower, a keepers dwelling, fog signal house, oil house, and carpenter shop. The landing featured a tramway which ran to the oil house.

The navigation light was a fourth order fixed lens lit by an oil lamp, 82 feet above mean high water. The square tower was attached to the westerly front of the keeper's dwelling, a two-story building with hipped cross gables. When the frequent fogs rolled in, the third class Daboll trumpet was placed in operation.

In 1926, the 600 candlepower light was upped to 1,600 candlepower and increased to even greater intensity three years later, following complaints from mariners. A year earlier, a short range radio beacon had been installed. In spite of improvements, the old frame station was doomed, for in the 1933-35 period it was replaced by a modern reinforced concrete lighthouse and fog signal building at a cost of $35,310. The tower projected from the roof of a two-story fog signal structure and was similar in many respects to the lighthouse at Five Finger.

Sadly, technological advances and inflation prompted the district to automate the facility in 1966, and dismiss its keepers. Due to vandalism and trespass, the Coast Guard burned down the keeper's dwelling in 1971, only the tower and fog signal house remaining on the six and a half acre island reservation.

Then, as suddenly as a touch of a feather, the Coast Guard elected to be even more economical in 1987 when the buoy tender *Woodrush* landed at the isle with a service crew that installed 15 solar panels to replace electricity at the lighthouse. The oldtime keepers, long

Cape Spencer Light Station, on a small barren isle off the cape, at the entrance to Cross Sound, Alaska, established in 1913 and rebuilt 1925. Photo courtesy of Official U.S. Coast Guard.

passed to their eternal rest, would have scratched their heads in wonderment at such an innovation. Even in our day, there's still a note of sadness in seeing unmanned lighthouses.

A navigation light and foghorn are still functional at the site.

SCOTCH CAP LIGHTHOUSE

This author always has a bit of a hollow feeling in the pit of his stomach when the Scotch Cap Lighthouse is brought to mind. Once, having put in for duty at the station in the 1940s, this individual instead was sent to Tillamook Rock. It was in that time frame that Scotch Cap Lighthouse was completely obliterated by a seismic tidal wave which took the lives of all five Coast Guard attendants.

But going back to the beginning: this station located on rocky, secluded Unimak Island was the first lighthouse to be established on the outside coast of Alaska, near the historic route of the ancient Russian seafarers. Situated some 70 miles northeast of Dutch Harbor, it's in an area where sea travel in winter often comes to a halt due to adverse weather conditions. Duty there was intensely lonely and cold, with no place to go unless one was brave enough to tackle the hazardous rock-ribbed trek by foot to the equally isolated Cape Sarichef Lighthouse, 22 miles to the southeast, facing the Bering Sea.

Serving at Scotch Cap was never a picnic, in fact the Lighthouse Service felt such sympathy for its keepers that each of the three who served there would get one year's vacation every four years. One of their number was once saved by a station dog in a blinding snowstorm while trying to get back to the dwelling from the tower after both hands were frozen and his feet frostbitten.

Standing like a tombstone for the lost ships and mariners, the old Scotch Cap light was at the southerly end of the brutal route along the Aleutian chain in a place that no Chamber of Commerce would ever recommend. It wasn't even easy to get contractors to bid on the construction of the station. All of the original bids were turned down as being excessive. Once bidders were apprised of the location and the problem of importing materials, most put in ridiculous bids to protect themselves in case they won the job. The Lighthouse Board, frustrated by the situation, was forced to hire laborers and to purchase the bulk of building materials themselves. As a result, the steam schooner *Homer* departed Seattle on June 23, 1902, casting off for Unimak Island with 30 workers, and a doctor looking for a new adventure. The building had to be erected during the better months as the bitter winter was out of the question. The men worked up until the first storm period and then retreated until the following season. Despite all of the difficulties, the station was finally established on July 18, 1903. That night the beam of light illuminated a very dark and foreboding sector of the world. Three days before the lamp was lit, the fog signal, of necessity, was placed in operation. Total cost of the facility was $76,571.

The lantern house was fitted with a third order Fresnel lens, originally developing 2,300 candlepower, and a ten-inch air whistle afforded the signal for fog-bound vessels. The structure was situated on a bench of a bluff near the beach. The lighthouse was 90 feet above the sea and 35 feet from the ground level. The basic structure reminded one of a Russian church, frame constructed, octagonal in shape with a pyramidal roof. The building was separated from three commodious dwellings, plus a barn and twin oil houses. Several safety factors were installed to protect the keepers on their daily rounds of the 8,852 acre lighthouse reservation.

Scotch Cap had few parallels in the history of pharology. In 1909, the sailing vessel *Columbia* was wrecked off Unimak Island. The 194 cannery workers aboard were forced to make their way to the lighthouse for survival. They reached their destination, and then exhausted most of the food supply at the station, as it was two weeks before a relief ship arrived to remove the castaways.

Among the other dramatic entries in the lighthouse log book was the wreck of the Japanese freighter *Koshun Maru*. She draped her shape over the rock-riddled beach in 1930 with the Scotch Cap fog siren blasting away a few cable's lengths distant. Again in 1942, the light keepers were host to the 60 survivors of the Russian SS *Turksib* after the vessel was wrecked near the station. Rough seas demanded their stay to be prolonged for several weeks.

One of the first acts of the Coast Guard after taking over jurisdiction from the Lighthouse Service was to construct a new light-house at Scotch Cap in 1940. It was a reinforced concrete facility supposedly built "stronger than a fortress," but which later proved no match for Mother Nature. The new lighthouse and fog signal cost $150,000 and was a stone's throw from the former frame structure. Initially, the old lighthouse was not dismantled, but only decapitated and its iron lantern house placed atop the new tower.

In all the annals of American lighthouses no single tragedy compared with what occurred at Scotch Cap on April Fool's Day in 1946. Despite its solid construction and a concrete seawall for protection, the facility was but a plaything in the throes of the ocean's seismic fury.

"Terrific roaring from the ocean heard, followed immediately by a terrific sea, the top of which rose above the cliff and struck the station causing considerable damage," so inscribed the man on watch at the Radio Direction Finding Unit located atop the cliff overlooking the light station. The one logging the entry immediately rang up the lighthouse and also attempted radio contact, without response. The light had gone out in the lantern house and the fog signal was no longer blasting. Suspecting the worst, and being familiar with the frequent earthquakes and high seas in the area, the officer-in-charge of the DF unit ordered his men to higher ground. The giant tsunami waves caused by an underwater eruption created 100 foot walls of water which drove into the cliff with the power of a thousand tanks, taking out the entire lighthouse down to its foundation, bringing instant death to the five Coast Guard lighthouse attendants within. The deceased at that regrettable moment in time were Chief bos'n's mate Anthony Lawrence Petit; Fireman first class Jack Colvin; Seaman first class Dewey Dykstra; Motor machinist's mate Leonard Pickering; and Seaman first class James Ness. So mangled were the body parts that identification was almost impossible, with bits of intestine, bridgework, and jewelry alone providing clues. It was a black day in the chronicles of the Coast Guard. Wiped out were all the old unused keepers dwellings and even the remains of the *Koshun Maru*, in addition to the lighthouse.

Never again would keepers man a navigation light at Scotch Cap. A temporary unwatched 375mm electric light was set up accompanied by a radio beacon in the aftermath of the tragedy, and that temporary aid to navigation was later succeeded by an improved concrete structure, 116 feet above sea level, boasting a modern beacon producing 240,000 candlepower, plus a Loran installation.

There were personnel elsewhere at the location to operate the radio-oriented facilities, but total automation came in 1971 when all personnel in residence were removed. A light on a skeleton tower was active at this writing.

Among the better known characters who manned the former Scotch Cap Lighthouse were Oscar Lindberg and "Uncle" Barney Lokken. Those veterans of the lighthouse service were tried and tested men who were faithful and resourceful, adjusted to secluded lifestyle, ready to face or tackle any emergency in their lonely corner of the world.

MARY ISLAND LIGHTHOUSE

Priority was supposed to be given to the erection of the Mary Island beacon, one of the first lights sighted by ships sailing northward through Alaska's Inside Passage. However, a classic act of foot dragging delayed its construction for well over a decade. As far back as 1890, the Lighthouse Board had recommended a lighthouse at the site, with an estimated price tag of $80,000. Even when a Customs House was built on the island in 1892, no funds were forthcoming, so the Lighthouse officials attempted to entice the Custom's people to build a small lighted navigation aid and man it for a fee, but there was no response from Congress, and no funds provided. Monies were then tight across the nation.

It took the Klondike gold rush to get action. The Lighthouse Board shortly afterward was provided Congressional approval for the financing of the facility, and the contract was awarded April 11, 1902. The building crew and supplies were landed at the site the following

Cape Decision Lighthouse was established in 1929 and updated in 1932. The tower located at the south end of the cape in Sumner Strait, is 75 feet high from the ground to the top of the lantern house and is built of reinforced concrete. Insert at right shows the landing area, circa 1933. At left, the fire suffered at the station which burned the boathouse and part of the dock and landing area, in 1989.

LINCOLN ROCK LIGHTHOUSE

Lincoln Rock Lighthouse had a rather unusual history. On a lifeless gnarled rock formation, Lincoln Rock Light was established at the western end of Clarence Strait, 54 miles northwest of Ketchikan.

A single bidder was awarded the contract in March 1902, but while transporting his building materials to the site the loaded barge was overturned in contrary seas and the recovery effort was for the most part futile. Several weeks passed before the contractor finally reached Lincoln Rock, in May 1902. The jinx continued, however, and construction was halted at the difficult location by a protracted series of nasty weather.

More trouble, in June 1903; the Lighthouse Service cancelled the contract on finding the builder was using substandard materials in order to recoup some of his earlier losses. At that juncture, the board was again forced to hire its own laborers, which generally was a more costly undertaking. At any rate, the station was finally completed in November, and on December 1, 1903, a light was aglow in the tower lantern room. Most of the small sea-girt rock was occupied by the structure, featuring a two-story frame dwelling with a square tower protruding at its western end. The tower was 41 feet high, and the light 58 feet above sea level. The beacon was a fourth order Fresnel, and the fog signal of the Daboll type, blasting through a trumpet. The entire structure was built atop a huge concrete pier, the rock itself inundated at high tide. A cutwater at the south side was built to split irascible seas from climbing up the side of the lighthouse. The idea had merit but proved ineffective, the structure often bathed and endangered in rough seas. In

month. The beacon was lit on July 15, 1903, and the entire station was completed two weeks later. It consisted of a one-story octagonal frame fog signal building with a pyramidal roof, surmounted by a black cylindrical lantern house atop the short tower. Shown by nightfall, sunset to sunrise, was a fourth order Fresnel lens displaying its light 67 feet above the sea and 45 feet above ground level. A third class Daboll fog trumpet projected from the easterly side of the structure. Two dwellings were situated 100 feet from the lighthouse, and other necessary units on the reservation included the derrick, boathouse, carhouse, and oilhouses. In 1926, among other improvements, the beacon's intensity was increased from 600 to 6,000 candlepower. Five years later, a third class radio beacon was installed.

As at other Alaska locations, the original frame lighthouse was replaced by a reinforced concrete tower, provided for in the 1936-38 budget. The cost was $54,792. Reaching skyward 61 feet from ground level, 76 feet from mean high tide, it was an impressive structure with modern equipment—the first floor containing engines, compressors, and generators. In the basement was an elaborate heating facility and fuel-storage. Numerous other buildings were on the reservation, all connected by cement walkways. The dwellings were more than adequate for the keepers at the 198 acre site.

After performing stellar manned service, the Coast Guard elected to automate the facility in April 1969, and at the same time install a minor light. Then a few years later even the radio beacon was discontinued, kind of a sad conclusion to the life of a lighthouse. It does, however, presently display a flashing white light every six seconds.

Official U.S. Coast Guard aerial photo of the Cape Spencer Lighthouse station located at the entrance to Cross Sound. The photo was taken before Coast Guard personnel succumbed to automation.

fact, both in November 1909 and in April of the following year the lighthouse received major damage. The beacon was put out of commission, and a temporary minor light installed. The keepers had to be evacuated via the Army steamer *Peterson* on December 1, and the imperiled lighthouse was for the first time without personnel.

It wasn't until March 1911 that Congress authorized reconstruction of Lincoln Rock Lighthouse at a cost not to exceed $25,000. A new fog signal was placed on another islet 440 yards from the original

TREE POINT LIGHTHOUSE

Tree Point was marked by a lighthouse which was first placed in operation April 30, 1904, just a year after its approval by the Lighthouse Board. Two weeks after the facility became operational, a sudden fire threatened to burn it down. Quick action by personnel controlled the blaze, and repairs got underway immediately. Nearly all

Another view of Cape Spencer Light Station with an insert of the first light displayed at the site before the lighthouse was built. It was an unwatched acetylene gas light that burned for long periods without being refueled. Photo courtesy of U.S. Coast Guard.

lighthouse site. In the interim, an unmanned acetylene light was placed in operation where the first light had been destroyed. The new manned station met the criteria set down by the Lighthouse Board, being completed for $24,774. It was commissioned on October 10, 1911. The site of the fog signal installation was also the locale of the keepers dwelling, boathouse, and landing, while the light fixture on the small piece of rock eventually became a skeleton tower with a light at its summit, last updated in 1961.

The entire station was eliminated from manned operation in March 1968, and the 1995 Light List showed Lincoln Rock West Light of a flashing white character every six seconds. An NR day mark (a diamond shaped day mark with color sectors) was also affixed to the skeleton tower.

the original Alaska lighthouses were of frame construction and the danger of fire was always a concern. Oil houses were always placed a safe distance from the towers, but using fuel to burn in the lamps was always a worry, despite precautions.

The lighthouse was situated at the entrance to Revillagigedo Channel, 40 miles south of Ketchikan and was very familiar to ships negotiating the Inside Passage. The service thought the station important enough to rate a third order light, fixed, but with a red sector warning of dangerous nearby Lord Rocks. To compensate for the frequent fogs, the installation was provided a first class oil burning air siren which could really pierce one's ears. The unique frame structure was octagonal in shape with the tower surmounting the center of the structure, 56 feet in height and over 86 feet above the channel. A

Point Retreat Light on Lynn Canal was first displayed in 1904 and reestablished in 1923. The insert was the first light shown at Point Retreat, a gas-powered fixture which flashed every three seconds for five months without attendants. Many similar minor lights marked the Inside Passage in the early part of the century. Photo courtesy of U.S. Coast Guard.

sizeable landing dock with a derrick installed gave ready access to the station from the water. Adequate living quarters were provided for the attendants on the 1,207 acre reservation.

The pioneer structure was replaced by a modern reinforced concrete lighthouse in 1935. Construction began in 1933, and the result was a handsome, square-shaped tower 13 x 13, rising majestically 66 feet, and 86 feet above sea level. The light was visible for 15 miles. The attached fog signal building was above an 18 x 36 foot basement containing a 5,000 gallon fuel oil tank, a water heating boiler, storage space, and air receivers. The first floor housed both fog compressors and generators plus a small office. There was also a diaphone operating room on the third floor in the tower. The lantern house on the original structure was removed and placed atop the 1935 lighthouse. By day time the cylindrical lantern house was easily identified by a gray paint with a black dome, later changed to all black, while the tower and out buildings were white with brown trimmings, similar to the other Alaska lighthouses.

The station was automated in 1969 and reduced to a minor navigation light. In the 1995 Light List, Tree Point still showed a flashing white light.

CAPE SARICHEF
LIGHTHOUSE

Undoubtedly the best known keepers who manned Cape Sarichef Lighthouse were Ed Moore and his assistant Ted Petersen who later took over the helm of the station. Moore put in many years of lighthouse service before retiring in 1933 at age 63. Petersen's tenure was similar, both having served Sarichef well on a reservation of 1,845 acres, the most westerly of America's lighthouses, a close relative to the ill-fated Scotch Cap sentinel.

Located on the northwestern coast of Unimak Island, a light was still shown there at this writing, (unmanned) displaying a flashing

white characteristic every two and a half seconds from an elevation of 170 feet. The navigation aid is above the locale of the original lighthouse. The closest settlement is Dutch Harbor, 78 miles away, which isolates Sarichef keepers from the world, especially from December 1 to March 1 when icy seas and howling blizzards were the order of the day.

Petersen recalled that the icebound station once went without mail for five months. Still he liked the peacefulness and freedom of the place. It was seldom visited by lighthouse inspectors which were often the bane of keepers who feared the "white glove" inspections, prior to the Coast Guard takeover.

The original bids for construction of the Sarichef facility were all rejected as "too excessive" in March of 1902. Again, the Lighthouse Service had to resort to hired labor early in 1903. Despite all of the obstacles and contrary weather, the station was completed by October 1, 1903, except for the lantern housing which had failed to arrive. The tower sat empty through the harsh winter as the laborers retreated until the following May when they installed the lantern, lens, and lighting apparatus. Official light up time was on July 1, 1904. The beacon was a third order fixed Fresnel producing 2,300 candlepower, visible about 15 miles at sea. The completed station, including the first-class compressed air fog siren, and other outbuildings, cost $80,000. The tower was 35 feet high and 127 feet above sea level. Of wood construction, it was octagonal in shape, the tower rising from the fog signal unit. The three dwellings, oilhouses, and barn were separate from the lighthouse building and in later years the old barn was used to house the station surf boat.

Isolation was the name of the game at Sarichef. It was said that two of the three dwellings were never used. The Lighthouse Board must have figured wrongly that more visitors would come to that outpost. Keeper's families were forbidden to live in such a secluded locale. Storms severely damaged the boathouse, engine house, and derrick in 1904, all of which had to undergo major repairs.

An overall view of the Point Retreat Light Station. Note how high the landing area, derrick, and derrick house are above the sea level. A DCB type beacon, exposed, is atop the tower. Circa 1961.

Above and at right: *Point Retreat Light Station under construction. Above photo shows Keeper Charles E. McLeod and his two year old son at the Station in 1928. McLeod kept the light from 1926 till 1930 when he died suddenly.* Photo courtesy of U.S. Coast Guard.

Not all of the keepers took to the island, and the isolation often prompted requests for transfer or forced removal of one who had gone crazy. One keeper desiring to see individuals other than those he worked with at the lighthouse attempted the 22 mile hike over the frigid terrain to see the keepers at Scotch Cap. He almost froze to death before he reached his destination.

In my book *Lighthouses of the Pacific* readers will find the story of the keeper who attempted the 22 mile trek between the two lighthouses. He took off his clothes at a swollen stream and tried to throw them to the other side so they would be dry when he swam across the frigid barrier. In heaving the clothing it fell short and was swept down the creek. Stark naked and feet bleeding he had to run for miles over rough terrain to reach the other lighthouse, much to the amazement of the keepers. His name was Lee Harpole, uncle of Doug Newman, feature writer for the Register Guard in Eugene, Oregon. The late lighthouse keeper passed away in 1942 and is buried at Dutch Harbor.

The daily log of events kept while Sarichef was a manned station told of one of the keepers, while out hunting, finding two dazed men wandering about the island. They were shipwrecked seafarers from the schooner *Gladiator* that had stranded 18 miles from the lighthouse. Dispatched to the wreck scene was the Coast Guard cutter *Chelan* which sent out a boat to rescue the schooner's Captain and remaining crew members. The lifeboat unfortunately capsized and the occupants were all thrown into the water. On reaching the beach they set out on foot, making for the light station. Once there, they spent nine days before the seas calmed enough for the *Chelan* to take the survivors aboard.

For fear that the Cape Sarichef Lighthouse might one day suffer the same fate as the Scotch Cap facility, the Coast Guard furthered

plans to replace the "senior" lighthouse at the site. The new structure was an unimpressive concrete rectangular one-story affair with an exposed 375mm (9,000 candlepower) light atop a small turret on one side of the roof. It was lighted in 1950. Several other structures were also on the reservation for necessary purposes including a radio beacon and fog siren. The original keeper's dwellings were dismantled. As automation eventually took over, the 1950 light structure was eliminated and replaced by a light on a utilitarian skeleton tower, as of June 15, 1979. Shortly afterwards the lighthouse reservation reverted to use by the U.S. Fish and Wildlife Service, all 1,845 acres. It also served as a National Weather forecasting center. At this writing a navigation light was still shining at the location.

POINT SHERMAN AND FAIRWAY LIGHT STATIONS

Thirty-eight miles north of Juneau, on the sea route to Skagway, lie the remains of the old Point Sherman Lighthouse. It became a reality on October 18, 1904. Its story was not one that made history but it was once a manned station, its small 230 candlepower light shining from a mini-tower, hexagonal in shape. Its significance was reduced in 1917, and the light abolished in 1932. Only part of former keeper's dwelling with a caved in roof marks the spot today, but a small navigation light is still maintained at the location.

The Fairway Island Lighthouse became operational on September 1, 1904, inside the eastern entrance to Peril Strait, marking an important turning point for ships arriving and departing from the port of Sitka, 28 miles away. In fact, the light had been recommended

One of the darkest days in U.S. Coast Guard history was on April Fool's Day in 1946 when a voluminous seismic tidal wave, 100 feet high, slammed into Scotch Cap Lighthouse and completely demolished the concrete structure, killing the five Coast Guard attendants inside. Photo courtesy of U.S. Coast Guard.

as early as 1900. Like others, however, there were the usual delays. An unmanned system of stake lights were later erected between 1917 and 1925 in various sectors of Alaska. With the closure of the manned facility, a small light continued to shine there and is still marking the spot at this writing. "Light No. 32" is atop a former dwelling.

GUARD ISLANDS LIGHTHOUSE

One of the favorite lighthouse assignments for Coast Guardsmen and their predecessors was Guard Islands. Its close proximity to Ketchikan, just nine miles away, made it certain that attendant's diets would never suffer or isolation become a problem. There are two Guard Islands marking the easterly entrance to Tongass Narrows. The station was built on the most exposed. It was in the summer of 1903 that hired laborers began construction of the station, but four months later only the preliminaries had been completed on the rough terrain. Thus, the winter ended further construction until the following spring, when the building crew came back to finish the project. It was on September 15, 1904, that a fixed lens-lantern was installed. The white square frame tower was topped by the traditional round iron lantern housing, 34 feet from the ground level and 79 feet above the narrows.

Ironically, the structure on which the tower stood was initially planned for sophisticated fog signal equipment, but a shortage of funds reduced the station to a minor light and a fog bell, struck by clockwork machinery every 20 seconds.

Complaints about the inaudibility of the bell came from fog-bound mariners on that busy marine highway. It was not until 1922, however, that funds were made available for a 20 x 35 foot concrete fog signal building with an air diaphone mechanism. It became operative in February 1924, and never again was a complaint heard by mariners, who often put their fingers in their ears when in the vicinity of its raspy voice emanating from the ten acre isle.

That same year, a new lighthouse of reinforced concrete replaced the old sentinel. A new dwelling was also erected providing quarters for two keepers and their families. Family stations, unlike the bach-

elor units, were always much preferred. The reestablished station cost $46,586, and gave added importance to the lighthouse. Radio telephones and a radio beacon were added in the late 1930s.

Finally, as must happen to all lighthouses in our generation, with the rising costs of maintenance and new self-operating signals the Coast Guard automated Guard Islands Light Station in 1969. The lighthouse and fog signal building remain today, but it was with no small amount of nostalgia when the last Coast Guardsmen locked the doors of the popular station. All of the outer buildings were eventually dismantled. Guard Islands at this writing is displaying a minor white light flashing every ten seconds.

POINT RETREAT LIGHTHOUSE

Hit and miss might be a description for Point Retreat Light Station. It was given only minor status when built on Admiralty Island on the northerly point of Mansfield Peninsula in 1904. Fitted with a lens-lantern, it was lighted September 15, 1904. The stubby tower was only six feet above the ground. One of the twin keeper's dwellings burned to the ground a few months after completion of the station. The facility didn't even rate a fog signal originally. Some even wondered why an aid to navigation was established there. In 1917, the Lighthouse Service pondered its effectiveness. It was then unmanned and reduced to a minor aid.

Oddly, the lighthouse came back to life in 1923-24 when the entire station was reestablished as a vital navigation unit. A combined light and fog signal building, 63 feet above the water, was constructed of reinforced concrete. All the outbuildings, including two modern dwellings, a fully equipped landing wharf with derrick, a cistern hollowed out of solid rock, oil houses, and boathouse were all first-class. The station had risen from rags to riches on a price tag of $58,242.

In 1966, one of the residences was demolished to create a helicopter pad. In all respects, the station took on an entirely new role, updated with radio beacon facilities in later years. In fact, it was not until 1973 that automation knocked at the a door and the attendants were transferred to other duties.

Then again, riches to rags. The abandoned station was reduced to a minor light category with a battery-powered fog signal. A flashing white light was still displayed at this writing. Solar panels have been placed on several Alaska navigational facilities in recent years where ever sufficient sunlight is available to generate cheap electricity.

ELDRED ROCK LIGHTHOUSE

Most keepers of the former Alaska lighthouses had pets for company during their long and lonely vigils. Birds, dogs, deer, cats, and even abandoned cub bears were adopted. Sam Olsen, keeper of Eldred Rock Lighthouse in the 1920s, had a pet cat that was with him constantly, even when he went fishing in the station boat. It was quite amazing how felines and canines adapted so well to their masters—perhaps it was the love and affection afforded such animals by those stuck in their lighthouse seclusion.

Eldred Rock Lighthouse was durable. Though most of the original Alaska sentinels were later replaced by reinforced concrete facilities, Eldred Rock's lighthouse is still standing in its same position, unaltered from its origin. It is the only one of its kind still existing in Alaska. It is also one of the most photographed, standing proudly on the southeast portion of the rock in Lynn Canal, 50 miles north of

This is the way the Scotch Cap Lighthouse looked before being destroyed by the 1946 seismic wave. The strong reinforced concrete structure was no match for the wrath of Mother Nature. Lower photo shows the entire station including the original lighthouse at far left, established in 1903, and years later replaced by the concrete lighthouse. To the right are the three spacious keepers dwellings, two of which were hardly ever used. On the beach is the wreck of the Japanese freighter Koshun Maru *wrecked in 1930 just off the lighthouse reservation. Everything seen in the lower photo was wiped out by the seismic tidal wave.* Photo courtesy of U.S. Coast Guard.

Juneau. Even today, many cruise passengers aboard the growing fleet of luxury ships photograph the lighthouse in its beautiful setting.

Completed and commissioned on June 1, 1906, it was one of the last of the originally planned major light "stations" established in Alaska. Set for completion in November of the previous year, a severe winter put the skids on construction for six months.

The original fourth order light put out 2,100 candlepower from an elevation 91 feet above sea level. The tower and lantern house projected from the roof of an octagonal fog signal structure. Perhaps one reason for the longevity of the lighthouse in Alaska's damp climate was that the lower story of the fog signal building was of concrete and the upper story and tower of frame construction. The building is 56 feet high and originally built to house the light, fog signal, and living quarters.

Eldred Rock's original fog signal was a first-class automatic siren which was more than adequate in warning ships in the Inside Passage. The boathouse, derrick, and tramway were located about 150 feet north of the lighthouse.

About the only major change in later years was the installation of a radio telephone in 1939. Even though the station was automated

and placed in the category of a minor light in 1973, its outside appearance remained unchanged and is still showing a flashing light characteristic at this writing.

There was the usual melancholy connected with the automation of the station, especially by the folks of Haines, whose fishermen were well acquainted with the antiquated structure. A reporter on the local newspaper wrote, "Haines has been made more isolated than ever before from its nearest neighbor to the south. A cold, lifeless lighthouse stands guard amidst the whims of wind and weather in Lynn Canal. The most important facet of this facility is gone, the human observer."

CAPE HINCHINBROOK LIGHTHOUSE

Cape Hinchinbrook has been a ship killer down through the years. No incident was more indicative of the treacherous waters and rocky obstacles off the Cape's perpendicular walls than was the wreck of the U.S. Lighthouse tender *Armeria*, once the largest and best equipped of her breed. It was on May 20, 1912, while endeavoring to bring in coal and supplies for the station, that the vessel ran aground. Ensign upside down, distress flag fluttering in the breeze, the helpless vessel was doomed. Her tall black stack puffed its final burst of smoke, and the ship's telegraph indicated "finished with engines." She was impaled on an uncharted rock ledge. Though her crew reached safety, there was no reprieve for the vessel. The station keepers aided in the rescue.

Earlier, other problems had faced Cape Hinchinbrook Lighthouse. Slated to mark the entrance to Prince William Sound, 55 miles south of Valdez, it was to become the most important sentinel in the south central sector of Alaska. Construction was prompted by the news of the tragic loss of the passenger steamer *Oregon*. Congress always took notice of shipwreck. A sum of $125,000 was provided by a Congressional act in 1906, but receiving the money was another thing. As the elements reduced the wreck to junk, only $25,000 had been coughed up by Congress in 1906, $50,000 the following year, and the remainder in 1908. Construction didn't get started until Seattle contractor A. B. Lewis arrived with his building crew in April 1909. Forty skilled workers labored long and hard, but the weather turned sour and supplies were badly delayed. To make things worse, a scow laden with $12,000 worth of materials got away from a tug and drifted out of sight in a wind storm. Two Indians discovered the runaway craft ashore on Montague Island, and alerted officials.

By September 1909, more inclement weather closed down further work for the season, the lighthouse only completed to the first floor. A temporary fixed light was put in operation on the uncompleted building, and a man and his wife remained at the site to refuel the oil lamp each week.

Construction resumed in June 1910, as 30 workers labored long hours. Their work was praised by chief draftsman, C. W. Leick, designer of not only Alaska lighthouses, but many in the Pacific Northwest as well.

It was a momentous day when the long delayed project was finally finished at a cost of $100,323, slightly below the bid price. The light tower atop the two-story 47 foot octagonal fog signal building contained living quarters and had a base diameter of 52 feet. The lantern house, equipped with a third order lens and lighting apparatus, was 12 feet in diameter and 18 feet high. The flashing white light of 20,000 candlepower was visible more than 20 miles at sea, Alaska's most powerful marine beacon in that time frame. The focal plane of the light was 235 feet above sea level, one of the loftiest in the territory. The main building was unique, with the housing generator and compressors operated by twin kerosene engines. Housed in the lower floor was an engine room, workshop, and storage areas along with bathroom facilities. On the second floor were four bedrooms, sitting and dining room, pantry, and kitchen. Heat was provided by a hot water system, plus an underground cistern to hold 15,000 gallons, free from the winter freeze. The entire edifice was virtually fireproof. Every other structure on the 5,000 acre reservation was modern in every respect, including the carpenter shop, storehouses, and oil houses. Above the steep cliff was a large derrick for hoisting boats and supplies. Tramways and concrete walkways were also provided.

Said one official who inspected the station, "It has to be one of the finest in the nation with every convenience and safeguard a lighthouse could have."

There was even an emergency landing area at the end of a six mile trail leading to the protected waters of English Bay, usable when no landings were possible at the lighthouse site.

Despite its out of the way location, Cape Hinchinbrook station was the "darling of all Alaska lighthouses." Some even described it as indestructible in the same vain the SS *Titanic* was claimed unsinkable. Don't ever fool with Mother Nature! Man's best efforts are often inadequate. The culprit this time was erosion caused by earthquakes in 1927-28. Earth movements caused slides on the seaward side of the 180 foot cliff where the lighthouse stood. The cave-in progressed toward the "dream" sentinel, and the authorities, recognizing the danger, decided that the lighthouse would have to go. Its replacement would stand on a nearby rock foundation 130 feet away. Moving the old structure was considered not feasible, so in 1931, Congress afforded monies to get the project started, but only $30,000 was immediately available. The usual delays and slow shipment of materials saw the construction linger aggravatingly. Not until 1934 was the re-established station in full operation.

The former lantern housing was moved to the new 67 foot tower. Modern in every respect, the concrete reinforced one-story building measuring 44 feet by 54 feet was fitted with a two-tone diaphone fog signal extremely effective from its high perch. The super intensity light source produced 200,000 candlepower. New residences were built separately, for the three keepers, but families were forbidden.

Ironically, the old lighthouse building, decapitated and empty, refused to fall over the cliff but was gradually dismantled, with only its concrete foundation remaining. Unlike other lighthouses, the new structure received a coat of medusa paint in place of the usual white. The light and fog signal were a blessing for the growing number of commercial steamships that utilized Prince William Sound. Ships carrying copper ore from the Kennecott mines and oil and coal from the Katalla area, as well as the commercial fisherman, all depended heavily on the Cape Hinchinbrook light and fog signal.

The station succumbed to automation in the 1974 summer season but the tower still stands proudly, fronted by a helicopter pad where Coast Guard maintenance crews can land periodically to service the light, fog signal, and radio beacon.

CAPE ST. ELIAS LIGHTHOUSE

The same time that the Cape Hinchinbrook station was automated in the summer of 1974, the Cape St. Elias Lighthouse suffered a similar fate.

It was at that location, considered by some to be a very dangerous sector for navigation, that debate lingered for years before an aid to navigation became a reality. Located on a lonely piece of terra firma at the south end of Kayak Island, 60 miles southeast of Cordova, few ever came to the place before a light station was established. Aboard the ill-fated tender *Armeria* was a temporary lighted gas buoy which was to be tethered off the Cape to mark the treacherous Southeast Rock. It never arrived, but was lost with the ship. It was further suggested that a lightship should be placed off the cape, and that plan also fell by the wayside.

With added importance placed on the Alaska Railroad construction, the Bureau of Lighthouses recommended and got an appropriation of $115,000 for a lighthouse at Cape St. Elias in 1913. In the interim, a temporary lighted gas buoy was finally positioned offshore.

The following year, preliminary work of survey was completed and an acetylene blinker light installed. Construction began in 1915, and a large portion of the station was completed by the termination of the season. Even with government funds reaching rock bottom, the lighthouse was finally placed in operation on September 16, 1916. In addition, the ocean buoy with a light, whistle and a submarine bell was retained off Southeast Rock on a permanent basis, the dark St. Elias area at last well marked.

The beacon on the cape displayed its light at an elevation 85 feet above the sea, the square concrete tower extended from the corner of the fog signal building. Even the nearby keepers dwelling and outbuildings were all of concrete construction. The builders named the cape "Big Baldy."

Another distinction for the station was that its light and fog signal apparatus, prior to installation, had been displayed at the Panama Pacific International Exhibition in San Francisco, to show the latest improvements in the field of pharology utilized by the service.

Another first for St. Elias was the installation of a modern wireless service in charge of the three lighthouse keepers, whereby the citizens of Katalla could be alerted of incoming ships. After automation, the unmanned station was reduced to a minor light status. The feet of the keepers no longer roamed the 490 acre reservation. The unaltered 1916 structure still stands at this writing, flashing a white light every ten seconds from the 55 foot tower visible 15 miles at sea.

CAPE SPENCER LIGHTHOUSE

It was a long, arduous task to reach Cape Spencer Lighthouse when it was a manned installation. Barren of vegetation, it sits on a small basaltic upheaval offshore. The lifeless island at the entrance to Cross Sound is located 70 miles west of Juneau. Before it was crowned with a lighthouse, the Bureau ordered an unwatched acetylene light installed in 1913, 90 feet above the roaring ocean. For the seven previous years maritime interests had pleaded for an aid to navigation on the seagirt isle.

A small temporary light had to satisfy until Congress finally agreed to fund a major lighthouse, but not until 1923. Construction began a year later. At a whopping cost of $174,881, the station was opened for operation December 11, 1925, just in time for the keepers to spend their loneliest Christmas. They couldn't even grow a dandelion on the solid rock.

The lighthouse tower rose from the center of the fog signal building, which was 51 feet by 62 feet. The reinforced concrete structure not only housed the fog signal and its apparatus, but also had comfortable quarters for the "bachelor" keepers. Station buildings were all built to withstand hurricanes. Landings were most difficult in contrary seas and often Herculean efforts were necessary to get fuel and supplies topside via the derrick at the landing platform.

It was rugged duty for the Cape Spencer keepers. One visiting Coast Guard high-ranking officer claimed it to be the most difficult of all the district lighthouses to reach. A 200 mile range radio beacon was placed there in 1926, the first of its kind in Alaska. The light intensity was also raised to 20,000 candlepower.

Personnel were removed in 1974, when the facility was automated, but the original buildings are all intact even today, and as at other such locations helicopters can land maintenance personnel to check the navigation aids periodically. Things were much different when the keepers had to arrive and depart by the intricate sea route. At this writing a light was still shining from the tower, more than 105 feet above sea level, visible for than 20 miles. There is also a foghorn and radio beacon on the island, all of which operate with hi-tech automated accuracy, without human hands.

CAPE DECISION LIGHTHOUSE

As a result of a careless act, of human origin, fire broke out on October 11, 1989. It destroyed Cape Decision's boathouse, part of

Replacement for the formidable but ill-fated Scotch Cap Lighthouse on lonely Unimak Island. Photo courtesy of U.S. Coast Guard.

Dressed in their lighthouse workclothes, keepers Oscar Lindberg, left, and "Uncle" Barney Lokken pose in front of the camera with a scrawny Christmas tree behind them. Although Unimak Island has no trees, this tree was left off by a passing ship. The keepers had an easy time decorating the tree for Christmas at Scotch Cap Lighthouse in the 1920s.

the landing platform and a portion of the tramway and trestle. The blaze started in a 55 gallon garbage drum next to the light station's boathouse. It was intended as a controlled fire by the Sitka-based aids to navigation team visiting the facility for routine maintenance. However, the burning garbage in the drum got out of control and despite extinguishers and a bucket brigade it turned into a minor conflagration. The ANT staff was spared, as was the lighthouse.

Cape Decision Lighthouse ceased being a resident facility in 1974, most of the buildings kept intact, and Coast Guard maintenance crews arrive periodically, usually by helicopter, to check the aids to navigation and grounds. As of 1996, a powerful navigation light was shining from the lighthouse, 75 feet above the ground and 96 feet above the sea, visible for 20 plus miles. A foghorn blasts every 30 seconds and a radio beacon nearby sends out its dot dot dash, pause dash signal.

Cape Decision Lighthouse, located on the southwest end of Kuiu Island, is 63 miles south of Sitka. It was the final lighthouse constructed under the Bureau of Lighthouses prior to the Coast Guard takeover. Not until March 15, 1932, did the facility cast its beams. The Lighthouse Service received its first allocated monies from Congress, some $59,400, in the summer of 1929, but the preliminaries were even frustrating before the project was completed. The final figure of $158,000 was three times the original appropriation. Costs

Circa 1927, Scotch Cap Light Station keepers under the former U.S. Lighthouse Service. From left: Charles Shepardson, Barney Lokken, and Oscar Lindberg.

45

of construction were always considerably higher in Alaska than in the contiguous United States, and are still higher in our day.

A light at Decision had long been agitated for with the increasing ship traffic in the canned salmon industry, reduction plants, and herring salteries spread along the shady Chatham and Sumner Straits. Lighthouse officials had long insisted that deep sea vessels steaming through the Inside Passage were threatened when fog closed down in the narrows, and were forced to take a substitute route near Cape Decision where a light and fog signal were urgently needed.

Better late than never, the classic station when finally completed featured every modern convenience for long duty keepers. A derrick was placed at a lofty height and was used to lift supplies, station boats, and personnel up to the rocky plateau. From there, a lengthy bridgework walkway and tram led to the lighthouse. The structure was a 46 by 47 foot reinforced concrete building surmounted by a lofty tower rising from its center. Two Typhon horns were mounted on the roof of the building to warn of fog. A class A radio beacon was also in place.

Lincoln Rock (Rocks) Light Station gets a seagull's eye view in this U.S. Coast Guard photo. The station got off to a rocky start in 1905, later suffered major damage. The station was rebuilt in 1948 for the final time. It is located on the east side of the north end of Clarence Strait in southeastern Alaska. Photo courtesy of U.S. Coast Guard.

Landing at the 216 acre reservation was often hazardous when the weather was contrary, and delays were common. In addition, the nation was still suffering from the Depression and keepers were admonished to be conservative in everything by keeping machinery free from unnecessary repairs. Had the early appropriations to build the lighthouse not been made before the big stock market crash, the sentinel at Cape Decision might have been much less formidable. It was, however, a first-class station in every respect, and a tribute to its builders. The three keepers assigned, for the most part, were satisfied with their home away from home and were proud to keep the 350,000 candlepower flashing light in spit and polish condition.

When the Coast Guard took over in 1939, tours of duty were eventually cut, and transfers of personnel become more frequent, as was the case elsewhere. Hopefully, the Cape Decision Lighthouse will remain on its lofty perch for many more years.

The status of all the remaining Alaska lighthouses are constantly subject to change. Many of the buildings on the lighthouse grounds not utilized as aids to navigation are in some cases occupied by visitors from other government agencies for varying purposes. The navigation lights are constantly being updated, and to cut costs, solar energy is being widely utilized. Coast Guard buoy tenders have a tremendous job in keeping the numerous lights, foghorns, buoys, and allied aids, including day marks, in proper repair due to the elements and from vandalism. Coast Guard helicopters have lessened some of the burden, but in many places landing pads are not available. The 17th U.S. Coast Guard District headquarters at Juneau and the Ketchikan depot station has the largest area to cover of any of the

other districts in the nation. They carry out their duties with impunity, and with little publicity and notoriety they get the job done, often under the most difficult conditions.

True, the buoy tenders under the Coast Guard are shifted around much more often than were the faithful lighthouse tenders under the Lighthouse Service, but the requirements are much the same with the exception of the increasingly growing hi-technology equipment in our present day. Will there be a time when traditional lights or fog signals are no longer necessary? It could happen; only time will tell. The old lighthouse keeper has been relegated to history.

There were many excellent and faithful keepers who maintained the aids to navigation in Alaska during the old days, but none stands out quite as much as the late Ted Petersen, perhaps because he had a part of Alaska living in him. His mother, who died when he was one year old, was part Aleut and part Russian, leaving him and his six year old sister to become tenants of the Jesse Lee home in Unalaska, the village where Ted was born on February 24, 1905. His father Christian Petersen, successful whaler and trader, occasionally visited his children between trips to the north.

In 1916, Ted's father took him from the orphanage and out to sea as a cabin boy aboard the whaling vessel *Hermann*, and why not? Ted was a quarter Aleut, a quarter Russian and half Norwegian, which qualified him for a rugged life on sea or land.

When he applied to the Bureau of Lighthouses for a keepers position in 1927, there were no openings, so he was given a job as a deckhand on the lighthouse tender *Cedar*, and kept his application for a lighthouse keeper valid, with preference for Unimak Island. After a six-week tour on the *Cedar*, the third assistant keeper at Cape St. Elias Light Station had gone crazy from the isolation and Ted got the job as his replacement.

Within a year, the second assistant keeper at Cape Sarichef was removed because of insanity after learning his wife was cheating on him. Ted got the nod and a station of his choice. He arrived at the lonely domicile in July 1929, and four years later relieved head keeper Ed Moore, a former buffalo hunter, who had served at Sarichef for 20 years.

At the station on the other side of Unimak Island, (22 miles) Ted recalled that the ashes of the late keeper Barney Lokken were spread near Scotch Cap Lighthouse by the tender *Cedar*. Lokken had put in 20 years at that lighthouse—and remember, these were two of the world's most isolated navigation aids. Such men found peace and solitude in a separated lifestyle despite the unbearable weather conditions. They learned how to communicate with nature and be satisfied with a seclusive existence. The often ice-chocked Bering Sea was Sarichef's front yard and in the other direction were smoking volcanoes, which the Russians called "The Roof of Hell."

Once Ted experienced an earthquake so powerful that it doused the beacon, jammed the lighthouse door, and stopped the clock's pendulum.

The light was revolved as a 150 pound weight descended down the trunk of the tower. The fog siren was turned on frequently, and each of the three assigned keepers took turns housecleaning and cooking plus gardening, doctoring, plumbing, engineering, and barbering. In an emergency, a cutter from Dutch Harbor would respond.

Keepers often hunted caribou for meat or caught fish. Mail came once a month weather permitting, and pay during Ted's duty at Sarichef was $120 per month. The *Cedar* arrived annually with food and supplies.

In January 1934, Ted set out on a 263 mile trek around Unimak Island to see a woman school teacher working at the False Pass Cannery. The trip took 14 days in weather so cold at times his beard froze solid. Another woman once visited the station selling magazine subscriptions. The keepers, enthralled with seeing an attractive woman in such an isolated spot, bought several subscriptions without even knowing what they had purchased. In 1935, Ted was sent to San Francisco on his second years paid vacation, a benefit granted those who served three years straight at Sarichef, after which his dad insisted he make another Arctic sea voyage. He couldn't say no to his dad, so off he went. In 1937, he tried to get on again at Cape Sarichef Light Station but no openings were available so he had to settle for second assistant at Cape St. Elias. While there he was offered a job on the *Cedar* if he'd get a third mate's license, but though he got the license

the Coast Guard in the interim took over the Lighthouse Service. He then tried to get assigned to Cape Sarichef once again, but the new service had different plans.

In 1940, Ted became first assistant keeper at Point Sur Lighthouse in California, then transferred to Oakland Harbor Lighthouse and finally to Rowe Island. In all his years, he preferred the lonely life at Cape Sarichef the most. "Out there," he said, "I was part of the elements and I was an individual. I was at peace. I wish I had never left."

Old Ted finished out his days at the senior citizens home in Seldovia, his tanned weather-beaten face, white hair, and beard marking him as the kind that one would term not only a model light keeper but a true Alaskan in every sense.

The automation of Alaska light stations was probably best described by former Coast Guard overseer ET 2 Kevin Anderson. "This has been the best job I reckon I will ever have the pleasure of doing. I just hope these lighthouses are never forgotten."

Not all agreed with Anderson's analysis, but most had respect for the old sentinels. Jack D. Gorhring who served at Eldred Rock Lighthouse during World War II stated, "I must admit, I don't have any particularly fond memories of my lighthouse assignment, but it was better than getting shot at."

A private aid to navigaton was built at the entrance to Sitka Harbor in recent years. It is called Cape Edgecomb Lighthouse and acts as a bed and breakfast unit.

Another view of Lincoln Rock Light Station. The upper right photo shows the original frame lighthouse which was destroyed by adverse seas.

Principle complaint of the lighthouse keeper under the former Lighthouse Service, prior to the Coast Guard takeover in 1939, was the frequent inspections. Brass work was the constant lament of the keeper, for everything had to be spit and polish at all times. The following lines by an unknown poet tell well the frustration:

Oh, what is the bane of a lightkeepers life,
That causes him worry and struggles and strife
That makes him use cuss words and beat up his wife?
It's Brasswork.

What makes him look ghastly, consumptive and thin,
What robs him of health and vigor and vim,
And causes despair and drives him to sin?
It's Brasswork.

The lamp in the tower, reflector and shade,
The tools and accessories pass in parade
As a matter of fact the whole thing is made
of Brasswork.

The machinery, clock-work and fog signal bell,
The coal-hods, the dust pans, the pump in the well,
Now I'll leave it to you, mates, if this isn't—well
Brasswork.

I dig, scrub and polish, and work with a might,
and just when I get it all shining and bright,
In comes the fog like a thief in the night
Goodbye Brasswork.

Oh why should the spirit of mortal be proud
In this short span of life that he is allowed
If all of the lining in every darn cloud
Is Brasswork?

And when I have polished until I am cold,
And I'm taken aloft to the Heavenly fold,
Will my harp and my crown be make of pure gold?
No, Brasswork.

A 1948 Coast Guard photo of lonely Cape Sarichef Light Station on Unimak Island. The station was established in 1904 and updated in 1950. Today the beacon is a small light on a skeleton tower.

Upper photo, the original Cape Sarichef Lighthouse. Lower left is its replacement in 1950, placed on a bluff above the original light. At the right, the lighthouse is seen surrounded by snow in the early 1930s. Photo courtesy of U.S. Coast Guard.

The original Cape Hinchinbrook Lighthouse built in 1910 as Alaska's finest in later years was threatened by erosion as can be seen in this Lighthouse Service photo. In the 1930s, a replacement lighthouse was constructed and the structure seen here above to its fate. Photo taken in 1933.

Put in operation in the 1934-35 era is the beautiful new Cape Hinchinbrook Lighthouse near the entrance to Prince William Sound. Situated 235 feet above sea level, the 67 foot tower is still maintained by regular visits of the Coast Guard aids to navigation crew. Insert shows the first light placed at Cape Hinchinbrook before the 1910 lighthouse. Photo courtesy of U.S. Coast Guard.

It was always a major job to hoist oil drums and supplies up to the landing at Cape Hinchinbrook Light Station which was 150 feet above the beach. The sea cliff to the right juts up 1,400 feet. Automation put an end to the chore. In the photo at left taken in 1950 the ice-breaker Northwind *delivered the station fuel cargo. Photo courtesy of U.S. Coast Guard.*

Cape Hinchinbrook Light Station. Insert shows the new lighthouse nearly completed in 1934 and the threatened original lighthouse in the background minus its iron lantern house which was placed atop the new Hinchinbrook structure. Photo courtesy of U.S. Coast Guard.

An overall view of the Guard Island Light Station taken by a Coast Guard photographer in the 1950s. Insert: Back in the days of the U.S. Lighthouse Service, keeper George West is pictured with his wife Alma and assistant keeper Waltenberg in the dining room of the keepers dwelling.

The original Guard Island Lighthouse placed in operation in 1904 under the U.S. Lighthouse Establishment. A host of visitors to the frame tower are seen on the gallery surrounding the iron lantern house. Note the fog bell mounted on the tower. Photo courtesy U.S. Lighthouse Society.

Guard Island Light Station as seen from the air. The station was established in 1904 and rebuilt in 1924 to accommodate ship traffic in Tongass Narrows. In the above photo, the lighthouse, located on the north islet of the Guard group was equipped with a diaphone fog signal and radio beacon as well as a distance finding station in the 1950s. Photo courtesy of U.S. Coast Guard.

	1890	1895	1900	1905	1910
Lights	0	1	1	15	37
Fog Signals	0	0	0	8	9
Buoys	27	57	57	68	84
Daymarks	15	26	25	30	30

	1915	1920	1925	1930	1940
Lights	112	196	260	350*	457**
Fog Signals	10	11	13	14	15
Buoys	167	224	303	309	316
Daymarks	39	94	140	178	181
Radio Beacons	0	0	0	3	9

*Figure includes 311 minor lights, 13 light stations, and 26 lighted buoys.

**Figure includes 387 minor lights, 14 light stations, and 56 lighted buoys.

Number of navigation aids in Alaska 1890-1940 compiled by the U.S. Bureau of Lighthouses and its successor, the U.S. Coast Guard.

Mary Island Light Station, showing the original 1903 tower in the insert and its replacement in 1937. The first lighthouse was of frame construction, the latter reinforced concrete. The beacon was the first major light seen by ships entering the Inside Passage of Alaska northbound. Photo courtesy of U.S. Coast Guard.

Above and right: *These pictures surround the events of Ralph Edwards' radio show "Truth or Consequences" (sponsored by Duz soap). Robert Livingston, the contestant, could not answer questions on the show and his consequence was to deliver a bucket of ice to a light station in Alaska, "Operation Ice Cubes." He came to Guard Island with representatives from the show and a photograher. These pictures are the result. Taken 1949.*

This is Scotch Cap Lighthouse on Unimak Island shown during the period of its construction shortly before the tragic seismic tidal wave destroyed it. The upper insert shows the original frame lighthouse established in 1903. Most of that structure was still in place when the newer lighthouse was completed. It was also wiped out by the great wave. Lower insert, the unwatched replacement navigation aid installed after the tragic episode. Photo courtesy of U.S. Coast Guard.

The new Tree Point Lighthouse marking Dixon Entrance, nears completion in 1935. Below, the station's small boat is pictured at the Tree Point landing in the 1950s. Photos courtesy of the former U.S. Lighthouse Service.

Remote and scenic is this site of the U.S. Coast Guard Light Station at Cape St. Elias on the south end of Kayak Island in the Gulf of Alaska. To the left in the background is 1,800 foot Pinnacle Rock where eagles gather at its peak and sea lions frequent its base. When this photo was taken in November 1950 the lighthouse was displaying a one million candlepower light. Photo courtesy of U.S. Coast Guard.

Dwarfed by the precipitous sea cliffs of Kayak Island, lonely Cape St. Elias Lighthouse keeps its vigil. Photos at left shows the lighthouse under construction in 1916 and just after its completion. The Coast Guard photo at right was taken in the 1950s.

Five Finger Lighthouse under construction in 1935, a reinforced concrete structure.

Tree Point Lighthouse—father and son—1904 and 1935. The original lighthouse is pictured in the upper left hand corner and its replacement as seen from the air in the 1960s. Photo courtesy of U.S. Coast Guard.

Above: *Five Finger Lighthouse, the first Alaskan primary light station went into operation in 1902, culminating the end of a long agitation for more and better aids to navigation on the territory's Inside Passage. That pioneer lighthouse is pictured in the insert, upper left. The main photo, taken in the 1960s, shows the new lighthouse which was built in 1935 and equipped with light, diaphone fog signal, radio beacon, and distance finding apparatus.* Photo courtesy of U.S. Coast Guard.

Below: *An alternate view of the Five Finger Light Station taken by a U.S. Coast Guard photographer in the 1960s.*

Zooming in on Sentinel Island Light Station in 1951. The tower was completed in 1935 replacing the one established in 1902. Note the spacious keepers dwelling and the lengthy tramway going up from the station landing.

Below: *This is the pioneer lighthouse erected on Sentinel Island. Although the USLHE sign on the tower dates it as 1901, it was not officially placed in service until the following year. Note the keeper and his family in their vintage garb and the rocking chair on the front porch. The ornate structure succumbed to its successor in the mid-1930s. From files of the former U.S. Lighthouse Service and Alaska State Library.*

Cape St. Elias gas powered whistle buoy is seen being lowered into Orca Inlet from the lighthouse tender Cedar in July of 1918.

Crewman unload a scow laden with construction materials for the Cape Spencer Light Station in May 1924.

Buoys at the lighthouse depot in Ketchikan in December 1916, ready for placement in Alaska sealanes.

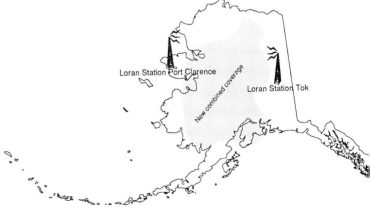

Loran Station Port Clarence

New combined coverage

Loran Station Tok

Modern aids to navigation—major Alaska LORAN stations in remote locations are a far cry from the lighthouses and foghorns of yesteryear.

Loran Station, Attu, marks the frozen terrain of the most westerly Aleutian Islands land mass. It was commissioned in the 1960s.

Lighthouse Service Depot, Ketchikan, Alaska, in 1916.

Above and below: *The venerable and dependable U.S. Lighthouse Tender* Cedar *performed yeoman service in Alaska along with her longtime master, Captain John W. Leadbetter. He was given command of the vessel right out of the builder's yard in 1917. The* Cedar *is pictured here in drydock for her annual overhaul in 1919.*

Alaska was still in Russian hands when the steamer Shubrick *visited New Archangel (Sitka) in 1865, two years before the purchase. She was the first U.S. government vessel to do so. The sidewheeler was the first lighthouse tender, revenue cutter, and all around government police vessel on the Pacific Coast performing her duties from California to Alaska. Insert shows the vessel at the Flavel pier near Astoria, Oregon, in 1860.* Photo courtesy Columbia River Maritime Museum.

U.S. Lighthouse Tender Hemlock *performed admirably in Alaskan waters.*

Sleek little U.S. Lighthouse Tender Rose *put in several years of service on the inland waters of Alaska.* Bouchers photo.

Weatherbeaten and nostalgic, veteran Alaska lighthouse keeper Ted Petersen holds the map showing the route he took around Unimak Island when keeper at Cape Sarichef in 1934. Photo by Ed Moreth, U.S. Coast Guard.

Pogromni Volcano and Faris Peak; Red Hill and Cape Sarichef Lighthouse (in left foreground).

Tragic ending for the U.S. Lighthouse Tender Armeria *wrecked May 20, 1910, off Cape Hinchinbrook when bringing in supplies and construction materials for the Cape Hinchinbrook Lighthouse. She is seen here with inverted ensign and distress signal flags. Note the boats removing the crew.*

U.S. Lighthouse tender Columbine *was a workhorse for the U.S. Lighthouse Service in bygone years. Built at Cleveland, Ohio, in 1892, the* Columbine *performed stellar service in the Pacific Northwest, Alaska, and Hawaii.*

Brilliant Gold to Black Gold

*No mineral in all the
world shines with as
much brilliance as "Gold".
It can make or break the finder.
—Anon*

Seldom has there ever been more excitement than was generated after the passenger steamer *Portland* arrived at Seattle with its famous ton of gold. The news was electrifying, and even with slow communications at that time in history (1897), the word got around the world in record time. Gold-hungry humans from far and wide endeavored to reach Seattle and other Puget Sound ports, and even in some cases Oregon ports, willing to pay most any price to book passage to Alaska. The economy of the Pacific Northwest picked up almost immediately. Seattle became the principal jumping off place for the Klondike and Yukon.

Ships of every kind and description pointed their compasses northward, the majority navigating the poorly marked Inside Passage to Juneau and Skagway with the latter port becoming the northern terminus for gold seekers, who unbeknownst to most would have to haul their equipment by foot over the treacherous Chilkoot Pass to Whitehorse and on to the gold fields by riverboat to the Klondike. The mountainous struggle took its toll, some never reaching Whitehorse where river transport was available up the Yukon River to Dawson. Just north of Whitehorse is the site of Lake Laberge, a locale that gave Robert Service his theme for the classic poem "The Cremation of Sam McGee."

Some of the ships took the outside passage to Nome, where gold was being panned from the beaches. Little mining camps cropped up in many places and men with picks, shovels, and pans were everywhere. Along with the makeshift settlements in the Klondike came the saloons and brothels, and money passed around freely. Those who ran the stores charged outrageous prices for everything. For the few years of the big gold discovery those who cashed in big with their gold dust and nuggets were basically the exception. Many others lost everything. It would have been better if they had never left the security of their homelands. Gold, however, will do that to mankind. The Klondike strike was a close runner to the California gold rush of 1849,

Coast Guard wins DOT gold medal

The Department of Transportation awarded the Secretary's Gold Medal to the Coast Guard for the service's "outstanding servicewide response to the Exxon Valdez oil spill disaster, which exemplifies their 200 years of courageous national service and devotion to duty."

"This year, breaking tradition, I awarded the medal, for the first time, to an organization; to the United States Coast Guard for their efforts in Alaska," said Samuel Skinner, secretary of the Department of Transportation. "That was because I thought their effort was so extraordinary."

"Your commitment and dedication in responding to the largest oil spill in our country's history played a key role in being recognized for this distinguished award," said CAPT David A. Worth, the Seventeenth Coast Guard District's chief of staff.

"While this award is not something that you can hang on your chest, it is something to be very proud of, and you will have the knowledge that what you do in Alaska does count," he said.

Gold medal awarded the U.S. Coast Guard by the Department of Transportation for the outstanding service rendered in the wake of the Exxon Valdez *disaster.*

and the results were mostly the same, some becoming multi-millionaires and others left to pick up the pieces.

Skagway, which in the mid 1890s was little more than a fishing village, was somewhat shaken by the great armada of ships that filled its harbor. Other southeast Alaskan ports such as Dyea were also cashing in on the bonanza.

Only four major steamship companies provided passenger service to Alaska prior to the gold rush. The discovery prompted new interest in Alaska and there were those beside gold seekers who wanted to visit the great territory in order to enjoy its scenic grandeur, and its fishing and hunting opportunities. There was also interest in the native Alaskans, their culture, and totem poles. Eskimos were also a source of curiosity.

The Pacific Coast Steamship Company had entered Alaskan trade as early as 1877 with the 266 foot sidewheel steamer *Ancon*, and to the *Ancon* must go the honor of being the first vessel to promote the Alaska cruise industry. Unfortunately, she met her fate on August 28, 1889, in command of Captain D. Wallace. While leaving the dock at Loring, at three in the morning, she swung around on her stern to keep free of foul ground, one line holding her to the wharf. A Chinese long shoreman then cast the hawser off prematurely. The ship drifted broadside on, punched a hole in her wooden hull, and with the receding tide broke her back on the rocks. Pacific Steamship Company valued her at $100,000. The loss was beyond the control of Captain Wallace and the pilot, H. H. Lloyd. Passengers and crew reached shore safely. The *Ancon* gradually fell to pieces as she lingered helplessly astride the rocks like a dead whale.

The SS *Idaho* was probably the first Alaskan passenger ship to offer shore excursions. Henry Villard, American industrialist, with interests in travel, tourism, and transportation, organized the initial excursion party in 1881 to Alaska aboard that steamer, in command of Captain James Carroll. The *Idaho's* lifeboats were used to take passengers into places of interest while the ship waited at anchor.

Two years later, Villard completed the Northern Pacific Railroad across America, terminating at Tacoma on Puget Sound. He then purchased the Oregon Railway and Navigation Company to provide ships for river and northland excursions on a regular basis. Said he,

"Now an East Coast American, tired of Europe's spas and scenes can take a railroad west and a passenger steamer north."

In the early years, ports like San Francisco, Portland, Seattle, Tacoma, or Port Townsend were the places to book cruises to Alaska, and most of the fleet made calls at Victoria or Nanaimo before sailing for Juneau, Douglas, Wrangell, and Sitka. Such a cruise would last for three or more weeks at a cost between $130 and $150, all inclusive.

Of course, such vessels were also used on regular liner service as the mode of common transport. Most of the cargo carriers always had limited accommodations for those who didn't desire the comfort of the liners.

How passengers should attire themselves was also addressed in the Pacific Coast Steamship Company folders of yesteryear. It read: "An umbrella is a convenient companion. A gossamer for a lady and a mackintosh for a gentleman...you have no use for your swallow tail or court dress, or Sunday go-to-meeting clothes in Alaska. Ladies skirts should be short so they will not draggle over the wet deck of the steamer...If you intend (as you no doubt will and certainly should) to climb up on to and take a run over a glacier, you will find much advantage to have spikes on your shoes—"

The die had been cast. Out of an abundance of ship lines formed almost overnight after gold was discovered, most flourished until the excitement began to wane. Many of the ships ran into navigational problems, especially on the Inside Passage. Some of the firms eventually were purchased by the larger companies and others went bankrupt.

Perhaps the most successful of all was the Alaska Steamship Company, established in 1897, with the SS *Willapa*, a stout little wooden passenger vessel that began her days as a bar tug when built at Astoria in 1881-82. A decade later at Portland, she was lengthened and converted, eventually becoming an Alaskan passenger vessel in direct competition with Pacific Steamship Company, lowering the cost of a passenger to as low as $12, Seattle to southeast Alaska. Wrecked in Alaska near the turn of the century, she was later salvaged and rebuilt as a unit of the Canadian Pacific Navigation Company. Still later, the *Willapa* came back under American operation and was renamed the *Bellingham*. In her wake came the SS *Dolphin*, in the Alaska Line's bid for first-class passenger service. The fleet grew by leaps and bounds with passenger liners and freighters dominating Alaskan trade until 1954, when the SS *Denali* made the last trip for the company, ending more than a half century of valuable service. The Alaska Line was long involved with copper ore shipments from the Kennecott Copper Company which had built a railroad to handle the rich deposits, first discovered in 1899 and lasting until 1938.

The venerable little *Bellingham* (ex-*Willapa*) continued a brilliant career not only being the first ship of the Alaska Steamship Company, but after coming back under the American flag was the first ship of the Black Ball Line (later Washington State Ferries), and the first ship of the Northland Transportation Company. In her later years she was converted to a diesel powered cargo ship, and after sinking at Deer Harbor in the San Juan Islands, was raised and purposely burned to the water's edge at the Seattle Seafair celebration in the summer of 1950.

In 1907, the renowned H. F. Alexander founded the Pacific Steamship Company, better known as the Admiral Line. It competed with coastal and Alaska service provided by the Pacific Coast Steamship Company. The two firms later merged under the Admiral houseflag, and steamers like the *Admiral Sampson*, *Admiral Evans*, and *Admiral Rodgers* became household words on the Alaska run.

Canadian Pacific Railroad entered the coastal shipping trade in 1901 when it purchased the Canadian Pacific Navigation Company. Its historic roots went back to the Hudson's Bay Company which brought the first steamer to the North Pacific, the sidewheeler *Beaver* in 1835. That vessel sailed out from England, and didn't have her paddlewheels attached until reaching the Hudson's Bay settlement at Fort Vancouver on the Columbia River.

Canadian Pacific is still a factor in our day with rail, air, and allied interests. The firm played a large role in Alaskan maritime trades for many decades, including Alaskan cruise ships.

As late as 1963, the State of Alaska, in response to an increasing demand from its citizens for an inexpensive passenger, car, and truck route by sea to Southeast Alaska (from first Seattle and then Bellingham) established the Alaska Marine Highway System and financed the construction of large, modern, seagoing ferries. The popular service attracted locals and tourists from far and wide as a way to see the inside scenic passage in an informal manner, featuring utilitarian accommodations with all the necessities.

Little did John Muir, the famous California naturalist who traveled the Inside Passage by steamer and canoe in 1879 (accompanied by missionary S. Hall Young and four Tlingets), realize that his words would be the springboard in alerting the public to the grandeur of the Great Land. Said he: "To the lover of pure wilderness, Alaska is one of the most beautiful countries in the world."

His remarks were truthful in every way. The naturalist continued by insisting that "no excursion that I know may be made into any other American wilderness where so marvelous abundance of noble, newborn scenery is so charmingly brought to view as on a trip through the Alexander Archipelago to Fort Wrangell and Sitka. Gazing from the deck of a steamer, one is borne smoothly over the calm, blue waters through the midst of countless forest-clad islands. The ordinary discomforts of a sea voyage are not felt, for nearly all the whole, long way is on inland waters that are about as waveless as rivers and lakes."

Muir's comments were well taken and his discourse pointed many visitors to the pristine waterways, which, though generally smooth, can get mighty riled in the winter season as many victims of shipwreck could well attest to. Muir saw the land at its best under very favorable conditions. Everything that has a good side can also have an adverse side.

The cry of "Gold in the Klondike" lured thousands to the Yukon Territory's settlement at Dawson (a former Indian village) from 1896 through the summer of 1898. Soon, however, the call was echoing in Nome and Fairbanks, and Dawson's boom collapsed almost as quickly as it began. The town remained sparsely populated and today has become an historical tourist destination. Skagway, which sprang up as the jumping off point to the Yukon gold fields in 1898 boasted nearly 15,000 population, far more than call it home today. Back in 1898, John Muir described it as "A nest of ants stirred up by a stick."

As the gold deposits began to decline, many people tested the other prospects offered in Alaska. For instance, the Norwegian Peter Buschmann settled in Petersburg, about the turn of the century, and built a salmon cannery. Many of his Scandinavian cohorts also moved there, which was the beginning of an industry that still exists in Alaska today. Petersburg became known as "Little Norway", what with its Nordic citizens and the similarity of the surrounding mountains and fjords so emblematic of Norway.

Old Fort Stikine near Wrangell, a Russian stockade in 1834, was manned by principals of the Hudson's Bay Company when it leased the site from the Muscovites in 1839. It became the supply point for fur traders, and in more recent years Wrangell became a fishing, lumber, and tourist area.

Coal mining became a big factor in the Alaskan economy in the late 1800s on the Kenai Peninsula near the present town of Homer, and copper mining, as earlier mentioned, gained ground starting around the turn of the century and flourished for many years at the Kennecott Copper holdings. Kenai, established as Fort St. Nicholas by Russian fur traders in 1791, became a U.S. garrison in 1869. A Russian Orthodox church is still there today.

As the territory grew in the early years, the religious movement was not idle. After a disagreement with the Church of England, the Reverend William Duncan moved nearly 1,000 Christianized Tsimshian Indians from northern British Columbia to an Indian reserve on Annette Island at Metlakatla.

A Presbyterian mission was founded at Haines in 1881, and at the Eskimo village of Bethel a Moravian mission was founded in 1885. Various other denominations also started churches in Alaska in the 1880s and 1890s.

With so much emphasis on the Klondike gold rush, the gold strike at Anvil Creek (near Nome) in 1898 played second fiddle, but that discovery along with the yield from the nearby beach sands the following year attracted no less than 20,000 prospectors, housed in endless rows of tents. There is still some gold to be found there today, but it is mainly the Eskimo handicrafts that attract tourists to that northern outpost facing the Bering Sea. About 200 miles east of Nome on the Yukon River is the village of Nulato where the Alaskan natives still boast of their victory over the Russian invaders, a fact seldom mentioned in Soviet history books. The place began as a Russian trading post in the late 1830s. In 1851, there was an Athapaskan uprising. The settlement was destroyed and the Russians driven out. The native stick dance performed at Nulato and Kaltag (downriver) commemorates the event to honor their native ancestors.

Ketchikan, originally an Indian fishing camp from ancient times, later became the salmon capital of the world. Tlinget and Haida totem poles still hearken of the past there, but in more recent years lumber, pulp, and tourism joined the fishing industry to increase the commercial value of the port.

Though Alaska's population growth was small by comparison with the lower states, the percentage has accelerated in recent times. From an estimated 28,000 in 1867, including 500 nonnatives, the population reached 75,254 by 1940, with 32,400 Eskimos, Indians, and Aleuts. Half of the whites were congregated in five of the largest towns.

Since World War II, the population of the state hit the 600,000 mark, and as mentioned earlier, is no longer the least inhabited of the 50 states, that designation going to Wyoming. Anchorage, for many years a very small town, has become by far the largest in all of Alaska. It was plotted in the early 1900s as a camp and supply center for the crew building the Alaska Railroad. Its importance came during World War II with construction of Fort Richardson and Elmendorf Air Field. Nearby oil production and the city's prime location as an international air crossroads, plus its portal for shipping, make it Alaska's number one metropolis. Even the devastating 1964 earthquake, which took a heavy toll, could not slow the growth of Anchorage. An added bonus is the Port of Whittier, in Prince William Sound, which the U.S. Army created as an ice-free deep water port in the

1940s. It also is a rail terminus for the Alaska Railroad, and though built to get military supplies to interior bases, it can also be a port of call for Anchorage should ice hamper Cook Inlet.

Seward also became a rail terminus. It bears the name of U.S. Secretary of State William H. Seward, responsible for Alaska's purchase from Russia. The city received major damage to its port dock facilities and oil storage area in the 1964 earthquake.

Valdez grew rapidly in the early 1900s as a port of entry to Alaska's interior, but was also devastated by the massive 1964 quake. The town was rebuilt four miles to the west, and today has regained prominence as the major port for supertankers picking up crude oil at the southern terminus of the trans-Alaskan pipeline, stretching all the way from Prudoe Bay, where massive oil fields were discovered in 1968. The estimates are 9.6 billion barrels of oil and 26 trillion cubic feet of natural gas.

The discovery turned Alaska into a treasure trove of black gold, far more valuable than the former Yukon gold fields. Near Prudoe Bay, the Kuparuk River field with reserves of one billion barrels began producing oil in 1981. Though exploitation of the untapped Beaufort Sea petroleum is estimated to be costly, geologists believe that as much as 17 billion barrels of recoverable oil and 72 trillion cubic feet of natural gas may exist there. Perhaps only a national shortage of petroleum will prompt an all-out effort to tap that reserve. Research and controversy continues over the opening of that field.

Another source of Alaskan oil, some five billion barrels, is said to exist in a 37,000 square mile area designated by President Warren G. Harding in 1923— a huge piece of real estate on the vast North Slope. Alaska's first commercial oil production was in 1902, in the south central sector. The northernmost town in the United States is Barrow, (Point Barrow) largely inhabited by Eskimos. Petroleum exploration during the 1940s drew increasing numbers of people, the 1968 oil strike establishing Barrow as the northern capital. Many of the natives still hunt whale by treaty off Point Barrow and caribou are still plentiful there.

Chief mate Bill Ike of the Salvage Chief *shows off the souvenir life ring presented to the crew of the famous salvage ship after the superior work performed in the saving of the 211,000 ton tanker* Exxon Valdez. *Upper left, the veteran master of the* Salvage Chief, *Captain Reino Mattila.* Photos courtesy of the Daily Astorian, photographers Kent Kerr and John Fortmeyer.

The Alaska National Interest Lands Conservation Act of 1980 established ten natural preserves, and designated or enlarged eight national parks. It also granted Alaskans who live off the land the right to continue traditional fishing, hunting, and gathering practices. Today, the National Park System encompasses 14 per cent of the state which guarantees the future of the natural wonderland. The nation's highest peak, Mt. McKinley, was established as a national park in 1917. Today, it is officially part of the Denali National Park and Preserve. As earlier mentioned, the massive mountain rises 20,320 feet and is snow-capped the year round. In the huge park fish and wildlife are in abundance—grizzly bears, caribou, moose, wolves, and Dall sheep, to name a few.

Fairbanks was also a gold mining settlement in the early 1900s. Now referred to as Alaska's "golden heart," with interior focus on trade, it blossomed again in the 1970s as the construction base for the trans-Alaskan pipeline. It boasts military installations and the nation's most northerly university.

Attempts were made in recent years to have the state capital moved to industrious Anchorage, but resistance has kept that from occurring. Sitka served as U.S. territorial capital after the territory's purchase from Russia and remained so until 1906, when Juneau was accorded that honor.

Shipping costs have always been a bugaboo for Alaska. Seattle replaced San Francisco as its commercial gateway in the wake of the Yukon gold rush. Wagon roads covering five miles in 1867 to a thousand by 1920 supplemented river and rail travel. Bush pilots pioneered a new era in the following decade, as air transport ousted dog sleds. In the southeastern sector so many settlements are on islands that air flights have become a blessing in recent decades, both domestic and commercial.

Congress gave the green light to the building of the Alaska Railroad in 1914. The rails favored Anchorage as a shipping point, especially for coal. Such shipments could come by river boat on the Susitna, Nenana, Tanana, and Yukon River system, all the way to Anchorage.

Alaska's great farming potential was brought to the public eye in the 1930s in the wake of the Great Depression., when 202 families arrived to pioneer the Matanuska Valley Project, under the Federal Emergency Relief Administration. That 1935 epic was one of several designed to boost the sagging economy in the Great Land. The Matanuska colony raised a healthy crop of vegetables and livestock in their new surroundings. Other government aided work included road building, airfields, and radio beacons. Though the Matanuska project produced some good results the overall series of performances failed to cause a hoped-for land rush. Markets for farm produce were limited, and distant. Many of the settlers were obviously inexperienced.

Through the years, the salmon industry remained steady in southeast Alaska. It was mainly the Tlingit and other Indian tribal members that were the laboring force in the canneries. As fishing fleets increased, more Asians, both Chinese and Japanese, along with Filipinos and Mexicans took over. By 1940, half the fishing and cannery crews were foreign-born workers. The Alaska Packers and Columbia River Packers ran fleets of outmoded commercial sailing vessels to bring the cannery workers to Alaska each season in conjunction with company steamers, right up until World War II. There were also firms like the Loman Commercial Company that among other items were involved with reindeer products. In the 1890s, Bering Sea coastal natives hunted the caribou to near extinction after being introduced to repeating rifles. Then they turned to the reindeer which were numbered at about 700,000 in 1931, but protectionism by U.S. cattlemen, plus range management problems combined with the Depression killed off a promising export industry.

On the plus side, Alaskan natives had reclaimed title to lands as sovereign nations (after the purchase), unlike Native Americans in the lower contiguous states. The missionaries of the Protestant, Roman Catholic, and Orthodox churches were saddled with the job of education for the natives under government control in 1884. By 1930, Federal health programs at last reversed nearly 200 years of population decline among the natives, which has continued to the present time.

Alaska Land Act of 1980 classified 103 million federal acres, more land than the state of California as under government control, a somewhat controversial piece of legislature. As earlier mentioned that single

act doubled the nation's parks and refuges, and tripled the wilderness areas. Environmentalists were overjoyed, industrialists agitated. By 1983, nearly 73 million of the state's 104 million acre entitlement had been transferred, and the native corporations under ANCSA had received 28 of their 44 million. Prime stands of western hemlock and Sitka spruce enriched Sealaska, one of 13 native regional corporations, through sales to Korea and Japan.

Little did George Carmack realize what effect he would have on the future of Alaska when he staked his Klondike gold claim in 1896, nor did the first miners who found gold on the beaches of Nome. Until the White Pass and Yukon Railroad opened to Whitehorse in 1900, gold seekers from Juneau and Skagway followed the ancient Indian routes to Dawson and nearby camps. Valdez was an early gateway to gold deposits around Fairbanks, via the Valdez Trail and river routes. By 1923, the federal government completed the 412 mile Alaska Railroad to Nenana, and finally the Richardson Highway followed the former route of the old Valdez Trail. But with all the emphasis on Alaska's interior, people still were slow to settle the newly opened lands, there being only 117 homesteads on the route.

Alaska was still dependent on Puget Sound and Canadian ports. Again it was back to the maritime industries to support the territory with the exporting of Alaska's salmon, timber, and furs.

World War I termination and the end of the gold boom drained many settlers away from Alaska by the early 1920s, despite improved communications, federal colonization, and a thriving salmon industry. White settlers were somewhat sparsely positioned.

The effort to turn things around got off to a slow start. In 1934, a congressional delegate had real foresight when he pleaded loudly, "Defend the United States by defending Alaska." His words fell flat, and when the real test came in 1942, with the Japanese invasion of Alaska, the U.S. was basically unprepared. Only God's grace kept the invaders from making great inroads into the territory. After the war, many Japanese military officials admitted they never realized how vulnerable Alaska was. America's ability to finally rally its war cause eventually throttled the invasion, but had Uncle Sam heeded the words of the congressman in 1934, Alaska would have been ready. When Japan invaded the Aleutian Islands in 1942, Alaska took the stage by necessity. Not since the gold rush days had so much emphasis been placed on the territory. This time, however, it was an all-out effort to thwart the enemy in the aftermath of the Pearl Harbor bombing, December 7, 1941. Military bases began to dot the empty Alaska spaces. Airfields, roads, and the modernization of port facilities brought thousands of construction workers and military men to the northland. The once remote frontier suddenly became a strategic front line. Ships by the score laden with war materials and general cargo descended on Alaska in waves, with the announcement that, "Japan must be stopped at any cost." Considerably more attention was focused on South Pacific war actions than on the Alaska defenses, but certainly if the North Pacific operations by the allies failed, the war would have taken a whole new course.

The battle for Alaska was on when the Japanese landed on, and occupied, Attu in June 1942. From the "Land of the Rising Sun" the invaders planned to have that sun shine on their Alaska trek, hop-skipping from one island to the next until they could strike the heart of Alaska and raise their flag over conquered lands. Japanese invaders landing on Attu immediately captured 40 Aleuts. When the U. S. military forces fought back in 1943, in a bold effort to retake the island, they suffered 3,800 casualties, many of whom were victims of exposure from the harsh elements. In the interim, the Nipponese had established a strong garrison on Kiska Island in 1942. U.S. bombers descended on that island, and the enemy having already lost Attu, remained on Kiska for only a year longer before pulling out their troops.

U.S. military bases, established in 1942 after the initial Japanese invasion played a major role in the Aleutian campaign. Important bases still remain in the Aleutians today.

American forces, poorly prepared at first, showed what our country was made of with a cooperative all-out effort in seemingly doing the impossible. There was, however, a price to pay. Ships and planes on both sides were lost through war action and from natural causes, and lives were sacrificed. By and large, the American military forces did remarkably well in combating the enemy. A good example was the prime usage of the military port of Whittier, served by the Alaska Railroad, where millions of tons of valuable cargo was handled. The port was ice-free which was a great advantage in the winter season.

By November 1942, the 1,428 mile Alaskan-Canadian Military Highway (ALCAN) connected Alaska to Canadian railheads. The project piped Canadian oil to fuel trucks and aircraft.

By 1943, work began on the Eielson air base which was to not only be a huge factor during the World War II era but a strong deterrent against the Soviets had the "Cold War" with Russia have become a hot one. The United States and Canada strung the distant early warning (DEW) line of radar stations across the continent's ice rim in the mid 1950s, which was followed later by a missile-detection facility near Fairbanks. Even today, such facilities have great importance to our military. The surveillance must continue. That the revitalized Russian nation cannot be taken lightly is still evident by the on-going shadowing of our nuclear submarines. One of the nation's prime nuclear submarine bases is located at Bangor on Puget Sound and those submarines often enter Alaskan waters, some having navigated the frozen northland ice beneath the surface through the fabled Northwest Passage at the top of the world.

Many more American ships were victims of stranding and other natural calamities in Alaska during World War II than by enemy action. The USS *Gilmore* was sunk by Japanese submarine *1-180*, 120 miles southwest of Kodiak, and the USAT *General Gorgas* was shelled by the Japanese submarine *1-9* in the Gulf of Alaska, but was saved from destruction. The Japanese submarine *1-25* in a bizarre incident in the North Pacific, torpedoed and sunk the Soviet submarine *L-16* October 11, 1942, believing it to be an American submersible.

Two US Coast Guard cutters claimed the sinking of a Japanese submarine off the west coast of southeastern Alaska in 1942, but the Japanese War Ministry claimed it never happened.

Even more unusual was the bombing by Japanese planes of the old SS *Northwestern* which served the Alaska Steamship Company for many years. She was serving as a barracks ship at Dutch Harbor when the bombing occurred in June of 1942. Survivor of numerous strandings during her long tenure as a passenger liner, she had the reputation of an indestructible ship with a somewhat voodoo reputation. The vintage vessel always bounced back from each accident.

Ironically, she was identified by the Japanese as a major fighting ship. One of the bombs struck her a blow amidships—some reports saying it went right down her stack.

Few were aboard at the time and fortunately so, as she was buckled and smoldering after the attack, but as always remained proud as a peacock and refused to sink. Later, the wreck was towed to nearby Captain's Bay and shoved ashore where she remained for many years, a monument to the war. Many claimed the *Northwestern* never died, she just rusted away.

Following the Pearl Harbor attack, the U.S. Navy took full command of all Pacific Northwest shipping operations. All sailings for foreign ports were cancelled and movements in the coastal, inter-coastal, and Alaskan trades were placed under security restrictions. At the same time, Admiral C. S. Freeman, commandant of the 13th Naval District, announced that armed escorts would be provided for "all important vessels from the Northwest and Alaska ports."

On the seacoast, including aids to navigation, a rigid blackout was ordered as rumors were circling hot and fast that a major Japanese naval fleet was poised off the Pacific Coast ready to strike. The phantom fleet never appeared but it did shock Americans of the possibility.

Japanese submarines were lurking off the Pacific Coast. Torpedoes ripped apart some cargo vessels and tankers. Land targets (other

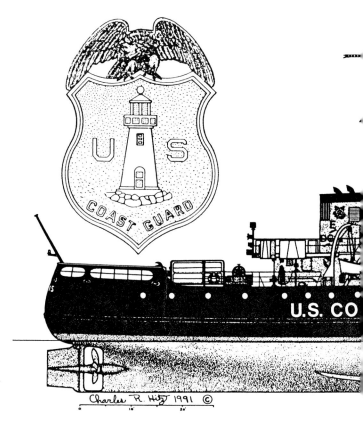

Outboard profile of the veteran Coast Guard cutter (buoy tender) Iris *which aided in the oil spill efforts in Alaska in the wake of the* Exxon Valdez *disaster. The 180 foot* Iris, *at this writing, one of the oldest units of the Coast Guard surface fleet has long been homeported in Astoria, Oregon, and will be replaced in the future. She has done yeoman duty in servicing navigation aids and in rescue work, though her twin diesels can only manage 12 knots at maximum speed.* Photo courtesy of U.S. Coast Guard.

than Alaska) were ineffective balloon bombs and harmless shellings of Fort Stevens in Oregon and the lighthouse station at Estevan on Vancouver Island's west coast.

Japan was more focused on Alaskan targets, starting with the Aleutians and working eastward. One of the first casualties on the Alaska supply route was that of the 40 year old cargo vessel *Kvichak*. The ship, formerly operated by the Alaska Packers Association, was one of the first commandeered by the U.S. Navy as a transport vessel. She was en route to Alaska with cargo when on January 27, 1942, she ground up on the rocky shores in Queen Charlotte Sound, 125 miles south of Prince Rupert. The naval gunboat *Charleston* came to the rescue and removed 23 passengers and the bulk of her 38 man crew. Master of the *Kvichak*, Captain W. W. Williamson, and a skeleton crew remained aboard the wreck for a time.

The need for every possible ship during the early months of the war was apparent, and salvage efforts got underway on the *Kvichak*. Pacific Salvage Company of Victoria, B.C., made a quick response, but while efforts were underway to remove the vessel she slipped off the rocks and sank in deep water. Still the work went forth, and after considerable expense, the wreck was raised and brought to port held afloat, by four scows, with pumps working full time. The flotilla reached Prince Rupert with the wreck half submerged.

Another early victim was the motor vessel *Tondelayo*, a converted lightship which had once served the San Francisco and Umatilla stations. She stranded on Twin Rocks, Clarence Strait, Alaska, on October 22, 1942. Stranding at high tide she slid off on the ebb and went down in deep water. A large number of small vessels were additionally lost in Alaskan waters in the 1941-42 era from natural causes.

A remarkable effort was put forth to build a huge fleet of cargo and military vessels in the Pacific Northwest at yards in Washington,

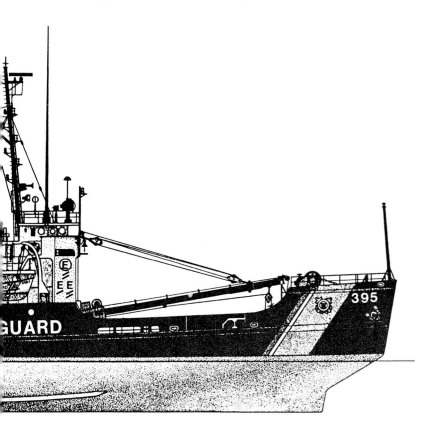

Oregon, and British Columbia. Many would subsequently see duty in Alaskan waters, especially the Liberty and Victory ships, along with numerous other types. More than 50 shipyards in the Pacific Northwest employed thousands of workers to build ships for the war effort.

The freighter *Arcata* was torpedoed in the Gulf of Alaska by a Japanese submarine in 1942, and the well known Alaska Line passenger ship *Mount McKinley* ended her days near Scotch Cap on March 18. The passengers and crew, headed by Captain Arthur Ryning, managed to reach shore safely. Salvage efforts failed.

Other well known ships lost in Alaskan waters during those early war years were the SS *Coldbrook*, operated by the American Mail Line, wrecked on Middleton Island June 28, 1942; the diesel tug *Edward Schenk* which foundered off Tree Point on October 14, with the loss of all hands, and the halibut schooner *Kingfisher* which capsized in a storm off Lazaroff Island on June 3, 1942.

Coast Guard cutters and tugs were successful in pulling the stranded USS *Branch* free in Tongass Narrows. Other victims of stranding, but later refloated, were the old sailing vessel *Scottish Lady* and the steamer *Bering*.

Each month during the war period there were strandings in Alaskan waters similar to the situation during the gold rush era.

Blacked out aids to navigation in the early months of the war undoubtedly caused some of the problems following Pearl Harbor, but after the tide of victory seemed within grasp, navigation returned to near normal.

Strange to say, it was the war that turned national attention toward the territory. Industry and population was accelerated to new heights. Alaska at last had come into its own, and the future appeared brighter than ever.

Still the war in Alaska was rough on shipping and many vessels left their bones to rot on the rugged shores of the northland. Vessel losses were heavy in 1943-44. The SS *Mapole* was wrecked at Cape Divine, Shumagen Island; *Elna* at Wide Bay; *Highway* in Lynn Canal; *Slocum* at Bold Cape; *Imperial* in Gasineau Channel; *Jeane* at Cordova; *Tyee Scout* at Icy Point; *Sprigg* on the Ugashik River; *Crusader* on Shumagen Island along with a series of barges and other small craft.

Down through the years vessel losses have remained substantial but greatly improved over earlier days. The Coast Guard has done a

yeoman job of safeguarding the waterways of Alaska with their buoy tenders, cutters, helicopters, and patrol planes. If you ask an officer in that branch of the service he just might tell you, "It's a big job but somebody has to do it."

Another area of major fishing activity in recent years has centered in Kodiak, the industrial center of Kodiak Island. The Coast Guard maintains an important center there. The area was important enough in World War II to demand both army and naval bases. Today, a big factor is King crab, which has become a luxury item for the palates of devotees in the lower 48. Large fleets of sophisticated fishing craft tap the local waters annually. Kodiak is rich in history, as it was founded by Aleksandr Baranov (Baranof) in 1792, replacing nearby Three Saints Bay as a fur trading headquarters. Tons of pelts passed through the port in days of yore and the place had a personality all its own. In addition to the Kodiak Coast Guard base, that service is also prominent at Ketchikan and Juneau where surface craft and aircraft are stationed, always ready to respond.

Navigation in southeast Alaska today is a far cry from yesteryear. Former Commissioner of Lighthouses, George R. Putnam, many years back described his initial experiences in analyzing Alaska's needs. Said he, "We marveled at the navigation of Captain Francis, the special pilot who had for many years been the mainstay of the government in guiding its vessels in these narrow, crooked and rock-strewn channels. When he could see nothing and had no aids to navigation, he blew his whistle and located the ship by the various echoes from the cliffs and mountains. His ability to identify these echoes with the localities which produced them was almost uncanny."

We today would call that pilot's ability, blind navigation, and where such an individual had a marvelous sixth sense, many counterparts were not so gifted, and without proper navigation aids got hung up on a rock, shoal or were involved in a collision with another vessel.

One writer of old described the Alaska coast "as wild as that of Norway, which indeed it resembles very closely, bristling as it does with fjords and islands, with rugged cliffs rising abruptly from the water to a height of several hundred feet. Navigation at night is extremely hazardous, as the path leads by devious ways through deep channels intersecting the outer barriers of islands where fogs hang, and thickly."

Alaska has a general coastline, measured in 30 mile steps of 7,300 miles as compared with a total of 4,884 miles for the Atlantic, Pacific, and Gulf Coasts of the United States—exclusive of Hawaii and the Great Lakes. With a hefty rainfall, frequent fog, extreme tides, and strong currents, one can readily see the difficulties in safeguarding Alaska's vast waterway system. Modern hi-tech electronic navigation devices have greatly countered the loss of ships and personnel in recent decades.

In modern times, regularly scheduled jet passenger planes such as those of Alaska Airlines make frequent flights to major Alaskan ports from the Pacific Northwest and California, but sea transport continues to be the most important factor in supplying Alaska with basic essentials.

The important role of air transportation, both by jet and by the smaller planes of the bush pilots, is vastly improved, but neither have the grace of the Alaska state bird, the Willow Ptarmigan which has been flying over and nesting in the Great Land since well before the advent of man in the frozen northland.

CHAPTER SIX
Regrettable Shipwrecks

*With strong convulsion rends
the solid oak: Ah Heaven! - behold her crashing
ribs divide! She loosens, parts and spreads
in ruin o're the tide.*
—*Falconer*

Without doubt, the most terrifying episode in Alaska's maritime history was the tragic loss of the SS *Princess Sophia* and her entire complement of passengers and crew. It was the North Pacific's version of the *Titanic* disaster, for though the *Princess Sophia* was about a third the size of the *Titanic* and only had a fifth as many aboard, there was not a single soul that survived to tell the tale. Had there been 1,500 aboard instead of 343, they too would have undoubtedly perished.

Just before midnight, the proud Canadian Pacific steamer pulled away from her wharf at Skagway, Vancouver bound. It was a miserable night and the usual frivolity was noticeably absent. Bitingly cold, a light snow was falling, as was the barometer. When the liner pulled out into the bay, the often calm waters were riled and angry. Most of the passengers; families of service men, miners, and draftees for the Army, were among the 268 who had booked passage. It was a capacity passenger list. As the steamer began to roll and pitch most had retired to their staterooms. On the bridge there was concern about the worsening conditions sweeping the ebony waters of Lynn Canal. Four hours out of Skagway the snow was driving against the windows of the wheelhouse in blizzard fashion. Captain Louis P. Locke, the *Sophia's* experienced shipmaster, grabbed the speaking tube and after an order to the chief engineer rang up slow on the ship's telegraph.

The signal was answered in the engine room and the liner moved through the murk like a phantom ship, her black hull like a ghostly shadow in the driven snow. As a precaution the shipmaster doubled the watch.

Ten lives were lost when the Liberty ship John P. Gaines *broke in half off the Alaska Peninsula south of Chirikof Island, November 25, 1943. The men on the after half of the vessel were rescued. The part of the ship that remained afloat drifted ashore on Big Koniuji Island. Built in 1942, structural weakness in the welded hull was given as the cause for the demise of the 7,167 ton vessel. Painted in her wartime gray, she had 90 persons aboard when the vessel broke up. Naval patrol craft came to the rescue.*

In the wee morning hours of Thursday, October 24, there was a terrific jolt as the vessel ploughed into inundated Vanderbilt Reef and stuck fast. Some of the passengers were rudely thrown from their bunks, and in the galley, dishes smashed onto the deck. There was confusion among the passengers; some ran out into the passageways clad only in night clothes.

Those on the bridge were flitting about, and down in the engine room there was concern as the valves and steel plates were checked.

"What's the situation down there?" hollered Captain Locke through the speaking tube to the chief engineer.

"Doesn't look too good," was the chief's retort. "Looks like we have leakage."

Orders had already been given to the wireless operator to send out an SOS. Juneau was 40 miles away and the ship four miles from Sentinel Island Lighthouse. It was off Sentinel Island in 1910, that the *Princess Sophia's* running mate, the *Princess May*, had stranded in much the same situation. She, however, was later refloated and there were no casualties. Would history repeat itself or would there be dire consequences?

The distress call alerted vessels in the vicinity. Three rushed to the scene, despite the turbulent seas. The *Sitka, King and Winge,* and Army steamer *Petersen* were standing by. The U.S. Lighthouse tender *Cedar,* Captain Leadbetter, didn't receive the message until noon, October 23, and then made full speed to render assistance. When she arrived, the *Estebeth, Amy,* and *Lonefisherman* were standing by, all endeavoring to hold their positions in the irascible waters, but to little avail. Earlier distress calls had been received in Juneau where Carey Tubbs at the U.S. Wireless Station tried to contact the Army post at Haines. Ironically, 45 minutes passed before he got an answer, as there was no night operator on hand. One of the personnel, however, heard the calls and summoned the officer-in-charge who finally tapped out the SOS responsible for getting ships to the rescue.

Meanwhile F. F. Lowle, general agent for Canadian Pacific at Juneau, received a dispatch from Captain Locke that the *Sophia* was in no immediate danger, that he had full assurance that her double bottom and bulkheads had withstood the impact with the reef. The dispatch also said that because of the heavy seas it would have been dangerous to try to transfer the passengers to the *Cedar* which was the logical vessel for such a purpose. Captain Locke preferred to wait until the seas calmed.

Other opinions were also expressed. Ed McDougal, master of the *Amy* who returned to Juneau to get supplies, noted that two feet of snow had fallen in Lynn Canal in 24 hours and that a strong northwest wind persisted. He reasoned that the *Cedar* should attempt removing the passengers from the wreck via a breeches buoy and that the ship's owners should dispatch a salvage tug to assist the wounded liner.

The *Sophia* was cradled high on the reef on the ebb tide almost as if balancing on a tightrope.

Postponing an attempted rescue of the passengers proved a fatal mistake. That night the worst possible scenario became grim reality. As the blizzard slashed the waters about the reef like a wild serpent, the force suddenly lifted the bulk of the liner clearly over the reef. Drowned out by the screech of the wind, the rending of steel against rock faded and the vessel plunged to her grave in the dark shadows. The sea opened for a dreadful moment and swallowed its victim, hook, line, and sinker.

The MS Zapora *is seen here trying to climb the hill after wrecking February 14, 1937, on the west shore of Alaska's Admiralty Island. Seven passengers and 19 crewmen were rescued. The cargo-passenger vessel operated between Puget Sound and southeastern Alaska ports.*

Only one terse message was sent out as the liner went down. "For God's sake come! We are sinking!" A message from the *Cedar* was received at Juneau with the breaking light of the new day.

"*Sophie* driven over reef during night. Only tops of masts showing. No Survivors. Will cruise Lynn Canal to leeward. Blowing storm. Started snowing this morning. *King & Winge* assisting."

The search for survivors was on. The *Cedar* plowed into the seething seas to where the doomed liner should have been. Sheets of spume drove against the tender as bits and pieces of wreckage bobbed about the surface. Nor could the other rescue vessels find any survivors.

Ah! a survivor at last. He was discovered on the rocky shores of Lynn Canal, a setter, his paws bleeding, had somehow managed to escape the sinking ship. Soaked and frightened the dog was given loving care by the finders. It was later learned that he was being shipped from Skagway to Seattle. If only he could have talked, what a sad story he would have told.

In the aftermath of the awful tragedy many who were on the would-be rescue vessels had varying accounts. Hindsight is always better than foresight. Many expressed opinions of what should have been done, but the die had been cast and placing the blame could accomplish nothing. It was a melancholy scene when the seas finally calmed in Lynn Canal. One broken mast left standing was the grave marker protruding from the wreck site. Captain Leadbetter stated that on receiving the distress message, he headed the *Cedar* into the northwest gale proceeding to where the *Sophia* should have been, but could find no trace of her. The wind was creating heavy swells and the snowstorm was blinding. The *Cedar* was forced to seek shelter and retired to an anchorage where she lay until Saturday morning. When the tender returned to the wreck scene the liner was deep in her grave.

Captain L. H. Bayers was returning from Peril Straits in his gas schooner *Anita Phillips* when he was signalled by Captain McDougal in the *Amy* about the *Princess Sophia* wreck. He in turn followed in the wake of the vessel to Lincoln Island. There the two craft lost sight of each other in the raging snowstorm, but the *Phillips* proceeded to Vanderbilt Reef, arriving there on Thursday night. The following account was given by Captain Bayers.

"We picked up the lights of the *Cedar* cruising nearby and made out another vessel as the *King & Winge*," he commented. "We bucked the storm up to a point between the wreck and the buoy, intending to drop the hook and ride her out until morning, but could not hold bottom, so made a run for shelter in Tee Harbor. She was pretty tough

crossing the canal as we fought a blinding snowstorm and heavy northwest wind, accompanied by giant seas, but were able to make it with only two broken windows on the port side of the wheelhouse. Come daylight we left Tee Harbor and had fairly good going to Vanderbilt Reef. The lighthouse tender *Cedar*, the *King & Winge* and *Estabeth* were there but due to their size were unable to get within hailing distance of the *Sophia*. I saw a flat bottomed skiff leave the *Estabeth*, which had tied to the (nearby) buoy. Its occupant was able to row nearly to the *Sophia*, but then was forced to turn back. All this time it would have been an easier matter to launch all the lifeboats of the *Sophia* and come to where we could have picked them up. I ran the *Phillips* up to within 100 feet of the *Sophia* and spoke to Captain Locke, her master. I told him to launch his lifeboats and we and the *Estabeth* would pick them up by the buoy, but he refused, saying that the *Princess Alice* (another unit of the Canadian Pacific fleet) would arrive the next day, and that he was in no immediate danger.

"We cruised around until about noon, when the wind began to pick up again. We were again forced to run for shelter in Tee Harbor where we had to work on the engine—my plugs and coils were wet," continued Bayers," Saturday morning we again left Tee Harbor for Vanderbilt Reef. The weather had flattened out pretty good. When we arrived at the reef, only the masts of the *Sophia* were showing. We began cruising around Lincoln and Ralston Islands looking for possible survivors, but saw none, so we left for town to get gas and supplies because we were about out. On the way, we picked up 48 bodies floating in an oil slick between Shelter Island and Shoal Point," concluded Captain Bayers.

The vessel *Monagham*, skippered by Captain Bob Griswold arrived at Juneau with 26 more bodies recovered around Shoal Point. Other vessels, including the *Cedar*, also picked up corpses from the general area, some that had been swept from the wreck scene by the strong currents.

As the seas calmed, Captain Griswold and deputy marshal Harry Morton visited Vanderbilt Reef at low tide and examined the cradle that had once held the *Sophia* prisoner. The grinding effect had left both smooth and broken sectors of rock from the weight of the ship which ironically rested on the sea's bottom in the opposite direction from the way it balanced atop the reef. With the top of the foremast still visible, one could see that the guy ropes were still taut.

It was theorized, even though no witness saw the vessel slide off the reef, that the storm quartered on the liner's stern which was free from the reef, swung her slowly around, the bow holding until the steamer faced in the opposite direction. With only her bow holding, the *Sophia* floated free and filled from a hole in the forward part of her hull.

What caused the stranding? Again theory enters in. It was believed by the experienced navigators on the Alaska run that the *Princess Sophia* had overrun her time from Eldred Rock, due to strong tail winds and was unable to pick up the buoy or fix her position due to the blinding snowstorm.

To add to the irony of the situation, a (lighted) buoy was on the deck of the lighthouse tender *Cedar* which was to have replaced the existing unlighted can buoy. Had the new aid to navigation been placed before the snowstorm, the terrible tragedy might have been averted.

Several months, even years after the calamity, bodies and body parts were found by fishermen and hunters along the Alaska beaches. A cemetery in Juneau has a plot where about 100 unidentified bodies have been buried, small mounds marked with wooden stakes as headstones.

Wreck of Str. "Mariechen". False Bay, Alaska

WP CO.

Above and right: Unfortunate wreck in a frigid setting. The German tramp ship Mariechen *hard aground at False Bay, Alaska, near Sitka. The hard luck steamer was en route from Puget Sound to Vladivostok with a $250,000 cargo when she was struck and disabled by a serious of gales. Her engine room flooded and the boilers went out. Drifting ever northward, the distressed ship came ashore at False Bay. In a major salvage job, the vessel was eventually refloated, patched, and towed to Seattle. The wreck occurred on January 19, 1906. When in Seattle's Elliott Bay on April 27, 1907, the* Mariechen *sank again before repairs were made. Raised, she was broken up for scrap. Photos courtesy of Winter & Pond.*

Wreck of Str. "Mariechen".

Among the dead were 87 employees of the White Pass & Yukon Route, including officers and crew of ten Yukon River boats, coming out of the north for the winter.

Among the dead was William Scouse, who, it was claimed, panned the first bucketful of gold-bearing gravel from Klondike Creek that started the gold rush.

Lynn Canal, deceptively calm in the summer months, frequently changed its personality in the off season, claiming its share of shipwrecks. In 1898, the steamer *Clara Nevada* went to her grave eleven miles north of Vanderbilt Reef taking with her 38 souls. The sidewheeler *Ancon*, already mentioned, was wrecked at Loring in 1889, and the schooner *William H. Dimond* became a total loss on Admiralty Island, 20 miles south of where the *Sophia* was lost, just to name a few.

Had it not have been for the stranding and refloating of the SS *Princess May* on Sentinel Reef in much the same manner as the *Sophia*

on Vanderbilt Reef, eight years earlier, there might have been an early attempt to rescue the passengers.

In the case of the *Princess May*, Captain McLeod, which stranded at 2 A.M. on August 5, 1910, the weather was not a factor, only a navigational error. En route from Skagway to Vancouver with 80 passengers and 68 crew, she rammed the north reef of Sentinel Island and took a poetic pose atop the barrier, embarrassingly within an earshot of the Sentinel Island Lighthouse. The seas were relatively calm. The ship's engines were stopped and the passengers told to dress and prepare to debark. There was no panic even though the decks were difficult to traverse, with the bow pointing 23 degrees skyward. The ship's officers assured the people that there was no danger as the sea was calm and the lighthouse nearby.

The liner, carried off her course by swift currents, straddled the reef at high tide, sliding over the barrier her entire length. On the ebb, she was perched high and dry on the reef, presenting one of the most spectacular wreck scenes ever caught in a camera's eye.

At the first opportunity the lifeboats were lowered. The first started to fill with water until someone remembered the plug had not been inserted. The lifeboats pulled away for the lighthouse and a hospitable greeting from its keeper Carl Peterson and his assistant Louis Betteker, who gave the passengers every courtesy during their stay. The keepers enjoyed the unexpected company at their lonely outpost. Widespread publicity on the *Princess May* incident brought up her rather unsavory past. Built at Newcastle-on-Tyne, England, in 1888, she had many an alias, first *Cass*, then *Arthur*, *Ningchow*, and *Hating*, then *Cass* again, until purchase by Canadian Pacific. She was much older than the ill-fated *Sophia* which was fashioned at a yard in Paisley, England in 1912. Under the name *Cass*, the *Princess May* was the scene of a mutiny en route to the Orient when English officers and Chinese crewmen mixed it up passing through the Suez Canal. The ship was once attacked by pirates off the China coast, and later was captured by a Chinese gunboat while slipping out of Shanghai in a state of bankruptcy.

Her best performance was under CPR, but the company, in the wake of the wreck, was none too happy with the cost of salvage and repairs. The American wrecking steamer *Santa Cruz* and the Canadian salvage tug *William Jolliffe* teamed up to refloat the *Princes May*. Repairs alone came to $119,000, big money in those days, especially for an older vessel.

Bark *Star of Bengal* Wreck

The salmon canning industry in Alaska had always been a thriving enterprise, but as in all such industries there are sometimes tragedies. From the standpoint of loss of life, one of Alaska's worst wrecks

They thought she was a total loss, but the SS Curacao *had a will to survive. The vessel foundered in 78 feet of water at Warm Chuck, Prince of Wales Island, in command of Captain William Thompson on June 21, 1913. Valued at $225,000 she was only insured for $118,000. She carried a cargo of coal and cannery supplies. A challenge to raise the vessel prompted a gamble that paid off after a lengthy endeavor. She was refloated and taken to Seattle for a complete overhaul and returned to service. She operated to Alaska until 1940 when sold to a Greek trampship firm who renamed her* Hellenic Skipper.

involved a veteran sailing vessel, a unit of the Alaska Packers Association. The *Star of Bengal* had seen her better days when purchased for a bargain price as an addition to the APA fleet of cannery ships. Company windjammers carried Asians north each year to work the canneries and then gave passage home after each season, along with a full cargo of canned salmon.

The *Star of Bengal* was built by Harland & Wolff at Belfast for the Cory fleet in 1874, and had some very creditable passages, mainly as a jute clipper. On one occasion her first officer was George Cupples, author of the literary sea classic *The Green Hand*. When the ship's Captain William Legg broke his leg in Calcutta in 1886, Cupples skippered the *Star of Bengal* back to England.

Now we find the aging vessel in what would be her final role, still dependent on the wind on her north and southbound voyages except when being towed in and out of ports. It was the latter that became her demise.

The big bark departed Wrangell, San Francisco-bound on September 20, 1908, under command of Captain Nicholas Wagner, with Gus Johnson as mate. Sitting low in the water the iron sailing vessel had 50,000 cases of salmon in her holds plus several thousand empty steel oil drums. Aboard were 134 souls, mostly Asian cannery workers. Before the crew could spread her canvas, she had to be towed out to open water by the steam powered cannery tenders, *Hattie Gage* (Captain Dan Farrer), and the *Kayak* (Captain Hamilton). While the vessels were moving through the restricted waters of the Alexander Archipelago, trouble brewed. By midnight, the glass had fallen and a strong wind was whipping the waters into a frenzy. Within two hours it was gale force. The unlikely towing craft had a tiger by the tail. Shallow-drafted, the *Kayak* was virtually useless and the strain fell on the *Hattie Gage* which herself was losing control. The trio of vessels were being swept toward the towering cliffs of Coronation Island.

Cut and run was the decision of the two assisting craft, both running for the shelter of Warren Island, 12 miles away. The *Star of Bengal* was left a sitting duck, dragging her anchors in ten fathoms less than 50 feet from rocky island ramparts. Imagine the panic among the Asians as they watched the tugs disappear in the murk and the threatening possibility of shipwreck. The *Hattie Gage* finally made a run for Wrangell to enlist the aid of the government cableship *Burnside*, then in port.

In the interim, the square-rigger strained at her anchor cables in the breakers off Helm Point. The tenuous predicament grew worse by the moment. Night was an eternity as the helpless vessel tried to hold her own on a lee shore in the teeth of the worsening gale. Seas were smashing into her side with a vengeance and there was no help in sight.

In desperation, sensing the gravity of their eventual plight, four men volunteered to attempt to get a line ashore. With great effort, seamen Fred Matson, Henry Lewald, Olaf Hansen, and cannery cook Frank Muir jumped into a ship's boat, launched with difficulty, and pulled for the narrow shelf of beach. Suddenly, an erupting breaker caught the craft broadside, threw out its occupants, and was promptly smashed to kindling. Ironically, the men struggled through the churning, frigid surf and managed to secure a line from the *Star of Bengal*.

Within an hour the big bark parted her cables and broke up on the rocks. Down came her rigging like a broken spider web, followed by her masts and yards. Over the crashing surf and howling wind the shrieks of the passengers could be heard. The hull split open throwing them into the vortex along with the oil drums and thousands of cases of canned salmon. It was an indescribable scene as a mass of helpless humans struggled to survive. In Captain Wagner's own words:

"When the final shock came, the *Star of Bengal* appeared to heave up her entrails in three sections. As I was thrown into the water I saw the midship beams of solid iron come out in a tangled mass. The force to produce this is scarcely conceivable. So strong had been preceding gusts that a five-inch iron davit was snapped short off. After I was thrown into the water any attempt to swim appeared ridiculous. As I struggled only to keep afloat, I was hurled toward shore among a thousand cases of salmon and hundreds of metal drums that constituted our cargo. I was practically unconscious when I reached the beach," concluded Captain Wagner.

Of the 134 souls aboard the *Star of Bengal*, only 22 survived in the bitter cold of the inhospitable shore. The *Kayak* finally returned to the wreck scene after the storm abated and picked up the miserable survivors. The tragic toll listed 110 who had lost their lives. Of the survivors 15 were Caucasians. Of the 74 Chinese aboard, only two were saved.

Bitterness arose in the wake of the catastrophe, with Captain Wagner charging the skippers of the towing craft with cowardice. They countered that they would have risked losing their vessels and crews by hanging on in the teeth of the gale. In the subsequent hearing, the criminal cowardice charges were dropped by the Alaska inspectors who in turn suspended Captain Wagner's license unjustifiably. The breach of justice was later reversed by Chief inspector Bermingham at San Francisco. Captain Wagner continued his seagoing career, always haunted by the terrible shipwreck of the *Star of Bengal*.

Tragic Loss of the SS *Islander*

Was it actually an iceberg that caused the sinking of the Canadian Pacific passenger steamer *Islander*? It may never be known for certain but it is generally believed that a runaway berg was in the channel when the liner plunged to her final resting place.

Having earlier departed from Skagway, the vessel had called at Juneau en route back to Vancouver, B.C. Steaming at her usual clip through Lynn Canal in the wee hours of the morning, everything pointed to a routine cruise through calm waters. Ahead was a fogbank, nothing unusual, and the speed was altered slightly as her triple expansion engines turned her twin screws slower just after passing Taku Inlet. Suddenly there was a severe impact with something unseen by the lookouts. The liner careened wildly. Veteran Captain H. R. Foote was on his feet in a flash, immediately concerned about the safety of his 77 first class and 30 second class passengers, five infants who didn't require tickets, and a crew of 81.

The impact had ripped a hole in the ship's skin and water was pouring in below. The black gang scurried topside even as the vessel began to sink by the bow, her propellers still spinning. Everything happened so suddenly that there was little chance for an organized evacuation, most of the travelers caught in their staterooms asleep. In a valiant last minute effort, Chief Stewart Simpson and some of the ship's officers slopped through the half flooded passageways knocking down jammed doors and rushing people out of harm's way. On the boat deck efforts were quickly made to get some of the lifeboats free from the davit cables as the liner sank lower and lower. Rushing sea water flowed like rivers down the slanting decks, dim lights reflecting weirdly. Many in night clothes had no opportunity to grab their belongings. It was now or never. Some unable to find a place in the lifeboats jumped overboard into the frigid waters and perished. As the *Islander*'s stern rose higher in the air, many lost their footing and fell headlong into a rush of water. There was confusion and panic but the ship's officers did everything possible under the dire circumstances.

In true fashion, Captain Foote went down with his ship, ending an honored maritime career. In fact, the death toll reached 42 in that nightmare drama. Fortunately, some of the boats got away before the liner went down in a whirlpool of churning brine.

Among the passengers and in the cargo was a reputed treasure in gold, being brought back from the Yukon, much of it reputedly in the ship's safe. It is told that one passenger rushed from his stateroom, then insisted on going back for his suitcase full of gold. Against strict orders, he returned to his flooded compartment, and in a Herculean

effort managed to find the suitcase. He then hurried back to where one of the last lifeboats had floated free. The occupants yelled at him to leap overboard and be picked up from the water.

"Leave the suitcase behind and jump!" they shouted. The man clung to it, white knuckled and would not part with it.

"Jump!" they urged again, one final time as the ship began to sink under his feet. Finally he did jump but failed to release his gold. The weight carried him beneath the black waters and he was never again seen.

As the ship plunged in the depths, all her lights went out, After a brief disturbance on the sea there was a silence amidst the wraithlike fog. The *Islander* was gone. Of the 183 persons aboard it was fortunate that only 42 perished. It could have been much worse.

Chief Engineer Brownlee, one of the survivors, gathered a party together once on the beach and led them to the Treadmill mine where the tenders *Lucy* and *Flossie* were dockside with steam up. After taking the castaways aboard, the vessels put out for the disaster scene, and later took the survivors to Juneau.

Bodies were recovered and considerable wreckage washed up on nearby shores, as the terse message of the loss echoed across the country. The publicity generated as much interest in the lost gold as it did over the dead. Some stories told of fabulous amounts of gold that spurred many to think of ways it might be recovered from the sunken ship. True, there was gold aboard, but the amount was perhaps greatly exaggerated.

At any rate, the loss of life was regrettable and one of the most popular passenger ships on the Alaska run was gone from the scene.

In the aftermath of the disaster many Alaska pilots and navigators were of the opinion that the *Islander* never struck an iceberg but that she had veered off course and sideswiped the outcrops of Point Hilda. A solid conclusion was never reached.

Rumors of gold, however, continued in maritime circles and reached fever pitch in the depression days of the 1930s, after several earlier efforts at recovery of the treasure had failed. An elaborate plan was then devised. The Curtis Brothers, Seattle house movers, purchased the idle five-masted barkentine *Forest Pride* and the ocean barge *Griffson* for salvage work on the *Islander*. The plan was to raise the sunken vessel from Davy Jones' Locker by dragging it over the sea bottom.

P. G. Waddell, who was part of that salvage team, tells in his own words the results of that operation.

"One fine day what was left of superstructure of the Islander hit the keel of the *Griffson* (which had been working with winches and the tides to raise the wreck from the bottom off Douglas Island). That's when we put the Forest Pride into action. Instead of 20 lines running

The SS Curacao *in her near death throes June 21, 1913, as seen in the upper photo. In the right photo she is seen going to her final grave under the Greek flag as the* Hellenic Skipper *on July 10, 1940, after suffering a mysterious explosion 125 miles off Grays Harbor, Washington. The vessel had just changed registry when the fire broke out that caused the explosion. The steamer, as the* Curacao, *was built at Philadelphia in 1895 for passenger service, later becoming a freighter.*

to 40 winches on the *Griffson* we left half the lines on her and ran the other half to the *Forest Pride* and then made a cradle between the two. In the end we did drag the *Islander* well up on the beach," said Waddell.

Continuing his account, he lamented, "We saw some funny things and some tragic things when we got that wreckage up into the sun and wind. The salt water had gotten into the bottles of whiskey; that was one of the first things we learned. There were any number of cases of champagne. For some reason it was as fresh and bubbly as ever. One day I found an old oil lamp, still with bracket and chimney and trimmed the wick and applied a match, and danged if the thing didn't light. (33 years under water.) We found woolen suits and the press in the trousers as sharp as it had been in August 1901. Shoes that still carried the polish of 33 years. We found the remains of a coal passer in one of the bunkers. He had been working there when the ship hit, and she had tilted crazily, no doubt of that. The sliding door of the bunker had slipped down almost to the bottom and jammed and trapped him in there in the darkness. He pushed the shovel handle under the door and pried, and the handle snapped. He had tried again and snapped the butt. Then, we suppose, the ending."

According to Waddell, "We set up some sluice boxes on the beach and ran all the in'ards of the ship through them. There was $7,000 in the ship's safe, some silver and some gold. We found one 17 pound poke on the floor in the men's room. That was the main and almost the only treasure. Say we took $100,000 out of the *Islander* all told. The expedition ran us over a quarter of a million!" pined Waddell.

Experts theorized that the strong currents sweeping the sea where the *Islander* had lain for over three decades may have carried large amounts of gold dust into oblivion. At any rate, the fabulous treasure so long sought proved a great disappointment, the salvagers coming out on the losing end, a sad conclusion to a story that received news coverage the world over.

The *Clara Nevada* Chronicle

Above and right: *The Pacific Coast Steamship Company's SS* Spokane *had more than one stranding in Alaskan waters. Steaming north with 160 tourists on June 29, 1911, she struck an uncharted rock in Seymour Narrows in command of Captain J.E. Guptill. Her hull opened up and a run was made for Plumper Bay where the ship was beached 40 minutes later. One lady passenger was drowned by the rising water and another died of a heart attack. As the vessel reeled, panic stricken passengers began jumping overboard like a bunch of sheep. The pilot, Captain R.D. McGillivray, took out a lifeboat crew and hailed the Grand Trunk passenger ship* Prince George *for assistance and later the SS* Admiral Sampson *picked up the passengers. The vessel was later refloated and repaired.*

One might fable her a jinx ship. The steamer *Clara Nevada* was often involved in controversial situations and bizarre incidents. One of many vessels of the gold rush years, she was the lone ship of the newly formed Pacific and Alaska Transportation Company, one of nearly 100 such steamship companies seemingly formed overnight in the big rush to the northland.

Southbound from her initial run under the PATC houseflag, on the Seattle, Skagway, and Dyea run, she went unreported. On the night of February 5, 1898, she was believed to have encountered trouble in the midst of near hurricane force winds. Pitching and rolling in her struggle to make headway, the terse call of "Fire" echoed through the compartments of the ship. Perhaps an oil lamp had been knocked from its brackets. Whatever the cause, the steamer was in jeopardy and her distress signals, if any were sent out, were not received. Her location was believed to have been off Berners Bay. Reported overdue, fears of a possible tragedy prompted a wide search. A week later came the report that a battered

Ready to slip into Davy Jones' Locker, the SS Edith *is seen foundering off Cape St. Elias while under command of Captain E.B. McMullen. Southbound from Nome and Latouche with copper concentrates, her cargo shifted and the 37 souls aboard were forced to take to the boats August 30, 1915. The SS Mariposa made a failed attempt to take the derelict in tow but she went down in deep water and was irretrievable. The* Edith, *built in England in 1895, was valued at $225,000, her cargo at $150,000.* Photo by Thwaites.

wreck had been sighted balanced on a reef off Eldred Rock (which a few years later was the location of a lighthouse). It was the steamer *Rustler* out of Juneau that found the wreck, deserted of all life, only her spars above the water at low tide. Searching the area, the *Rustler's* crew pulled a corpse from the water identified as George Foster Beck, one of the founders of the neophyte shipping company that owned the *Clara Nevada*.

Aboard the ill-fated steamer were known to have been 39 officers and men, and the ship's master, Captain C. H. Lewis of Portland. Inasmuch as no passenger list was made before the voyage, the death toll was undoubtedly much greater with an estimated 65 additional travelers which would have brought the regrettable toll to around 100. So lax were the records and rules in those hectic years that loss of life was usually greater than statistics showed. In virtually every case there were stowaways on the overcrowded vessels in the stampede to the gold fields.

When sailing from Seattle on her last trip north, on the afternoon of January 27, the steamer backed square into the government revenue cutter *Grant* in Elliott Bay.

Charges that the passenger vessel was unseaworthy and had incompetent officers were circulated.

A passenger that had booked passage on the *Clara Nevada* on her initial run to Skagway, Charles Jones, reported that, "I was afraid the *Clara Nevada* would be wrecked from the time she left Seattle until Skagway was reached. We not only smashed into the cutter *Grant* when backing from Yesler's dock; we rammed almost every wharf at which we tried to land; we blew out three boiler flues; we floundered around

in the rough water until all the passengers were scared almost to death; we witnessed intoxication among the officers and heard them cursing each other until it was sickening."

Others recalled that a stop at Port Townsend on the voyage north resulted in the ship's bowsprit being damaged after she bumped the dock there.

Rumors, charges, and counter charges flew wild and high in the aftermath of the tragedy—everything from boiler explosions to mutiny, none of which could be authenticated. The union supported the reputation of the ill-fated ship's chief engineer David Reed, who some had called incompetent. Captain Lewis was also the butt of criticism, as was pilot Edward Kelly. Unfortunately in such catastrophes, charges are always largely unfounded when there are no actual witnesses. The details of the tragic episode will never be fully known.

Inspectors were sent north to check out the wreck's remains but could give no actual reason for the vessel's demise, though the wreckers who removed machinery, donkey engines, fittings, and other gear rendered their own conclusions. Said they:

"It is now believed that the steamer caught fire, and during the frantic fight to keep the flames from the place where was stored powder and dynamite, the officers lost their bearings and incidentally control of the ship. The fierce, blinding storm in a few minutes drove the vessel on Eldred Rock, broadside on, and the *Clara Nevada* was split wide open." The findings of the wreckers went on to say: "The theory that the ship caught fire is borne out by the fact that along the deck of

The steamer Bertha *on fire after being grounded at Harvester Island near Uyak in July 1915. Captain Glasscock and his 24 man crew were cared for at the Uyak cannery. The Pacific Alaska Navigation Company vessel was totally gutted before the fire burned itself out.*

the wreck is strewn the ship's fire hose, attached to the hydrants and coupled to the pumps."

The *Clara Nevada*, named for a popular western actress of that period, was the former iron-hulled government survey steamer *Hassler*. Condemned for further service, she was later sold to the Pacific and Alaska Transportation Company and converted to a passenger vessel. Accommodations were provided for 100 first class, 100 steerage class passengers and 300 tons of freight. Despite the disaster, there was no slowdown in the onrushing to Alaska.

The *Discovery* Tragedy

Following almost in the wake of the ill-fated *Clara Nevada* was the passenger cargo-steamer *Discovery* whose sad chronicle was somewhat similar.

Built as a large steam tug at Port Townsend in 1889, the *Discovery* was placed under the capable command of Captain Thomas Grant. The vessel established an enviable record in the towing industry for nearly a decade until the discovery of gold in the northland. She got the call and underwent conversion to a passenger and cargo vessel, remaining under the command of Captain Grant.

Though she had a couple of profitable years on the Alaska run, as did all ships at that period, the *Discovery's* voyage in April 1898 almost came to an end after she ran hard aground on a reef near Berners Bay. Passengers were safely removed to the beach where they noted pieces of wreckage identifying the *Clara Nevada*. Fortunately the tides were running high and the crew managed to get the *Discovery* afloat again. Lifeboats brought the passengers back.

As the steamer moved southward under a slow bell, a fierce gale was in the making as they reached the vicinity of Queen Charlotte Sound. The storm became a blizzard. Then suddenly, a gasket blew out of the boiler and the ship drifted aimlessly while Captain Grant and his chief engineer worked tirelessly to make repairs under stressful conditions. In the interim, fearing for their lives, the rest of the crew as well as the passengers started a bucket brigade to bail out the water coming through the opened seams in the wooden hull. The combined effort of all hands paid off, and soon the wounded vessel was underway again, pushing ever southward, Seattle-bound. There was great relief by all when the little steamer finally reached her destination. The strain on the vessel had been so great that a few days later she suddenly sank at the Pacific Coast Company coal bunkers.

The Seattle fireboat *Snoqualmie* was ushered to the scene and pumped her out. Afloat once again, she was given an overhaul, and later found a new buyer in the fledgling White Star Line. That firm saw possibilities for the steamer for local service out of Nome during the open navigation season. In turn, she was placed in drydock, cut in two and lengthened for her new role as a freight and passenger vessel. There were some questions raised as to her seaworthiness following the conversion, but soon she was off to her new role in the far north.

Later, we find the *Discovery* in the Nome-Golovin Bay service. It was early fall in 1903, under command of Captain Marshall Walters. She was owned by Captain Harry Ramwell and Associates). The steamer's operating season had ended and the vessel was heading south for Puget Sound for the winter before the Nome Roadstead froze over. Aboard were 34 passengers; four others were working temporarily for passage back home, and the crew numbered 22. The voyage turned into a nightmare, the storm-tossed vessel forced to call at the secluded port of Unga. While there, all but two of the passengers quit the ship claiming that she was unseaworthy. The two that remained thought better of their decision after the leaking vessel called at Kodiak. They too left. Steaming out into the Gulf of Alaska, the *Discovery* became a plaything with the forces of nature, battling gargantuan seas and driving winds which proved her Waterloo. The vessel vanished along with all hands. Conflicting reports varied on just how many lives were lost. Though the original passengers had left the ship others reportedly booked passage at Kodiak and Unga. Whatever the situation, there were no survivors. Had not part of the *Discovery's* pilot house and one of her battered lifeboats washed ashore on Middleton

Island she would have been listed as lost without trace. No bodies were ever recovered. Many members of her crew were well known in maritime circles on Puget Sound and in Alaska.

State of California Wreck

The California sun was not shining on the SS *State of California* as she went to her final resting place in Gambier Bay on August 17, 1913.

Superstition has always been a problem with seafaring personnel, especially when it comes to the number 13. For many years ships never departed on a voyage on the 13th of any month; even more so on Friday the 13th. Right up until recent times the tradition prevailed. Olson & Mahony, a line that operated a fleet of steam schooners in the earlier decades of the century never allowed its ships to sail on the 13th, a superstition that goes back to Judas, the 13th apostle who betrayed Jesus Christ. Little thought was given to such a superstition when the *State of California* departed Seattle, Alaska-bound on August 13, 1913. However, it was to be her final voyage.

Dating from 1879, the iron vessel had established a good record and was popular with tourists on the Alaska run. As a unit of the Pacific Coast Steamship Company, she departed Seattle on her final voyage with a capacity passenger list due partly to the fact that a new gold strike had occurred in Alaska's Shushanna district.

Commanding was Captain Thomas H. Cann, Jr., whose rabbit's foot was with him seven years earlier when he relinquished command of the SS *Valencia* just before her tragic voyage in January 1906 when the vessel crashed into the rocks near Cape Beale, B.C., with the loss of somewhere between 117 and 126 lives.

On this voyage Cann's luck would run out even though the loss of his ship was neither blamed on him nor the Alaska pilot, but on the fact that the area of the wreck was not only poorly charted but had a dangerous unmarked barrier.

A large cannery had recently been erected on Gambier Bay by the Admiralty Trading Company, 90 miles south of Juneau. Pacific Coast Steamship Company had agreed to make a scheduled call there, the first for a large vessel. Narrow quarters in the bay made it a tight squeeze for a big liner. After a brief call at the cannery dock, the vessel pulled out into the stream, made a sharp turn and began to increase her speed. Pilot Robert MacGillivray and Captain Cann were taking all precautions, but at 8:26 AM, there was the terrible grinding of iron against rock as the vessel's bottom plates were ripped wide open, where the chart showed 35 fathoms. It took only four minutes for the liner to slip off the unmarked obstruction and disappear in 240 feet of water.

Imagine the panic in that brief moment in time. No boats could be lowered, few lifejackets donned, and no chance for an organized evacuation.

As she went under, the bridge broke partially free of the superstructure and Captain Cann kept directing rescue operations from the floating wreckage. All was done that could be done, and miraculously, of the 146 persons aboard, only 35 perished. In the mournful aftermath, some bodies were recovered and the frightened survivors were cared for at the cannery until other ships came to pick them up. Shortly after the wreck, divers were sent to the scene to check out salvage possibilities, but the depths were such as to make raising the vessel hopeless.

Charles Stagger, an experienced diver, examined the reef where the *State of California* struck, noting that the highest point was 16 feet below the surface at low tide and that "the pinnacles of rock looked like a giant saw set at right angles in the course of the ship. When the vessel scraped over the rocks, a hole as wide as the ship itself and extending from stem to stern must have been torn in her hull."

Master of the ill-fated liner continued his seagoing career with Pacific Coast Steamship Company and Admiral Line. His eventual death did not occur at sea, but he died after being struck by an automobile at Des Moines, Washington in 1925.

Demise of the *Yukon*

One of the more dramatic shipwrecks in later years was that of the Alaska Steamship Company's SS *Yukon*. After 47 years of service the staunch passenger liner finally reached her last mile on the night of February 3, 1946.

Captain Charles Glasscock was no stranger to shipwreck. In charge of the SS Admiral Evans, the vessel struck a reef while inbound for the P.E. Harris cannery. She had to be beached in Hawk Inlet in southeastern Alaska where 91 passengers were evacuated. The Canadian salvage tug Salvor was called to the ship's side and after many weeks of salvage work refloated the vessel. The wreck occurred March 9, 1918. After being rebuilt, the Admiral Evans was in service till 1930 when scrapped in Japan. Photo courtesy of Winter & Pond.

World War II had ended. The *Yukon* had played a valuable role in servicing the northland in both peacetime and wartime. She still had her wartime gray paint when disaster struck.

Southbound and laboring in gigantic seas, 40 miles southeast of Seward, the steamer suddenly crashed violently into the jagged rocks off Johnstone Bay, much to the horror of Captain Christian E. Trondsen and pilot Amigo Soriano. So devastating was the impact that the stern section was twisted completely away from the forward part of the liner.

Frantic passengers, some 371 of them, plus a crew of 124, all feared for their lives. Fortunately the forward section remained cradled on the rocks upright and most of those aboard were on that part of the ship. The aft section was bowled over by the raging surf and soon reduced to a pile of twisted metal. Make no mistake about it, the *Yukon* was in a treacherous vice, and distress signals filled the night air as most of this drama unfolded in the darkness. The composure of those aboard was amazing under the circumstances. All were staring death in the face.

Fuel and water tanks had been ruptured, the boilers put out of commission, and most of the food supply lost. With no heat or lights, the terrified souls huddled together, trying to protect themselves from the biting wind inside the superstructure.

Rescue ships had picked up the SOS and were making full speed toward the wreck scene. As one after another arrived their respective crews were appalled at what greeted their eyes. Would-be rescue ships included the Coast Guard cutter *Onandaga*, the buoy tender *Cedar*, steamships *North Haven* and *Henry S. Failing*, plus the Navy salvage tug *Curb* and patrol boat *No.107*. The one question, how to rescue the survivors?

Here were the circumstances—a boulder-strewn beach, sheer cliffs, the icy face of Johnstone Glacier rising 300 feet above the wreck, and heavy seas crashing all around. After the alternatives were considered, it was determined that rescue efforts would have to take place on the seaward side of the *Yukon* where sea conditions were such that rescue craft could easily be overturned in the frigid waters.

Meanwhile the anxious passengers, partially cheered by the presence of the rescue ships, were cold, miserable, and hungry, waiting in prayerful hope to feel the warmth of dry blankets and hot coffee. However, their wait continued for 48 hours, which must have seemed to them an eternity.

Tons of fuel had leaked out from the wreck and had a calming effect on the waters. That coupled with slackening winds and seas gave the green light to rescue operations. Even under such conditions rescue of the survivors would be rough going. Out of every disaster heroes are born, and the *Yukon* wreck was not without exception.

A man nicknamed 'Screaming Swede' (Jimmy Johnson), a commercial fisherman out of Seldovia, then serving as a private in the Army, led rescue efforts by piloting an Army BSP. He worked his way among the rocks and wreckage to the side of the wreck and began the perilous evacuation of the passengers, ferrying them to the *Onandaga*. Next, with help, he made a line fast from the cutter to his power barge, then rammed his shallow-draft vessel up on the rocky shelf where more passengers anxiously awaited. The barge then was winched back to the cutter. By this method 485 persons were rescued by the evening of February 5. Ironically, all those on the fore part of the wreck were accounted for. On the after section, it was a different story. The 11 who had been trapped as the stern was wrenched free, twisted and broken, all perished in the maelstrom.

Though none of the survivors had escaped the terrible suffering following the wreck, they for the most part showed great courage. All were received with open arms when the rescue ships landed them at Seward.

Always after a wreck, details are brought to light, overlooked by the gravity of disaster. For instance, over and above the heroic duties of Jimmy Johnson, was an unnamed seaman on the *Yukon* who swam into a flooded stateroom in freezing water to find shoes for a barefoot child whose feet were freezing on the ice-streaked deck. Then there was a steward who braved the same freezing salt water to find bottled fresh water for a thirsty baby who was ill.

The press reported some negative occurrences during the melee aboard the wreck, citing incidences of drunkenness and looting. A fireman was later jailed in Alaska for trying to pawn jewelry he'd purloined from the wreck.

Still, with all the pros and cons, the dramatic episode has gone down in Alaskan maritime history as an epic of the sea. What might have been a terrible loss of life was held to a minimum.

Fatally aground on Bligh Reef in Prince William Sound (the same reef that almost claimed the Exxon Valdez), *the SS* Olympia *struggles in vain after running into the barrier on December 12, 1910, amid a gale at the midnight hour. The vessel was en route from Cordova for Valdez. The 75 passengers aboard were removed but the crew stayed aboard in the hope of getting the ship free. The finally stripped and abandoned wreck rested on her perch for many months thereafter, navigators setting their courses by her rusting frame.*

On November 1, 1917, the wooden steamer Al-ki stranded on Point Augusta, Alaska, broke her back and became a total loss. Built at Bath, Maine, in 1884 the vessel ran between Puget Sound and southeastern Alaska for several years. Winter & Pond photo.

Victim of an uncharted rock in Sumner Straits, Alaska, the steam schooner Delhi *under Captain C.P. McCarthy became a total wreck January 18, 1915. At high tide on a later date, the wreck was towed to Prince Rupert, but determined there to be a total loss, much of her bottom ripped out. Loss set at $140,000 for the 11 year old freighter.*

Cracked in half by the elements of nature, Alaska Steamship Company's SS Denali *met her waterloo May 19, 1935. En route to southeast Alaska from Seattle, she ran aground on Zayas Island, B.C., in command of Captain Thomas E. Healy. Among the cargo was 30 tons of dynamite. Shortly after stranding a fire broke out. All hands, including seven passengers and four stowaways, 42 in all, abandoned ship. The Coast Guard cutter* Cyane *answered the SOS sent out from the ship and sped south from Ketchikan. The vessel was valued at $650,000.*

The Strange Case of the *Aleutian Enterprise* and *Pacesetter*

In more recent years the pattern of shipwreck has greatly changed in Alaskan waters. Hi-tech navigational aids both aboard ship and on land afford much more safety at sea, unlike the yesteryears. In addition, surface rescue vessels, helicopters, and planes stand ready for immediate response on receiving a May Day distress call, and constant communication can be carried on by ship to shore phones, far removed from the days of the dot and dash wireless apparatus.

The toll in large seagoing ships has declined, but the fishing industry every year suffers some losses, especially in the Gulf of Alaska and Bering Sea where mariners often operate in giant watery acclivities.

Several large ships have had their hulls split in two in that sector of Alaska, especially when hauling burdensome cargoes. A typical example was the American cargo ship *Panoceanic Faith* which went down in the storm-tossed Gulf of Alaska September 29, 1967, en route to Yokohama. Thirty-six members of her crew drowned with the ship, and only five survived.

But our concern here is the sinking of the fish processor *Aleutian Enterprise*. She capsized and sank within minutes, taking nine crewmen to a watery grave in the Bering Sea during the 1990 fishing season. The case ended up in the courts, federal prosecutors claiming the deaths were the result of a conspiracy to send out unsafe fishing vessels manned by people without adequate training, credentials, or adequate fishing equipment. The defendants in this case pleaded guilty—one company and six individuals faced with more than two million dollars in fines and additional penalties, plus a possible ten year prison sentence. Even as this book is written the case was being tried.

The *Aleutian Enterprise* was a unit of a fleet managed and operated by Arctic Alaska Seafood Corp. The case was tried before U.S. District Judge Carolyn Dimmick in Seattle. The Arctic Alaska Seafood firm had been acquired by Arkansas-Based Tyson Foods Inc., in 1992.

Among those named was Northern Trawlers Inc., one of the limited partners that owned the ill-starred processing vessel. Terry Baker, Arctic Alaska's former president, chief executive and vice chairman of the board was put on the carpet for conspiracy, making false statements to the government, sending an unseaworthy vessel to sea, plus misconduct and neglect leading to loss of life. Survivor Captain Mark Siemons, master of the *Aleutian Enterprise* on her fateful voyage was also among those on trial.

The epic case pointed out ever more what can happen when rules and regulations set down by the U.S. Coast Guard and the Transportation Department are ignored by cutting corners to gain bigger profits. An inexperienced crew, lack of safety devices and inattention to the seaworthiness of a vessel becomes a

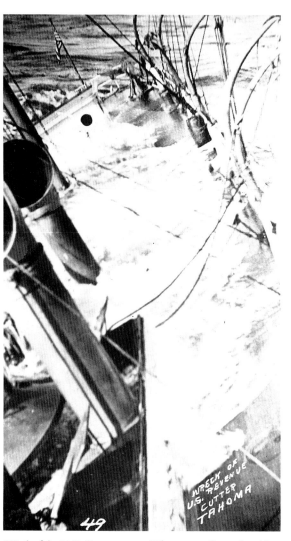

Wreck of the U.S. Revenue cutter Tahoma *on September 14, 1914, after striking an uncharted reef west of Kiska. The crew were forced to the boats and suffered privation as the SS* Cordova *of Alaska Steamship Company made full speed to the area. She rescued survivors from open boats aided by other vessels that searched out the survivors. The cutter, valued at $310,000, was a total loss, part of her skeletal remains clinging to the barrier.*

capital offense when lives are lost. Despite the tragic consequences, all companies involved in the salmon-King Crab and general fishing in the Gulf of Alaska and the Bering Sea watched closely the proceedings of the case and paid ever closer attention to abiding by all requirements for safety at sea, especially in Alaskan waters.

Those commercial fishermen who work in the Alaska Gulf and Bering Sea labor around the clock making good pay in a demanding but seasonal occupation, often battling contentious seas. Every precaution to provide for their safety is essential as danger constantly lurks about like a grim reaper.

In January 1996, the U.S. Coast Guard made a wide search for seven missing crew members of the 127 foot crabber *Pacesetter*. The vessel vanished in stormy weather and pulsating seas on a miserable Saturday night in late January in the Bering Sea. A distress signal was picked up by the Coast Guard. It pinpointed the location of the large fishing vessel, 60 miles south of St. George Island in the Pribilofs.

First to reach the scene was another commercial fishing vessel at 1 A.M. the following day. All that her crew found was an empty liferaft and a lifering with the *Pacesetter*'s name imprinted, and the attached emergency beacon that had sent out the direction signal.

Another fishing vessel picked up a second empty liferaft two hours later. Further Coast Guard surveillance found no other sign of the *Pacesetter* and the command center in Juneau revealed that all hope had ended for the entire crew of the vessel and her cargo of crab.

Goethe once wrote: The sea is flowing ever,
The land retains it never.
George Herbert wrote: Praise the Sea,
but keep on land.
Douglas Jerrold wrote: Love the sea? I
dote upon it from the beach.

The *Turksib* and *Rescuer* Case

One of the most colorful and yet disastrous Alaskan shipwrecks during the World War II era not only claimed a stricken Russian cargo vessel, but also the wrecking vessel that tried to save her. The salvage vessel, under Navy jurisdiction, was the SS *Rescuer*, a ship that had somewhat of a checkered career, including a role as a lumber carrier under the name *Casper*. Later she bore the moniker of *Nushigak*, and sank in Bristol Bay. Raised and taken over by the Quartermaster Corps, she sank once again off the California coast and had a long rest until the clouds of war fell over America. Raised the second time, she emerged from drydock and was eventually taken over by the Navy as *American Rescue Service Ship No. 18.*

Commanded by veteran mariner Captain William J. Maloney, a marine surveyor and master mariner, the vessel was diverted from a voyage to New Guinea and sent to Vancouver Island to refloat the stranded *MacArthur*. It took 18 days to refloat the vessel and put a patch in the 35 foot hole in her bow section. They

Passenger liner Yucatan *wrecked in Icy Strait, Alaska, on February 16, 1910, after striking an iceberg. Believe it or not she was resurrected, the passengers and crew were safely removed, and a commendable salvage effort refloated the badly damaged Alaska Steamship Company vessel. Her career under new owners was finalized three years later.*

Suddenly, the moderate seas kicked up, and within an hour a gale was in the making. Soon gusts were up to 80 mph and the lines holding the two ships together strained to the breaking point. Finally they were cast off, but before the *Rescuer* could gain headway, she too found herself on the rocks, water pouring onto the decks and power shorted out.

A navigating officer was trying to guide the *Rescuer* when she struck, but now an angered Captain Maloney took over. The Navy vessel *Oriole*, a minesweeper, attempted to assist as did some YP's, but the seas had mounted to liquid acclivities and danger abounded. All hands were clad in lifejackets, fearing the worst. The winds were freezing, and it was only a few degrees above zero.

When finally the seas calmed some and the wind gusts slackened, a port lifeboat was lowered, the starboard boat having been smashed at Kodiak where a gale had shoved the *Rescuer* into another vessel.

The position of the salvage ship worsened, and Maloney finally gave the order to abandon. It was a narrow escape getting the lifeboat away in such mountainous seas, but the crew managed to gain the awaiting *Oriole*. While grabbing the Jacob's ladder, Harry Kerwin, the *Rescuer's* yeoman, was dashed against the *Oriole* by an erupting wave and had his neck broken. Others did their best to comfort the victim with the available pills, but no doctor was in attendance.

Five days after the abandonment, the USS *Charleston* arrived on

were assisted by the fleet tug USS *Mahopac*.

Under the Navy, with a civilian crew, the salvage ship was then off to Alaska where in stormy seas in the Gulf of Alaska the vessel's rudder became disabled. The ship was finally towed into Kodiak for repairs where the crew spent Christmas in 1942, and a white, cold one it was.

Secret orders then came with the New Year 1943. Steaming out of Kodiak, the old vessel in the middle of her third decade of service was soon off the entrance to Unimak Pass. Then, rounding Seal Cape, their destination was reached. Orders were to refloat the stranded Russian freighter *Turksib* aground on a reef, 1,000 feet offshore. Her hull was punctured, her engine room flooded, and her decks a shambles.

Captain Mahoney lost little time setting off in a small boat to examine the wreck. He was greeted by a disgruntled Captain Mashnikov and a crew of 35, four of whom were women. The vessel was the victim of a blizzard, missing stays near Unimak Pass, making the turn too soon and ending up in jeopardy. The Soviet skipper was aware under the Communist government that the loss of a ship could mean a jail sentence or even death, depending on circumstances. His vessel was the former Dutch freighter *Der Schelde*. Purchased by the Soviet Union after many years under the flag of The Netherlands, the *Turksib* had departed Portland, Oregon, with lend-lease war cargo for Russia, including vehicles and weapons.

When the *Turksib* first struck, anchors were dropped to hold her position but with the rising tide, rather than being aided, she was swept higher on the unrelenting reef. By the time the *Rescuer* arrived, other vessels were standing by to assist and some of the cargo had been offloaded. The Soviet vessel stranded November 21, 1942.

The Russians were suffering from the cold in their badly damaged quarters. No time was wasted in getting salvage equipment and pumps aboard the wreck. The salvage vessel pulled alongside with only eight feet of water under her keel—a dangerous maneuver. With no steam power working on the *Turksib*, lines had to be sent from the rescue ship to afford steam to operate the deck winches. An effort would be made to pull the wreck free. Cables were sent out from her stern connected to four-ton anchors. Two attempts failed to free the freighter from the pinnacle barrier, although she moved slightly. A diver was then dispatched to consider the possibility of dynamiting her from the reef. The first diver to go down had his air line freeze. To lighten the ship further, remaining cargo was jettisoned, including stores of food—barrels of lard, cases of milk, meat etc.

Five million dollar loss. The Canadian Pacific SS Princess Kathleen *ran aground at Lena Point, Alaska, on her final cruise of the season, September 7, 1952, in command of veteran Captain Graham Hughes. The wreck scene was only 18 miles from Juneau and it occurred at 3:15 A.M., shaking up the 425 cruise passengers. Coast Guard vessels answered the distress call and within a few hours the passengers were being offloaded. All attempts to get the ship free failed and she slipped off the reef and went down in 150 feet of water, a total loss but fortunately with no loss of life. Photo courtesy of T. Davis.*

the scene, and the *Oriole* signalled for a doctor. In turn, Kerwin was taken to the *Charleston* and given immediate care.

As the storm blew itself out, assisting vessels removed all the equipment possible from the salvage ship, and a dispatch was sent to Seattle to enlist the salvage vessel *Discoverer*.

Volunteers were asked to go aboard the *Turksib* to ready her for another salvage try. The Russians were asked to assist in setting up a breeches buoy from ship to the beach—about 1,200 feet. The *Discoverer* failed to make an appearance, so other Navy vessels tried to free the *Turksib*, but to no avail.

Another storm was now in the making. Volunteers from the *Rescuer* had gone aboard the Russian freighter to assist with hopeful salvage work and were housed along with other Navy personnel in leaking quarters. For 35 days the wreck had been impaled and virtually no progress had been made. Fuel oil, black and gooey was escaping into the troubled waters, and combers sometimes swept the length of the wounded freighter. The radio room was flooded and the salvage operations brought to a halt. Auxiliary methods were employed for heat and the preparation of food, but time was running out. The survivors were trying to keep each other's spirits up but the mood was somber.

Giant seas kept battering the *Turksib* and alternative protective areas were constantly searched for. In desperation, an effort was made to seek the shelter of the ship's bridge but while an effort was underway to reach the wheelhouse, the men and women watched in horror as the bridge literally caved in before their eyes. The *Turksib* was fast breaking up. No place was safe. Captain Maloney and Captain Mashnikov were hurled about trying to gain a foothold, the Russian skipper suffering a broken hip and Captain Maloney a broken collarbone. It was chaos—every person for themselves. For three days the misery continued—no heat, no food, little shelter, and freezing temperatures. Suddenly a ship's engineer was washed overboard and drowned.

Frank French, diver's assistant, bravely slid down the breeches buoy wire and miraculously made a successful swim to the rock-bound shoreline in a hairbreadth escape. Then, even more alarming than his survival, was the fact that he hiked nine miles to the Scotch Cap Light Station for additional assistance. Another crewman who had attempted to follow French failed in his effort and almost drowned, but was later swept up on the beach and resuscitated. Those remaining on the wreck suffered terribly, constantly drenched, clinging desperately, and grabbing anything that floated by that appeared eatable.

Tragically, Captain Mashnikov, suffered a second fall after which he breathed his last. The others stood helplessly by, blue from the cold. At last, a surfboat from one of the naval vessels was able to get alongside the *Turksib* and in the pulsating waters managed to remove the injured, including Captain Maloney, three Russian women, and others.

Meanwhile, Coastguardsmen from Scotch Cap had traversed the nine miles to the wreck scene and managed to get the breeches buoy functional, after which one of the younger women on the wreck went hand over hand for the shore, all 1,200 feet, even before the conveyance was ready for use. By midnight the breeches buoy was intact, and 60 men from the crews of both wrecks were brought ashore, one by one. They were then escorted back to the lighthouse in small groups. All had only the torn clothing on their backs, and some walked the nine miles without shoes.

A Navy plane flew over and dropped warm clothing for the survivors. Coast Guard personnel managed to salvage some eatable food washed out from the wrecks, and then shot a caribou to afford meat. Hot meals were prepared at the lighthouse. Survivors spent up to 11 days at the lighthouse dwellings before the seas calmed enough for rescue. The nightmare was finally over, two ships were lost and two lives were taken.

The La Perouse Caper

By contrast, a little known but tragic episode goes back to the voyage of the intrepid French navigator and explorer Jean Francois Galaup comte de La Perouse, who headed a three-year, round-the-world expedition sponsored by the French government between 1785-1788. With the French frigates *Astrolabe* and *Boussole*, La Perouse cruised all around the Pacific and then set out to find the elusive Northwest Passage. His quest met with disaster when he reached Lituya Bay, Alaska. In a remarkable piece of navigation he guided his two cumbersome ships over the narrow bar entrance and anchored within the bay. Making a survey of the bay, his first lieutenant M. d'Escures was sent out in the *Boussole*'s pinnace with orders of caution to be aware of high breakers. Unfortunately, he and his men got trapped in the current and were overturned in the surf. To the rescue came the *Astrolabe*'s pinnace, but it too capsized and all were thrown into the surging sea, including De La Borde Marchainville, in charge of the second pinnace. Witnessing the tragedy prompted the jolly boat to be dispatched to the scene, under command of Bouton. He made a valiant but fruitless effort to rescue the ill-starred French sailors struggling for survival in the cauldron of confused, heaving waters. The strong currents and outgoing tide, however, swept the jolly boat seaward. In a Herculean effort the half swamped craft eventually gained

The Princess Kathleen *grinding on the reef which held her prisoner.* Photos courtesy of T. Davis.

the beach but by then it was too late. No less than 21 souls had drowned—no survivors. Among them were two valued officers plus the loss of two badly needed boats.

The saddened navigator erected a small monument and a copper plate on an island in the middle of the bay to commemorate the loss. He named the isle Cenotaph (burial place), and the funeral name stuck ever after.

The bay is seldom visited even today, but is a migrating area for scores of puffins and other sea birds. The copper plate is no longer there, perhaps purloined by the natives who prized copper, or maybe the Russians. Who knows?

La Perouse not only discovered and charted Lituya Bay but also La Perouse Strait, a 25 mile channel separating Hokkaido, Japan, from Sakhalin, Siberia, often called Soya Strait.

The valiant La Perouse, his two frigates and all the seafarers aboard strangely vanished without a trace after sailing from Botany Bay, Australia on March 10, 1788, a mystery remaining unsolved to this day.

Alaska's most tragic shipwreck from the standpoint of loss of life. The Canadian Pacific passenger liner Princess Sophia is seen straddling Vanderbilt Reef on October 24, 1918. She slipped off the reef during a stormy night before any of the passengers were evacuated. Into the depths she sank with her entire complement, 343 passengers and crew. There were no survivors except a dog found wandering on the beach. Note the lifeboats have been swung out in the davits. Photo courtesy of Winter & Pond.

Going, going, almost gone, as the Princess Kathleen *loses her grip on the rocks and slips beneath the surface on that fateful day in the late summer of 1952.* Photos courtesy of Schallerer's.

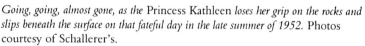

Upper photo: broadside view of the imperiled Princess Sophia *on Vanderbilt Reef with the can buoy in the foreground to mark the reef. Lower photo: only the mast of the ill-fated ship protrudes above the surface following the storm. The can buoy is still in place. Photos courtesy of Winter & Pond Company.*

Steamer Weiding Bros., a fisheries vessel in Alaska service, is seen stranded on Graham Island, British Columbia, July 29, 1913. Captain Otto Holstrom and his crew abandoned the Independent Fishing Company vessel, and she became a total loss.

The lone mast of the Princess Sophia *marks her grave following the 1918 tragedy. A man stands in her rigging surveying the situation. Photo courtesy of Winter & Pond.*

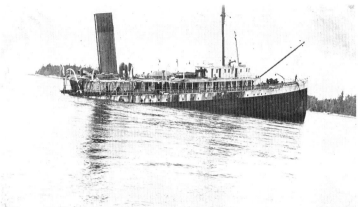

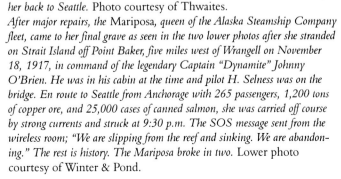

The Grand Trunk Pacific liner Prince Rupert suffered many strandings in Alaska and British Columbia during her years of service. One of her most serious and costly, she ran aground in a 70 mile gale on Genn Island, March 23, 1917. Captain Duncan McKenzie was in command. The vessel suffered major damage but was later refloated.

Three dramatic photos of the end of a graceful ocean liner, the SS Mariposa which came to her final resting place on October 8, 1915, at least that's what they thought, as seen in the upper photo where she was aground after striking a rock in Fitzhugh Sound, B.C., and landing at Llama Pass with a large hole in her hull. She was en route from Seattle for southeast Alaska and Cook Inlet. Passengers were evacuated and the Canadian salvage tugs Salvor and William Jolliffe spent weeks in refloating the wounded vessel, towing her back to Seattle. Photo courtesy of Thwaites.

After major repairs, the Mariposa, queen of the Alaska Steamship Company fleet, came to her final grave as seen in the two lower photos after she stranded on Strait Island off Point Baker, five miles west of Wrangell on November 18, 1917, in command of the legendary Captain "Dynamite" Johnny O'Brien. He was in his cabin at the time and pilot H. Selness was on the bridge. En route to Seattle from Anchorage with 265 passengers, 1,200 tons of copper ore, and 25,000 cases of canned salmon, she was carried off course by strong currents and struck at 9:30 p.m. The SOS message sent from the wireless room; "We are slipping from the reef and sinking. We are abandoning." The rest is history. The Mariposa broke in two. Lower photo courtesy of Winter & Pond.

In a fog at Ketchikan on September 22, 1945, a fuel tank exploded aboard the Canadian National liner Prince George, sparking a devastating fire that destroyed the vessel. Quick action by the Coast Guard managed to tow the steamer to nearby Gravina Island. Passengers were safely evacuated and despite a stubborn fight by the crew and others, the vessel was doomed. One seaman was killed when trapped in the engine room.

Perhaps the most legendary ship loss in Alaskan waters involved the SS Islander of the Canadian Pacific fleet. She sank in the depths off Douglas Island August 15, 1901, while in command of Captain H.R. Foote. Two questions remained unanswered: First, did she strike an iceberg after departing Juneau or did she scrape over Point Hilda? Secondly, did she really have the fabulous amount of gold aboard that has always been rumored? The twin-stacked vessel is seen here several months before her sinking. Forty-two lives were lost in that tragedy.

Above and right: After the fire finally burned itself out, the abandoned Prince George lay a forlorn, blistered hulk on Gravina Island. In 1949, four years after the conflagration, the hull was patched and the wreck towed to Seattle and scrapped.

S.S.Islander. WP©.

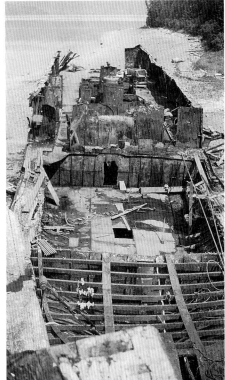

In 1934, after several failed attempts by others to recover the gold from the ill-starred SS Islander, the Curtis Brothers housemoving company of Seattle undertook a novel salvage operation to lift the wreck from the depths and winch her over the sea bottom to shore where her remains could be tooth combed to recover her treasure. The old barkentine Forest Pride and barge Griffson were purchased for the work and a salvage crew organized. The re-covery of the wreck proved successful but the yield of gold within proved a disappointment and the company lost considerable money on their endeavor. The photos here show the remains of the Islander on the beach after more than three decades beneath the sea. Photos courtesy of Winter & Pond.

Salvage workers examining the interior of the Islander *wreck in 1934.*

The steamer Dawson City *takes a broadside on the beach near Nome at the turn of the century. Her fate was sealed.* Photo courtesy of Hammond.

Broken in two and cradled against the snowy ramparts surrounding Johnstone Bay, the SS Yukon *of Alaska Steamship Company is pictured here with anxious passengers clad in life jackets awaiting rescue. The wreck occurred on February 3, 1946, the ship in command of Captain Christian Trondsen with Captain Amego Soriano as pilot. Eleven lives were lost on the section of the ship that broke free. In this photo, rescue craft can be seen along side the* Yukon.

Men checking out the yield from the Islander *wreck, panning for gold dust and checking every nook and cranny. In the lower photo, a worker holds a poke of gold found in the vessel's bilge.* Photos courtesy of Delano.

Remains of the veteran sidewheel steamer Eliza Anderson which made history on Puget Sound and the Columbia River in her heyday. Tired and worn out, the 1859-built steamboat was put back in service during the gold rush era and sent to Nome, Alaska, packed to the gunwhales with prospectors and freight. Never built for offshore service, the nightmarish voyage that followed aged the passengers ten years. It all ended on March 1, 1898. The steamer ran aground on parting her lines at Dutch Harbor and was left to die on the beach. Stripped and abandoned, the wreck is seen a few years later with only her massive sidewheels, walking beam, and part of the hull still intact. In the background in this vintage photo is the SS Centennial, a 325 foot iron-hulled passenger ship, originally the P & O Lines's Delta and later the Japanese SS Takasago Maru. She joined the Alaska fleet in her later years.

The SS Portland played a large role in the gold stampede to Alaska and the Yukon when she arrived at Seattle in 1897 with the "famous" ton of gold, a story that was flashed around the world. Her final end came on November 12, 1910, when she struck an uncharted reef near Katalla while in command of Captain Franz Moore. From Joe Williamson collection.

This was the famous ton of gold lifted in a sling from the SS Portland *at Seattle in 1897, an item that shook up the nation.*

Below: A voyage of discovery that ended in tragedy. LaPerouse's world voyage 1785-88 searched in vain for the Northwest Passage. He discovered certain geographical areas of Alaska and Siberia. After losing pinnaces from his French frigates, Astrolobe *and* Bossoule *at Lituya Bay, Alaska, along with 21 seamen, the two ships and their entire crew vanished from the sea without trace after sailing from Botany Bay, Australia, in 1788. In this artist's depiction, the two ill-fated vessels are shown at anchor at Maui (Mowee) in the Sandwich (Hawaiian) Islands.*

SS Admiral Evans, *Pacific Coast Steamship Company, in trouble at Hawk Inlet, Alaska, on March 9, 1918. Standing by is the salvage steamer* Salvor. *The vessel was eventually raised, patched, and returned to port for major repairs. She was built at Toledo, Ohio, in 1901.*

Tragedy personified. Disaster in Lituya Bay, Alaska, in the 1780s when pinnaces from LaPerouse's frigates Astrolabe *and* Boussole *were wrecked in the heavy surf, taking the lives of 21 mariners. The two French frigates are pictured in the background inside the scenic but often treacherous Lituya Bay.*

CHAPTER SEVEN
The Oil Connection

*It's amazing how such a sticky,
ickey black substance, repulsive
to the touch makes such an impact
on the wheels of industry! The world remains totally dependent
on black gold.*

From a minor commercial oil production begun in 1902 in the lower reaches of southwestern Alaska to the gigantic oil discovery in the Prudoe Bay-North Slope area, the Great Land has come into its own as the nation's chief producer of black gold. For nearly seven decades, oil production in Alaska barely made a ripple on the economy of the United States, but as of 1968 the entire scene changed. As mentioned earlier, not only is the present output gigantic, but the reserves are there if and when an even larger investment in its recovery and feasibility become a necessity.

Though the amazing pipeline from Prudoe Bay to Valdez continues its river of black oil, supertankers larger than any other ships that have previously traversed Alaskan waters run a steady operation to the lower 48 states and in some cases to foreign destinations. It is a multi-billion dollar business that has made Alaska wealthy, but has also brought about oil spills that have done great harm to the natural environment. It goes without saying that the tanker *Exxon Valdez* became enemy number one. When she draped her frame over Bligh Reef, in Prince William Sound (all 987 feet of the mammoth 214,680 deadweight ton vessel) more than 11 million gallons of sticky, crude oil spewed out of her tanks and caused a nightmare. None will ever forget that dark day in Alaskan maritime history. It was on March 24, 1989, that the curtain fell, throwing the state a bombshell which even today has an impact on the fishing industry.

Departing Valdez, San Francisco-bound, the huge tanker, in command of Captain Joseph Hazelwood, glided through Prince William Sound at 11 knots. Within her massive hull were 18 tanks, 13 of which carried crude oil and five for ballast. Captain Hazelwood was not on the bridge, the third officer in charge. As in all previous routine voyages, the crew were about their regular chores, the weather was moderate, and there seemed to be nothing of an unusual nature.

Suddenly, there was a jarring impact. The helmsman had shortly before received orders to turn to starboard. Had she turned one minute

Supertanker Exxon Valdez *hard aground on Bligh Reef, Prince William Sound, Alaska, where on April 5, 1989, her tanks spewed out 11 million gallons of crude oil that caused a nightmare for the Alaskan fishing industry and did considerable other environmental damage. The vessel was in command of Captain Joseph Hazelwood. In the photo, the* Salvage Chief *of the Fred Devine Diving and Salvage firm played a major role in the eventual removal of the 200,000 ton behemoth, her crew preparing the damaged hull for the tow to a San Diego repair yard. Photo courtesy of Fred Devine Diving and Salvage Inc.*

earlier or one minute later the tanker would have missed what turned out to be Bligh Reef. Drawing 56 feet, the bulk of the 166 foot wide giant scraped over the barrier with a sickening screech. Coming to a sudden halt, eight cargo tanks and three segregated ballast tanks were ruptured. Rock ridges ripped through three-quarter inch steel plating on the starboard side, stopping just short of the forward bulkhead of the slop tanks. Fortunately there was no damage to the ship's propulsion, pump room, or deck machinery, but she sat atop the reef totally immobile.

There was nothing wrong with the navigation charts and the reef was marked by a buoy. The little experienced third mate was totally flabbergasted by the sudden turn of events and the Captain, who allegedly left the bridge drunk, was shocked into the reality of his responsibility. Thick black goo was spewing out from the broken plates and the stunned crew were in a state of confusion wondering if the mammoth ship would split in two.

What had earlier been a peaceful scene was now a portentous situation. Radio signals were going over the airwaves constantly and several vessels hurried to the wreck site. Exxon officials reacted quickly, and before long three tankers rushed to the side of the wreck and immediately began lightening 42 million gallons of crude oil from the supertanker. In the interim, sticky crude oil was flooding the waters of Prince William Sound, one of the nation's prime fish and wildlife areas, a place where commercial fishermen had long made their livelihood from ports like Cordova, Seward, and Valdez.

Although the port tanks were intact, lightening those would take special measures, so as not to disturb the tanker's position and cause additional damage or spillage.

The west coast's premium salvage vessel, the *Salvage Chief*, was summoned immediately out of Astoria to speed to the side of the wreck where her experienced crew could direct salvage operations. Priority concern was given to the broken bottom plates to not only prevent further spillage but also to keep the ship from sinking. That job fell to Mick Leitz, salvage master with the Fred Devine Diving & Salvage Company of Portland, Oregon. He responded to a call from Exxon one day after the Good Friday stranding, and he arrived in Valdez on Easter Sunday. With 31 years of salvage experience Leitz was the man for the job. During his career he played a major roll in the salvage of 150 vessels, including the tankers *Chevron Hawaii* and *Sansonina*. He was willing and able to tackle any salvage job, win or lose. The *Exxon Valdez* would be one of his biggest challenges. By the time he was taken out to the wreck, the wheels of his brain had been spinning constantly as the facts were placed before him.

Throughout the operation, a naval architect calculated and recalculated the forces affecting the ship's position, draft, and keel. All such calculations had to be worked out in accordance with the American Bureau of Shipping, the U.S. Coast Guard, and Exxon's central engineering office.

Many experts initially believed the tanker could not be refloated, that she would end her days on Bligh Reef, eventually split apart, and sink into the depths.

Leitz and the salvage crew had different ideas. They studied a lot of interesting theories on how to refloat the behemoth. One theory was to empty her tanks of remaining oil and then secure smaller tankers to her side to afford stability.

Leitz countered that such a plan could end with three sunken tankers. The salvage master needed 8,000 tons of lift to refloat the *Exxon Valdez*. Systems had to be modified so that the tanker's own inert gas system could be injected directly into the tanks. All of the tank openings had to be blanked off. Adapters were built to take the

Classic photo of passengers aboard the steamer Ancon believed to have been taken at Portland, Oregon, in the 1880s just before the ship cast off for Alaska. The steamer was wrecked in Alaska in 1889.

a 1,000 square mile area. Even as the oil did its reprehensible damage, law suits were being filed by the score against Exxon, its tanker, and ship personnel responsible for the stranding.

After 13 days astride the reef the tanker would now wait a month at anchor being readied for the questionable tow south. Meanwhile, Alaska's governor asked the U.S. Coast Guard to take over the much criticized cleanup from Exxon Shipping Company. At the same time, Captain Joseph Hazelwood turned himself into authorities in New York, and in turn was held in lieu of a $1 million bond or $500,000 cash bail.

From the pen of George Bernard Shaw comes the following popular quotation:

Every drunken skipper trusts to Providence
But one of the ways of Providence with drunken
skippers is to run them on the rocks.

"These misdemeanors are of such a magnitude that has never been equaled," said Supreme Court Justice Kenneth Rohl.

Typical of the smaller passenger and cargo vessels serving southeastern Alaskan ports in the early days was the SS Al-ki seen here in the colors of the Border Line Transportation Company. When operated by the Pacific Coast Steamship Company, she carried 50 passengers in hardwood panelled staterooms plus a variety of cargo. The 210 foot 1,259 ton wooden-hulled vessel was built at Bath, Maine, in 1884 and immediately sailed for San Francisco via the Straits of Magellan, pushed along by her 600 horsepower engine. She was lost at Point Augusta, Alaska, in 1917.

inert gas and plumb it to the blowers to increase its pressure for injection into the tanks. The injected gas filled the holed tanks like a balloon.

Leitz recalled that they used a total of 13,000 feet of hose to hook everything up. The re-rigged inert gas system was pressurized just before low tide. After the tanks were pressed up to the predetermined level, the rising tide provided the last few pounds of pressure needed to refloat the ship.

Though there were two 7,000 horsepower tugs and four 9,000 horsepower tugs with lines to the *Valdez*, they never had to "pull" the ship off the reef for she essentially drifted off as if on a bubble.

After the refloating came step two. Ushered off to Outside Bay, and there anchored, she had to be prepared for a long tow without sinking en route. The only drydocks that could handle the burden were at Portland or San Diego. Before that could be attempted all the vessel's tanks had to be cleaned. The ship's own crude oil wash system was utilized, but neither chemicals or heated seawater could be applied as was the standard. Instead, cold seawater under pressure cleaned all tanks, and several washings were required.

It was then that divers working from the *Salvage Chief* went to work on the dangerous and difficult job of surveying the ship's bottom using among other things an ROV (remote operated vehicle). Excess material from the torn underwater plating was trimmed with cutting torches. Diving crews drilled holes in areas of the stress fractures to prevent spreading of the cracks. In all, more than 400 holes were drilled and $83,000 worth of drill bits were expended in the operation.

While all these activities were being performed to make the supertanker moderately seaworthy for the long tow, there was constant awareness of the possibility of her sinking en route.

At that juncture, however, greater emphasis was placed on the huge spill of oil, America's worst ever. Beaches were blackened and thousands of mammals, fish, and seabirds were dying in droves. It was almost like a floating avalanche. Oil skimming vessels and oil containment equipment were being utilized to the maximum, but even with an all-out effort the damage was unspeakable, reaching over

Hazelwood was arraigned on three counts, including operating the tanker while allegedly drunk.

"He's got to think about that. We have a man-made destruction that has not been equaled, probably since Hiroshima," the judge insisted.

A major role in the salvage endeavor was played by Captain Reino Mattila, master of the *Salvage Chief*, which was to become the wounded tanker's constant companion for several weeks. He and his 16 man crew worked tirelessly.

"We were able to transfer over 40 million gallons of oil to other tankers and save the $135 million ship", Mattila recounted.

Before the 203 foot *Salvage Chief* returned to her homeport she would spend almost five months tending the *Exxon Valdez*, doing everything possible to keep her from sinking. After the tanker was refused entrance to the Columbia River she was escorted to San Diego and finally allowed to pass through the Silver Gate and on to drydock.

As bad as was the huge oil spill, it could have been far worse had the ship gone down at Bligh Reef. Her entire cargo was 1.2 million barrels of North Slope crude, and the spill location was only 25 miles from her namesake port of Valdez.

The *Salvage Chief*, the number one salvage vessel in the Pacific, was equipped with large winches below decks, along with cranes, pumps, flotation gear, and a repair shop. There were also facilities for divers plus a helicopter pad.

When Mattila's ship first arrived at the Bligh Reef wreck scene, her crew was astonished by the immensity of the maritime response and cleanup effort. The Coast Guard buoy tender *Iris* was on the scene, along with other Coast Guard and Navy ships, 100 commercial fishing vessels, two Alaska ferries, and even a Soviet oil skimming craft. Exxon paid private boat owners $100 per foot of vessel per day for their help in scooping up the oil. In addition to the surface fleet, airplanes and helicopters hovered overhead.

For weeks, Exxon officials had considered sending the tanker to the Swan Island drydock in Portland for permanent repairs. That, however, would have required a stop at Astoria for divers to make a complete survey before allowing her to go up river. Exxon then sent the tanker to San Diego where she was kept well offshore while the *Salvage Chief* divers had to make another survey to the satisfaction of California port authorities to be certain of no further leakage or possibility of sinking inside the harbor. Finally on July 31, 116 days after the tanker was refloated in Alaska, she was allowed to enter the harbor and undergo a $25 million repair job.

Meanwhile, back in Alaska, the cost of the oil disaster ran in excess of $100 million. In addition, the Port of Valdez was temporarily closed down. Through its portals, 20 per cent of U.S. oil was shipped. Alaska Governor Steve Cowper declared a state emergency, and President George Bush designated the spill a Federal disaster.

Earlier Exxon admitted liability and promptly relieved the tanker's master Joseph Hazelwood of his command. He was in breach of both company and Coast Guard regulations in leaving the bridge in charge of the third mate who was not licensed to operate the vessel in those restricted waters. Blood and urine samples were taken from Hazelwood and other crew members who mostly admitted visiting bars before the vessel sailed from Valdez.

While marine insurance companies worked out liability problems, the *Exxon Valdez* was back home where she was originally built in 1986 by San Diego's National Steel and Shipbuilding Company. The final underwater survey indicated that eight compartments of the tanker's 13 sustained gashes up to 20 feet across.

The 76,813 ton tanker *Exxon Baton Rouge* had earlier offloaded most of the remaining oil from the *Valdez* while still in Alaska. Booms were used to contain the spill, while chemicals and burning methods were also utilized. Perhaps one of the most hazardous parts of the salvage effort was performed by the team of divers from the *Salvage Chief*. Their biggest concern was keeping clear of the giant walls of metal plating as they fell, after being severed from the ship with cutting torches. Further, alertness was necessary to keep lines from pinching, cracking, or getting wound around a jagged edge of heavy plating as it dropped away from the ship. Plates ranged from three to 70 tons. Some fell like rocks and others flipped away like a frisbee.

Divers, led by Mike Mangold, worked in 15 to 20 minute shifts with no more than three divers below the ship at once. The job was performed to perfection. The salvage crew all admitted that it was just short of amazing with so much structural damage that the tanker could float 2,200 miles on an air bubble and arrive safely.

Despite the presence of Greenpeace, who tracked the wounded tanker off the California coast, she was finally allowed entry into the harbor and a new lease on life despite her haunting past.

It is indeed true that the Exxon Valdez oil spill was the worst that had occurred in the United States. There, however, had been many heavier spills from tankers in the world tradelines. Few, if any, did more actual damage to the environment than did the tragedy in Alaska.

Perhaps the greatest of all spills occurred on July 19, 1979, when the *Atlantic Express* collided with the *Aegean Captain* off the Caribbean nation of Trinidad and Tobago. In that calamity some 88.2 million gallons of oil blackened that azure sea. On August 6, 1983, 73.5 million gallons of oil escaped when the tanker *Castillo de Bellver* caught fire off Cape Town, South Africa.

On March 16, 1978, France's north coast was plastered with crude oil when the supertanker *Amoco Cadiz* broke up on the rocky shore off Portsall. In that regrettable catastrophe 65.6 million gallons of oil flowed out of the vessel's ruptured tanks.

Then of course, many will recall the wreck of the tanker *Torrey Canyon* on March 18, 1967, off Lands End, England. Spewed out were 34.9 million gallons of oil. The supertanker was the first loaded giant oil carrier to break up and spill its cargo, calling attention worldwide to the horrible consequences of major oil spills at sea.

The *Torrey Canyon* disaster was followed by the tanker *Sea Star* just five years later, when on December 19, 1972, she dumped 33.8 million gallons into the Strait of Oman. On May 12, 1976, the *Urquiola* dropped 29.4 million gallons at LaCoruna, Spain.

In the North Pacific, the SS *Hawaiian Patriot* caught fire on February 25, 1977, and spilled 29.1 million gallons of oil in the ocean.

In the shoals off the Shetland Island in England, the grounded tanker *Braer* gutted her hull and spread 26 million gallons of oil, pol-

luting the islands. And the supertanker *Sea Empress*, though later refloated, spread over the beaches off St. Ann's Head, Wales, 21 million gallons of her nearly 38 million gallon cargo, blackening 120 miles of coastline, 26 important wildlife sites, and Britain's only marine wildlife sanctuary.

An undetermined amount of oil, somewhere between 18 and 29 million gallons sullied the sea when the *Othello* was in a collision in Tralhavet Bay, Sweden, on March 20, 1970.

Then, the *Exxon Valdez* was next in line with her spill of 11 million gallons.

Perhaps before you read these lines, another devastating oil spill will occur at sea or along its shores. First of all, it is amazing that the oceans of the world can absorb all this contamination and so quickly restore itself. Secondly, the spills will probably never cease because the world still runs on oil. Thirdly, with all of the elaborate safety factors that have been put in practice, accidents will happen, with human error the main cause, as was very evident in the *Exxon Valdez* case.

The oil spills from tankers plus minor spills from barges and shoreside facilities each year play havoc with nature as well as the economy in general. Spilled oil along with growing pollution from nuclear waste continues to contaminate the world's oceans and waterways. Fish and wildlife are already showing traces of such materials in their systems and fish consumed by humans may someday have a negative effect, leading to more cancer and other bodily defects.

No polluters are worse than the Russians who have ruthlessly dumped nuclear waste into Arctic waters, totally uncontrolled. Mankind appears to be highly indifferent to the wonderful natural blessings God has afforded and future generations will certainly suffer because of such carelessness with pollutants.

Now, let us take a look into the system of safeguards set up by authorities to protect against such tragedy as befell the *Exxon Valdez*. Those safeguards were in effect at the time of the stranding, but as mentioned, the cause was dereliction of duty within a danger zone. Valdez was the nation's first port set up to handle supertankers. Many of the American ports cannot handle the giants, especially if they are loaded, as some of the largest can draw up to 60 feet of water. The *Exxon Valdez* was not completely loaded, and she drew 56 feet.

Valdez Harbor, extending from Prince William Sound, is in a picturesque setting. Situated at the terminus of the giant pipeline, its relatively minor status as a port was lifted to major heights when it began catering to supertankers. Entry into the spacious harbor, bordered by mountain peaks that begin at the water's edge, is via a bottleneck less than 1,000 feet in width, titled Valdez Narrows. Were it not for an obstacle which the charts name as Middle Rock, the channel might not be fabled as a narrows. As it turns out, the pinnacle juts out like a sore thumb.

The waterway is no place for a neophyte navigator. Sometimes winds up to 100 mph roar over its surface and again it can be almost as peaceful as a lake. Like human beings, it sometimes has temper tantrums. There was no small amount of controversy about the advisability of Valdez becoming a super port before the first big tanker, *Arco Fairbanks*, of 121,000 tons, made the inaugural call in April 1977.

To prevent oil spills, a carefully augmented set of standards had been established prior to the parade of tankers that would eventually utilize the port. One of the most modern vessel-traffic systems in the world was set up in Valdez just across from the oil loading berths.

One way traffic only was permitted through the bottleneck (Middle Rock). Ships in Prince William Sound were made to follow traffic lanes, like a divided highway on the sea. In the narrows, high resolution radar constantly monitors the exact location of each ship, and the Coast Guard keeps constant communication with every ship in Prince William Sound. But, despite radar, traffic lanes and continuing communication, nobody can make an absolute guarantee of an accident-free port. And that was noted when the *Exxon Valdez* broke the safety mold, which until that time had worked well. Even before the spill, veteran navigator Captain William McKee, with 27 years experience, stated "You could be heading into the narrows and lose your steering mechanism. But what are you going to do, stop running tankers because of accidents? Hell no! People have decided that the damages are acceptable."

McKee was right in his perspective, but after the big spill some wondered if the risk was worth it. But as in all such cases, cool heads prevailed and the supertanker operations continued, following the temporary closure of the port of Valdez.

If any good came out of the disaster, an even closer surveillance over the port, Prince William Sound, and the narrows was instituted. Tanker skippers, officers, and pilots became ever more vigilant.

Will there ever be a similar catastrophe in the Alaskan waters where supertankers operate? Only time will tell.

In numbers of wrecks, the safety records of the behemoths is not that bad, considering the risks. Of the 1,513 tanker accidents from 1973 through 1976, only 77 involved tankers of 200,000 or more tons. The basic problem, however, is when oil spilled is generally monstrous on supertankers.

Even today, constant research continues in finding vessel safeguards. The tanker industry has expended millions of dollars in perfecting safety devices. In fact, a collision avoidance system alone costs more than $125,000. New tankers must have double bottoms as a protection should the outer skin be pierced. Twin screws for greater maneuverability are recommended. The fly in the ointment, however, is that the majority of the accidents are human error which means that better training and stricter regulations are absolutely essential. Even then, such things as emotions, fatigue, boredom, and anger can affect critical navigation judgment at sea. It has been documented that tension between the captain and the chief officers of the *Torry Canyon* contributed to the disastrous 34 million gallon oil spill when that ship cracked up off Cornwall, England, in 1967.

Simulators using computer images are among other innovations to prepare supertanker captains and officers for a variety of emergencies. In some maritime countries, small scale models are used for instruction of navigators in the petroleum trades.

From 1955, there was a competitive race to see what company could build the largest supertankers. They got so large that many became unsuitable for the trade, as ports and facilities were unable to handle such gigantic carriers, labled VLCC, (very large crude carriers) and when oil demands slowed many ended in lay up. For instance, a colossal such as French Marine Shell's *Bellamya* weighed in at 541,000 deadweight tons, and when fully loaded her keel was 94 feet below the surface of the water, her deck 24 feet above. Or to make it more visual, like an 11 story building, 206 feet wide and more than a quarter mile in length. Others such as the *Seawise Giant* and *Pierre Guillaumat* were even larger. The Liberian registered *Seawise Giant* of 564,763 deadweight tons, the world's largest, measures 1,504 feet in length. The *Bellamya* is rated fourth in size. At this writing,

more than 30 supertankers in the world were over 400,000 deadweight tons. Many have become too large and in some cases are a fast vanishing species, the dinosaurs of their trade. With more recent oil discoveries in Alaska, Mexico, and the North Sea, the hauls are not as long as from the Persian Gulf, and the 150,000 to 200,000 ton supertankers are more economical. The race of the giants that reached an apex in the 1980s has settled for economics, not size or prestige.

Oversized supertankers carry cargoes valued at more than $50 million, but cannot pass through canal systems. No such mammoth tankers will be used in Alaskan waters, in fact the 200,000 deadweight category, such as was the *Exxon Valdez*, is the largest practical size for the Alaska run in the supertanker tradelanes. Even vessels of that size, when hauling oil for the east coast, must offload their oil into smaller medium-sized tankers that can pass through the Panama Canal and continue to the final destination. The alternative is via Cape Horn.

As one can see, the oil connection in Alaska from its meager beginning in 1902 has come full circle to our present time. It now is one of the principal lifelines flowing through the industry of not only the United States but to other countries as well.

One other factor in the Alaska oil industry that received worldwide attention was the story of the tanker *Manhattan*. In 1962, this tanker at 115,000 tons was the largest merchant ship flying the American flag. She pioneered a sea route to Alaska's North Slope through the fabled ice-packed Northwest Passage. A reinforced bow section gave her ice-breaking capability. The 5,000 ton steel belt, 32 feet high and nine feet wide proved successful as her powerful engines drove her through a passage which had been sought from the early days of exploration. The effort proved successful, but was not continued, as a pipeline across Alaska to Valdez proved much more economical. Yet without doubt, the *Manhattan* will go down in maritime history for her epic voyage across the frozen northern seas linking east with west.

The practical transport of oil and allied materials has come a long way since 1886 when the initial prototype tanker, the *Gluckauf*, of 3,000 tons, carried oil from the United States to Europe. In that year nobody ever had the slightest idea that Alaska would become a major part of the petroleum industry; that oil existed on the North Slope, or that Valdez would become a supertanker port visited regularly by giant carriers of the sea.

In the spring of 1996, the nation was stunned by a remarkable rise in gasoline prices. Charges and countercharges were made concerning the major U.S. oil companies bilking the consumer. It was claimed that the increased use of petroleum had made our country overly dependent on foreign oil imports. The troubles in the Mideast only heightened the anxiety. Certain politicians urged the reimposing of a ban on Alaska's foreign oil exports to offset the dramatic increase in gasoline prices.

"It makes no sense to encourage oil companies to ship their product overseas when a shortage of domestic oil is driving prices into the stratosphere," insisted Representative Peter De Fazio.

Should problems continue, the untapped oil reservoirs east of Prudoe Bay may yet be developed.

At the age of 15, James A. Gibbs, the author's father, owned and operated the only grocery store north of the Arctic Circle in the Alaska goldfields. He is seen at the far right behind the cash register. This photo was taken around the 1905 period.

CHAPTER EIGHT
Epics of the Frozen North

*Iron men in wooden ships
faced untold challenge and
hardship in a battle to
conquer the frozen north.*

Exactly what is there in the makeup of humankind that urges us on to discovery, regardless of the odds? The challenge to tame the frozen northland, all the way to the pole, enticed many seafarers of old to risk all to make their mark in frozen wastes. Not even shipwreck, privation, starvation, or death-dealing cold kept discoverers from the challenge, not only to reach the North Pole but to crash through the Northwest Passage.

Ships of discovery battled every inch of the way in crunching the northern ice to attain goals. Who can forget the intrepid seafarers like Peary in the *Roosevelt*; Scott in the *Terra Nova*; Amundsen in the *Gjoa*, or Byrd in the *Bear of Oakland*?

One of the most famous ships ever to sail Alaskan waters was the U.S. Revenue (later U.S. Coast Guard) cutter Bear. *Built by Alexander Stephen & Sons at Dundee, Scotland, in 1873-74, this 198 foot steam-powered barkentine was fashioned of six-inch-thick strakes of oak bolted to Scottish oak ribs, decks of teakwood, and sectors of Swedish iron. Side sheathing was of Aus____ iron bark with a bottom of yellow pine, masts of Norway pine and hollow iron, and a bow reinforced with heavy oak timbers for smashing through ice. Her two-cylinder compound engine developed 500 horsepower. The* Bear *did yeoman work in Alaska for years in rescue, supply, law, and exploration, in places where few ships ever went in the often ice-choked seas of Alaska's far north.* Photo courtesy of Captain Theodore K. Thomas.

Epic voyages go back to 1819-20 when England's Lt. William E. Parry penetrated masses of ice as his 375 ton bark *Hecla* managed to make it half way through the Northwest Passage, wintering at Melville Island.

Sir John Franklin tried to penetrate even farther in the auxiliary bark *Erebus* in 1845, but his party perished after finding a link with the western channel. Searchers who followed found the skeletal remains of Franklin's crew, but no sign of the *Erebus*, nor her consort *Terror*, which were believed to have been crushed in the ice.

Sweden's Adolf Nordenskjold steamed around Siberia to Japan becoming the first to traverse the Northwest Passage, west to east in 1878-79, while earlier in 1875, England's Captain George S. Nares drove his steam-powered bark *Alert* up the coast of Ellesmere Island, the farthest north by that year.

The auxiliary bark *Jeanette*, under Lt. Commander G. W. Delong, endeavored to gain the North Pole from Bering Strait in the 1879-81 era, but ice claimed his command north of Siberia and nearly all of his party perished.

Next came the iron barkentine *Proteus*, steam-powered, in 1881, which gained Ellesmere Island and landed a U.S. meteorological party headed by Adolphus W. Greely. Bringing supplies two years later the vessel was lost, and Greely and six emaciated members of his party alone were barely alive when relief ships broke through the ice in 1884.

Then came the little giant: the auxiliary schooner *Fram*, under Norway's Fridtjof Nansen, pushing through the ice north of Siberia in 1893 with the hope of drifting across the Pole. The floes carried her to well past the 85th degree, the farthest north at that date. She broke out of the ice near Spitzbergen in 1896. That famous craft is presently enshrined at Oslo, while the small schooner *Bowdoin*, veteran of almost 30 years of Arctic exploration, is preserved at Mystic Seaport in Connecticut.

As the challenge to conquer the North Pole continued, an equal effort was being made to reach the South Pole in vessels of exploration.

One of the great sagas in the drive for the North Pole involved Commander Robert E. Peary and his rugged auxiliary schooner *Roosevelt*. Built to his specifications, she had a wooden hull 2.5 feet thick designed to meet the forces of the ice packs. Skippered by Captain Bob Bartlett, the *Roosevelt* penetrated as far north as Cape Sheridan on Ellesmere Island in September 1908. Pummeled about in the ice, battered by 1,000 ton bergs, Peary was forced to use dynamite. Finally breaking through, the *Roosevelt* offloaded her cargo, which was then sledded to Cape Columbia at the farthest northeast tip of the island, from whence Peary began his historic trek to the North Pole. It was then that the weather closed down with a vengeance. A six day blizzard howled like a banshee. The bitter cold halted Peary's party, and some were sent back to the *Roosevelt* for more supplies.

Reinforced, the discoverer and his half frozen cohorts got to within 130 miles of the pole. Captain Bartlett, among them, was needed back on the *Roosevelt* which had steamed farther north than any other ship that year. She was forced to winter amid the ice at Cape Sheridan, 500 miles from Peary's goal.

Meanwhile, Peary's sidekick Matt Henson and four Eskimos pushed on over the ice against overwhelming odds, every foot of progress gained with exhausting determination. Finally on April 6, 1909, after many previous years of Arctic exploration, Peary at last raised the Stars and Stripes over the North Pole. Shaking the hands of his faithful companions, the great explorer said of his accomplishment, "The Pole at last, a sufficiently unceremonious affair."

With the American flag waving, he built a cairn and remained at his coveted goal only 30 hours. In Peary's wake others would follow, some flew over the Pole; others drifted there on ice flows; still others utilized ice vehicles, and the Navy went under the Pole in nuclear submarines. Not since Peary, however, did another party sledge there until a quartet of Britishers did so in a 14 month, 1,300 mile trek by dog sled from Point Barrow, Alaska, in 1969.

This writer visited Peary's *Roosevelt* after she became a tugboat for the Washington Tug & Barge Company in Seattle. Her stout hull was as rugged as ever and she bore the same proud look, minus her sail power, as when she carried Peary's party to the place from where he sledged to the North Pole. The end for the *Roosevelt* came in 1937, when she broke down while towing the Naval collier *Jupiter* from San Francisco to the east coast. She was returned to French Canal in Panama, stripped of her machinery and allowed to rot away, an ignominious ending for an historic ship.

Earlier, the great Norwegian explorer Roald Amundsen was determined to negotiate the Northwest Passage. After serving in Polar sealing vessels for several years, he returned to Norway in 1899, and engaged the advise of his counterpart Nansen, who had considerable Arctic experience in his rugged vessel *Fram*. In turn, Amundsen pur-

chased an old fishing sloop of 50 tons, a rather unorthodox vessel with gaff and boom rig, jib boom, and bow spirit. Her moniker read *Gjoa*. Fitting her with a single square yard for a head sail on the single mast that also carried the fore and aft mainsail and flying jib sails, the craft was additionally given an underpowered 13 horsepower engine and tanks.

Talk about courageous abandon, Amundsen dared challenge the Arctic with that tiny craft packed with supplies to the gunwales and carrying a crew of seven. He departed Norway in June 1903 into the teeth of howling winds, pea soup fogs, tortuous channels, and ice floes. The vessel survived a stranding, an engine room fire, and perilous seas, but pushed ever onward, wintering on King William Island northwest of Hudson Bay. There, anchorage lasted for nearly two years, the ice refusing to break up. Wasting no time, the explorer made scientific observations, survey, and sledge trips over the ice. Without communication with the outside world, the seven man party existed Eskimo style, enduring much hardship, but never giving up.

Finally in August 1905, the little sloop was ice-free and continued her voyage westward amid intricate half frozen channels, ever seeking a breakthrough to solve the missing link in the Northwest Passage. Suddenly, a ship coming from the opposite direction. Ex-

Outbound for Alaska, towing out to sea, the old square-rigger Abner Coburn, *a former downeaster, spent several years in the Alaska canning operations, carrying cannery workers north annually and bringing back Alaska canned salmon. Unlike many of her counterparts, the old sailing vessel weathered many a storm without disaster. She was scrapped in 1929. From Joe Williamson collection.*

The auxiliary schooner Roosevelt *served as Admiral Peary's flagship on his 1909 expedition to the North Pole. The explorer reached his goal April 6, 1909. The* Roosevelt, *well known in the northland, later became a tug for Seattle's Washington Tug & Barge Company. Peary died in 1920, one of the great explorers of his day.*

citement reigned aboard the *Gjoa*. Her Norwegian flag was hoisted, but no response.

As they drew closer the excitement died. It was feared she was a derelict. But no! Suddenly the American flag fluttered from the gaff of the stranger. Jubilation at last. The *Gjoa* had made it through the passage from east to west, and the riddle of the fabled passage had been solved. The vessel they met was an American whaling ship hunting bowheads in the Arctic.

Still, the little *Gjoa* would have to spend one more winter in the land of ice, this time on the northern coast of the Yukon Territory. What a leader, discoverer, and skipper Amundsen was—and his small band of subordinates were loyal to the man. Finally, in August of 1906, the broken ice was such that the sloop, part with sail and part with her mini-engine, passed Bering Strait and was free as a bird in unobstructed waters. When she arrived at Nome, one of the biggest celebrations ever known at the small settlement took place. The heroes of the Northwest Passage did what many had claimed impossible. History will always remember the accomplishment, for all though Amundsen and his crew have all passed away, their rugged little vessel *Gjoa* lives on, enshrined at the Norwegian Maritime Museum at Oslo.

The epic voyage of the *Gjoa* in opening the Northwest Passage enlisted increased interest by both Canada and the United States. In later years, Royal Canadian Police Sergeant Henry Larsen piloted the small Arctic patrol vessel *St. Roch* through the fabled passage in both directions, east to Halifax in 1940-42 and west to Vancouver, B.C., in 1944. First to make the transit in both directions, the 104 foot auxiliary schooner is now preserved for future generations at a Vancouver museum.

Mentioned in the previous chapter was the voyage of the ice-strengthened supertanker *Manhattan* which put her 43,000 horsepower steam plant to work as she plowed her way, creating a channel over the top of the world from east to west to become the first commercial American merchantman to do so. Destination of the 1,005 foot monster was the valuable Alaskan North Slope oil fields.

In March of 1987, the *Manhattan* sailed from the Columbia River for the last time, bound for Valdez to load Alaska crude for Long Beach.

She then cleaned tanks and sailed for Korea to undergo repair and await orders. While anchored at Yosu, Korea, on July 16, she was hit by typhoon Thelma and blown ashore. Her starboard side was torn open and the engine room flooded. Damage was so extensive to shafting, propellers, and rudder that she was declared a total loss and sold to Chinese shipbreakers.

Had it not been for the Alaska pipeline, a regular tanker route would have been maintained through the Northwest Passage. The ice problems, however, coupled with severe weather conditions and the constant need of ice breakers and specialized ice strengthened ships, made the pipeline operation far more practical.

Having earlier conquered the Northwest Passage, Amundsen went back to Norway, fitted out Nansen's old *Fram* for a try at the North Pole, but on learning of Peary's having planted the American flag firmly at the coveted goal, he turned his visions of discovery toward the South Pole where he was triumphant.

In the 1918-20 era, as the world was involved in the great war, Amundsen, enthralled with previous successes, navigated over the northern extremes of Asia in the *Maud*. He followed in the wake of Nordenskjold in the *Vega* as more and more secrets of the frozen north were brought to light.

Meanwhile, more sophisticated polar exploration continued. Lincoln Ellsworth and Umbert Nobile flew a dirigible over the North Pole in 1926, with none other than Amundsen aboard. Two years later the Norwegian explorer was placed on the list of the missing when his plane crashed while searching for Nobile, whose dirigible had earlier met the same fate.

History records, however, that Admiral Richard E. Byrd preceded Ellsworth and Nobile's initial dirigible flight over the North Pole when earlier in 1926 he was first to fly by plane over the coveted landmark. Doubts as to Byrd's claim of being first to fly over the North Pole were unveiled in 1996, when the explorer's 1926 notes were brought to light from the archives of Ohio State University. Specialists in navigation have determined that Byrd fell short of his goal due to adverse weather, and that Amundsen, Ellsworth, and Nobile were first to succeed. The debate goes on. Byrd was first to fly over the South Pole three years later. He then went back to sea exploration in the southern pole latitudes using respectfully the *City of New York*, *Jacob Ruppert*, and finally the famous steam barkentine *Bear of Oakland*. The *Bear* had earlier rescued survivors of the Greely Arctic expedition in 1884, and then under the United States Revenue Service patrolled Alaska's sealanes to the Yukon in the 1890s.

While Byrd continued his South Pole discovery efforts, activity continued in Alaska's northern seas as they had since earlier times. Perhaps no Alaska vessel gained more fame than did the USRC *Bear*, (later Byrd's *Bear of Oakland*) along with the man who commanded her longer than any other. He was Captain Michael Healy, better known as "Hell-roar'n Mike," who started his seagoing career as a 15 year old cabin boy on an East Indiaman, sailing from Boston in 1855. He gained notoriety in 1886 when he took command of the *Bear*, transferring from the USRC *Corwin*. The *Bear*, as stout as a wooden vessel could be, was built at Dundee, Scotland. Some 200 feet in length, she had massive beams, strong oak frames, and Australian iron bark sheathing as armor against the ice.

Much better suited for patrol duty than the smaller *Corwin*, the *Bear* was capable of eight knots under sail and nine with her steam engine. During her long service in the Bering and the Arctic seas, when not under sail, she put her two cylinder compound steam engine to work. The sometimes cranky propulsion was often cursed by the "black gang" who saw to its whims. Until 1912, she had only a two-bladed propeller. Coal fired, the engine required 392 tons of fuel, some stored on deck.

The vessel was given a diesel engine in later years, developing 600 horsepower. Among her regular duties as police ship of the north was transporting a variety of federal agents, castaways, destitutes, missionaries, and felons.

Migration and sea activity to northern Alaska had increased when Healy took command of the *Bear*. Not only were whaling vessels abundant, but miners and hunters were seeking new haunts. One of the orders for the *Bear* was to "seize any vessel found illegally sealing in the Bering Sea." As the chapter on the sealer revealed, it was a tough job enforcing such a law. Sometimes Healy was forced to use harsh methods which brought international criticism, especially when he captured 12 Canadian sealing schooners in 1887. By 1892, the *Bear*, *Rush*, and *Corwin* had made so many seizures on the Bering Sea Patrol that tension grew hot between the United States and England, (Canada) over what was termed by the latter as illegal encroachments. It took an international arbitration tribunal to reach a decision. The findings were against Uncle Sam, holding that the Bering Sea was open water and available to ships of all nations. Not until 1911, did the sealing practices end when four maritime nations agreed to protect the diminishing herds on the North Pacific rookeries.

On the *Bear*'s annual visit to King Island in 1890, Healy found a shore full of starving Eskimos, so weak they could hardly stand. Too proud to beg for food or accept charity, they were nevertheless taken aboard fed and nursed back to health. Their chief told Healy that 200 of his people had perished during an unusually severe winter. Only 100 had survived. The usual walrus on which the Eskimos fed on during the winter had not returned, and they had been forced to kill their dogs for food, laced with seaweed.

The *Bear*'s crew helped inter the dead and provide supplies for the settlement before sailing away. Among those who witnessed the aftermath of the King Island tragedy was Missionary Dr.

Bull Terrier of Alaska was the name applied to the little steamer Dora *which made history in Alaska, breaking down after departing Cold Bay, and drifting for 63 days in the north Pacific in 1905-06, under Captain Zimro Moore. Given up as lost she amazingly arrived at Port Angeles, Washington, using rag-tag pieces of canvas for sails.* Drawing by Win Stites.

Sheldon Jackson. He, along with Healy, embarked on a plan to import reindeer from Siberia as a source of food to assist the diet of the Eskimo, a plan that proved a success in future years, the herds multiplying rapidly. In the next decade, 1,100 reindeer were imported into Alaska, and Dr. Jackson's Bureau of Education took charge of the distribution.

The Eskimos learned the value of the meat and took to it well. With regulated killing of the reindeer, the herds continued to multiply so fast that by 1940 they were 500,000 strong, turning out to be one of the most constructive measures ever carried out by the United States government. It was also one method that reduced the high rate of death among the Eskimos.

Healy's ship often served as a floating Court of Justice in trying cases of the law. One of the most remembered took place in 1893, and involved the murder of two Eskimo boys. The bizarre incident involved H. R. Thornton, a missionary and school teacher at Teller. A stern, self-righteous man, he had threatened to whip three boys, in-

cluding the chief's son, for minor infractions. Such physical punishment was not tolerated by the high-ranking Eskimos who dreaded humiliation. It was considered an affront to their dignity. Rather than submit to the whipping, the boys decided to kill Thornton. They in turn went to his abode and knocked on the door. When he opened it they shot him through the chest.

Villagers came running to the scene on hearing the gunshot and when they saw the missionary lying in a pool of blood, dead, they turned on the boys who seemed to know that their dastardly deed must be paid for. Two of the lads were immediately stoned to death, but the chief's son, on claiming to be thirsty, was escorted to his dwelling and given his last drink. Then, in complete submission, he was led back to his grave site where he obediently laid down. His treasures were placed with him. Picking up his rifle, the boy's uncle then shot him in the head and he passed into eternity.

Eskimo custom was not in tune with that of United States law, and Healy was confused about which course to take. Though he strongly disapproved of such methods of execution, he realized that justice had been done, Eskimo-style. Thus he passed no sentence, but harshly warned that such practices in the future would not be tolerated and that proper punishment would be dispensed after a legal (American) trial in a court of law. The Eskimos did not protest the warning and eventually accepted the white man's way.

Being the total authority in implementing harsh law, along with long strenuous years in the northern climes later turned Healy into a near tyrant, and charges were made against him concerning unfair treatment of his subordinates and of dealing out punishment on members of the whaling and sealing fleets.

One infraction got widespread attention when he took out his temper on some belligerent whalermen from the ship *Estella*. Healy insisted they mend their ways, and when they refused his authority, he had them brought aboard the *Bear*, put in irons, and triced up on the cutter's yardarm.

Later the man turned to heavy drinking and further abuse of his crew. After 20 years of service in Alaska, most of it commendable, Healy was brought up on charges of drunkenness and abuse of subordinates. Though only 50 years of age, his face had become hard and lined. He had long felt that his authority should never be questioned when far divided from the outside world. The whale ship crews hated him as well as they did the Revenue Cutter Service, inasmuch as it wanted to end the indiscriminate killing of whales. The outside world tended to favor the whalermen after news of some of the harsh punishment reached the lower states.

Ironically, despite bitter feelings between the *Bear*'s captain and his officers, the enlisted men stood by their skipper. Strong words and accusations were traded at the subsequent hearing in 1889, but Healy was found innocent of all charges.

In 1895, similar charges were brought against Healy by his officers, and this time the hearing was slightly less than torrid. He was found guilty of some of the charges and was given a black mark on his 30 year career. His name was accordingly placed at the bottom of the "Captains list," and he was sent back to San Francisco to await orders.

Healy took his licking with considerable remorse. In 1902, he was given command of the USRC *Thetis*, but the disgrace still weighed heavily on the man, and the following year he retired from the service. Several months later he died in San Francisco at age 65. His mostly brilliant career, tarnished by "Healy's law," and an overindulgence in alcohol had reduced him to a defeated individual at the end. Some said he died of a broken heart.

Healy was long outlived by the *Bear* which he commanded for so many years. After 90 incomparable years of service in the Revenue Marine, the Navy, and the Coast Guard, the vessel came to her final resting place in Davy Jones' Locker. Sold out of government usage, she was being towed to Philadelphia to become a floating restaurant. They say ships seem almost to have souls, and as if to protest the indignity, she parted her towline in a storm. Her hull opened up and she sank in deep water on March 19, 1963. Seafarers the world over mourned her loss.

Another of the widely publicized rescues in northern Alaska involved the *Bear* in 1897-98. A fleet of ice-trapped whaling vessels near Point Barrow were in trouble. Winter came early in 1897. Eight whaleships were trapped in the ice with only enough provisions to have carried them back to San Francisco at the end of the season. It was early November that the unexpected early freeze occurred, and the lives of some 265 on the whale ships were in jeopardy. They could not survive long without provisions.

President William McKinley ordered a relief expedition to rescue the marooned. The call went to the famous *Bear*, under the command of Captain Frances Tuttle. He would take only volunteers on the difficult mission. Because the *Bear* was unable to gain the northern limits of Alaska, the rescue party was still about 2,000 miles from the whaling vessels. Lt. David Jarvis was chosen to lead the overland expedition, assisted by 2nd Lt. E. P. Bertholf and ship's surgeon Dr. S. J. Call. The party was landed at the Eskimo village of Tununak on December 15, where they were met by Alex Kalenin, a half-breed trader who guided them 250 miles north to St. Michael. The *Bear* in turn had to reverse course and winter at Unalaska Island to also keep from being trapped in the ice.

Thirteen days later, the party at St. Michael picked up another dog team to sled them northward. There, the party split, with Bertholf going on alone and Jarvis and Call together. Each of the three acquired their own dog team from the C.O. of the Army post there. From then on it was a battle against bitter subzero temperatures. Finally reaching Point Rodney, they were able to obtain a herd of 138 reindeer from a local Eskimo named Artisarlook who agreed to join the party to care for the herd. The animals would serve as a food supply for the hungry whalermen.

Suffering extreme hardships, the rescue party reached Cape Prince of Wales where a government reindeer station was located. The station keeper, the Reverend William Lopp, turned over his herd to the "Arctic cowboys" and also joined the group which was still 700 miles from the stranded whaleships. History was in the making, as never before had a rescue team crossed rugged mountains and frozen tundra in midwinter when temperatures got as low as minus 70 degrees, amid blizzardous conditions and jagged walls of ice. Even a few of the deer perished from the demanding pace, and one was killed by a hungry pack of wolves. Still the gallant men pressed on.

Jarvis and Call rendezvoused with Bertholf near Kotzbue and exchanged news of their respective experiences. The latter had difficulties when some of his Eskimo companions and their dogteams turned back, forcing Bertholf to set up a way station for the whalermen in the event their escape south might not come to fruition. Moving ahead of the reindeer herd, Jarvis and Call mushed into their destination on March 29, 1898, the herd arriving the next day. What a reunion. The stranded whalermen had resigned themselves to death by starvation and freezing. At first some believed it only a mirage. Others were near death, suffering from scurvy and other diseases. Animalistic thoughts had passed through their minds, temporarily crazed from hunger. Some of the whaleships had already been crushed by the ice. The intact vessels were spread out over a long distance and there was much work to do to organize, care for, and to slaughter the reindeer for badly needed meat. Shelters were built, medical help offered, and food distributed in one of the greatest and grandest humane rescue operations in American history.

Not until July 28, 1898, was the *Bear* able to reach Point Barrow which still was rimmed with ice. The whaleships still in one piece, were well provisioned in order to make their escape, while 97 castaways whose ships had been destroyed were taken aboard the *Bear* for the voyage back to San Francisco. Lt. David Jarvis and all of his accomplices became folk heroes in their time. In 1905, following his advancement to Captain in the Revenue Service, he would later be named to a three-year term as Alaska's collector of customs.

After retiring from government service, he became an executive with the Northwest Fisheries Company. Then in 1911, to the complete shock of his family and friends, he tragically took his own life at the age of 48. What a sad ending for a great hero who left his legacy behind him.

Just after the purchase of Alaska in 1867, the USRC *Lincoln* carried the initial government inspection party into Alaskan waters, and without any special design features the vessel was to make recommendations for lighthouses, coaling stations, and customs houses. In addition, rich fishing banks were to be located, specimens collected, physical and geographic areas sleuthed out, and numerous other items tended to. The cutter's skipper, Captain W. A. Howard was accompanied by Professor George Davidson of the U.S. Coast Survey.

The *Lincoln* and the *Wayanda* provided the earliest data indicating the vast potential of Alaska's natural resources. A single haul of the *Lincoln*'s seine brought up 2,500 salmon and herring, while the *Wayanda*'s captain reported great veins of coal. Crews of both cutters brought back word of the predacious devastation of fur seals.

Those early exploits of pioneer cutters opened Alaska's doors to the far north, and the first regularly assigned Revenue cutter was the *Reliance*, headquartered at Sitka in 1868. In 1880 the *Corwin*, with an ice-strengthened hull, began the service's regular cruises in the Arctic Ocean and Bering Sea. Annually the responsibilities grew, and sister cutters like the *Thetis*, *Bear*, *Northland*, and *Storis* all played a role in early law enforcement, exploration, scientific research, and protection for the Alaska natives, which at times were cruelly exploited by some of the early white settlers.

In 1880-81, the *Corwin* was engaged in a dangerous but futile attempt to locate survivors of an Arctic exploration ship and two whaling vessels which had not been heard from for months. Before starting out on the mission the vessel's crew managed to careen their 145 foot vessel on the beach, and sheath her with ice-resistant materials. As the vessel sailed out on the rescue mission she penetrated as far north as possible, after which two officers, a coxswain, and two natives were dispatched by dog sled to search the area of Cape Wankerem. After a month of traversing through driving snow and slanting sleet, the team reached their destination. To their horror and disappointment they learned that one of the whaleships had completely vanished and the other vessel's crew members had died from cold and starvation.

Continuing her search amid breaking ice, the *Corwin*, sought out the exploration ship *Jeanette*. En route, her rudder snapped off in the pack ice. Despite driving snow, the crew managed a jury rig which allowed the cutter to work herself free. While still in the open sea water the crew fabricated a new rudder. Later, it was learned that the *Jeanette* had been destroyed by the ice well beyond the reach of the would-be rescuers. One of the lone survivors was George Melville who somehow managed to carry an injured fellow officer to safety in an incredible escape. Melville in later years became a rear admiral in the U.S. Coast Guard, which took over the Revenue Cutter service in 1915.

In the years that followed, the Revenue Marine and later the Coast Guard were to play a major role in ice-breaking and allied ac-

The mysterious, haunting art of the native Tlingit people is expressed in this totem pole image which never fails to captivate Alaska tourists. Photo courtesy Holland America Westours.

Framed against a glacier on Alaska's rugged coastline is the beautiful cruiseliner Crystal Symphony of Crystal Cruises. Offering the ultimate in Alaskan cruising splendor, the vessel is highly popular with tourists. Photo courtesy Crystal Cruises, Los Angeles.

Nobody knows how the Alaska natives gained their talent for carving totem poles, but they have become legendary and many are still seen today.

Map of Alaska showing the sea routes served by the Alaska Marine Highway System with its fleet of eight modern ferryliners. Insert, one of the big blue ferries at a southeastern Alaska port of call. Photo Courtesy Alaska Marine Highway System.

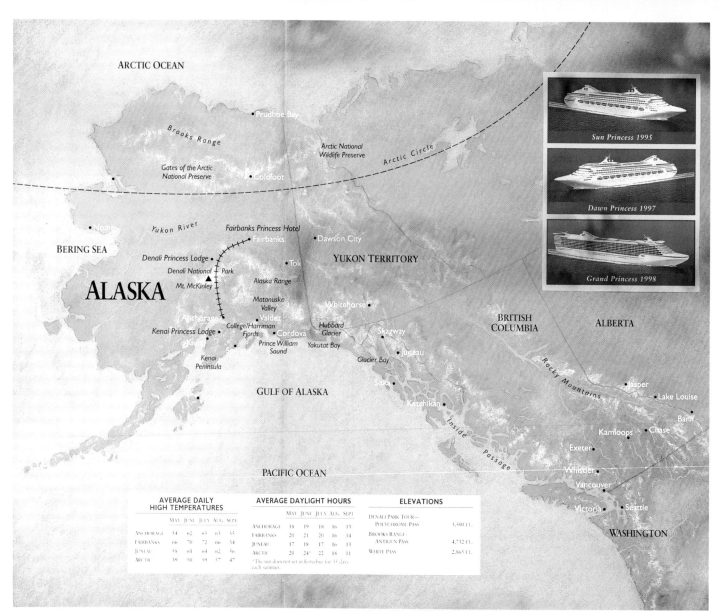

ARCTIC OCEAN

Prudhoe Bay

Brooks Range

Arctic National
Wildlife Preserve

Arctic Circle

Gates of the Arctic
National Preserve

Coldfoot

Sun Princess 1995

Dawn Princess 1997

Grand Princess 1998

BERING SEA

Nome

Yukon River

Fairbanks Princess Hotel

Fairbanks

Dawson City

YUKON TERRITORY

Denali Princess Lodge

Denali National — Park

Mt. McKinley

Tok

Alaska Range

ALASKA

Matanuska
Valley

Whitehorse

BRITISH
COLUMBIA

ALBERTA

Anchorage

College/Harriman
Fjords

Hubbard
Glacier

Skagway

Kenai Princess Lodge

Kenai

Cordova

Prince William
Sound

Yakutat Bay

Juneau

Glacier Bay

Jasper

Lake Louise

Kenai
Peninsula

GULF OF ALASKA

Sitka

Rocky Mountains

Banff

Kamloops

Chase

Ketchikan

Exeter

Whistler

Inside Passage

PACIFIC OCEAN

Vancouver

Victoria

Seattle

WASHINGTON

AVERAGE DAILY HIGH TEMPERATURES					
	MAY	JUNE	JULY	AUG.	SEPT.
ANCHORAGE	54	62	65	63	55
FAIRBANKS	66	70	72	66	54
JUNEAU	58	61	64	62	56
ARCTIC	39	50	59	57	47

AVERAGE DAYLIGHT HOURS					
	MAY	JUNE	JULY	AUG.	SEPT.
ANCHORAGE	18	19	18	16	13
FAIRBANKS	20	21	20	16	14
JUNEAU	17	18	17	16	13
ARCTIC	20	24*	22	18	11

*The sun does not set in Kotzebue for 35 days each summer.

ELEVATIONS	
DENALI PARK TOUR— POLYCHROME PASS	3,500 FT.
BROOKS RANGE— ANTIGUN PASS	4,732 FT.
WHITE PASS	2,865 FT.

Map of Alaska afforded by Princess Cruises shows an insert of the latest units of the fleet, facts, and figures on Alaska, and the rail route from Anchorage to Fairbanks. Princess Cruises inaugurated the "Love Boat" theme several years ago in the TV series. Alaska is one of the line's premier cruise areas.

One of the most popular cruiseliners to traverse the waters of Alaska is the SS Rotterdam, a 38,000 ton royal lady of the sea which may soon be replaced by more modern tonnage. The 748 foot vessel can carry 1,075 passengers. She is seen here cruising the placid waters of the Inside Passage of Alaska. Photo courtesy of Holland America Line.

Fabulous Glacier Bay, one of Alaska's foremost scenic attractions.

From the deck of Princess Cruises' initial Sun Princess *moving slowly through Glacier Bay, in the summer of 1979.*

Darkness falls over Lincoln Rocks on Alaska's Inside Passage.

A clever artist turns a rock formation on the Skagway waterfront into a toothy skull. Below are containers for the White Pass and Yukon rail route.

One of Holland America Line's earlier cruise ships moves slowly through ice-flecked Alaska seas in the 1979 cruise season.

The great Trans-Alaska Pipeline at Prudoe Bay in northern Alaska travels hundreds of miles down to the loading terminal for supertankers at the Port.of Valdez. Though not a pretty sight as it courses along the rugged natural terrain of Alaska, it serves a vital role in industry. As it has been said, "the world runs on oil."

The powerful Foss Maritime Company tug Craig Foss is shown underway for southeastern Alaska ports with a fully loaded modern container barge. Foss has long been a major factor in the towing industry throughout the Pacific and sometimes beyond. Its role in Alaska is substantial. Headquartered in Seattle, the company was formed before the turn of the century at Tacoma, and today has one of the world's largest and most modern fleet of tugs and barges. Photo courtesy Foss Maritime and Michael Skalley. Camera Craft Inc. photo.

At dockside in Seattle in 1897, crowds gather alongside the SS Portland on her arrival from Alaska on her epic voyage with gold. From the Williamson collection.

Below: In the 1970s, the Atlantic Richfield 121,000 ton tanker ARCO Fairbanks tests tricky Valdez Narrows on a test run for the shipment of crude oil from the southern terminus of the Trans-Alaska Pipeline. Since then, multi-millions of gallons of oil have been exported from Valdez, both to domestic and foreign ports. Photo courtesy of National Geographic Magazine and photographer Martin Rogers.

The Exxon supertanker Exxon North Slope ties up temporarily at the Port of Astoria before moving up the Columbia River for repairs in Portland. A near sister to the ill-starred Exxon Valdez, she too has hauled much crude oil from Valdez. Note the size of the 900 foot giant compared to the small craft in the boat basin.

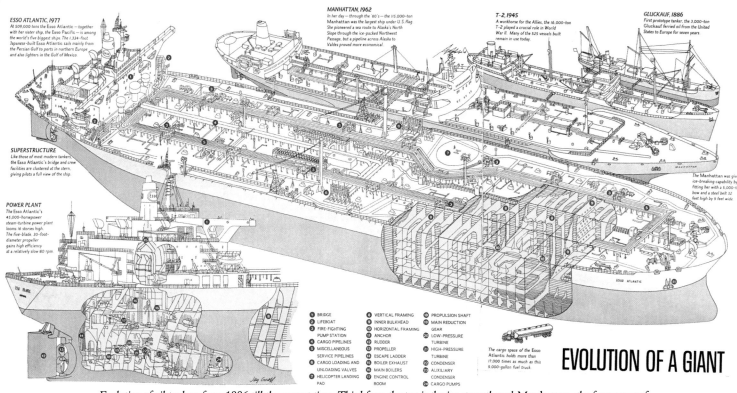

1. BRIDGE
2. LIFEBOAT
3. FIRE-FIGHTING PUMP STATION
4. CARGO PIPELINES
5. MISCELLANEOUS SERVICE PIPELINES
6. CARGO LOADING AND UNLOADING VALVES
7. HELICOPTER LANDING PAD
8. VERTICAL FRAMING
9. INNER BULKHEAD
10. HORIZONTAL FRAMING
11. ANCHOR
12. RUDDER
13. PROPELLER
14. ESCAPE LADDER
15. BOILER EXHAUST
16. MAIN BOILERS
17. ENGINE CONTROL ROOM
18. PROPULSION SHAFT
19. MAIN REDUCTION GEAR
20. LOW-PRESSURE TURBINE
21. HIGH-PRESSURE TURBINE
22. CONDENSER
23. AUXILIARY CONDENSER
24. CARGO PUMPS

The cargo space of the Esso Atlantic holds more than 17,000 times as much as this 9,000-gallon fuel truck.

EVOLUTION OF A GIANT

Evolution of oil tankers from 1886 till the present time. Third from the top is the ice-strengthened Manhattan, *the forerunner of supertankers in Alaskan waters. She managed to break through the ice-clogged Northwest Passage in 1962, but it was found more economical to ship Alaska oil by pipeline via Valdez. Artist Jay M. Groff and researcher Gunars J. Rutins fashioned the above, which appeared in an edition of the* National Geographic *in 1978 in an article by Noel Grove. Our thanks to the National Geographic Magazine.*

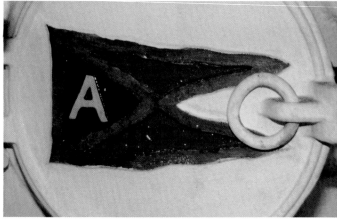

House flag of the Alaska Packers Association painted on the porthole storm cover of APA's Star of India. *Alaska packers ran a larger fleet of square-rigged sailing vessels out of San Francisco than any other firm in the canned salmon industry. Photo courtesy of Bob Schmemmer.*

Scuba divers photograph the remains of the SS Princess Kathleen *four decades after she went to her final resting place in about 150 feet of water off Lena Point. Photo courtesy of Bob Schwemmer.*

The MV Bartlett *passes through Alaska's pristine waters. The smallest of the Alaska Marine Highway fleet, she has been active since 1970 and continues to serve the Prince William Sound route.* Photo courtesy of James Thomson.

Totem Ocean Trailer Express (TOTE) fleet is depicted by an artist with the map of Alaska framed in the background. From left, the Westward Venture, Northern Lights, *and* Great Land, *all super big carriers to Alaska which would make the cargo ship of yesteryear seem pint-sized.* Photo courtesy of Alan J. Stark, TOTE.

Kathleen Brezina and Pete, Rachel, and Harry Johnson give a traditional Tlingit performance aboard an Alaska Marine Highway vessel. The Arts on Board program brings a variety of artists, dancers, musicians, weavers, carvers, and storytellers on sailings to share their talents with ferry passengers. Photo courtesy of John Hyde.

The Alaska Marine Highway's eight ferryliners cover some 3,500 miles of waterway, about the distance from New York to London. Here one of the sleek, blue-hulled "Glacier" vessels cruises through the Inside Passage. Photo courtesy of Alaska Division of Tourism.

Alaska Marine Highway vessels, from the 193 foot Bartlett to the 418 foot Columbia *are large enough to carry passengers and vehicles, be it a bicycle, motorcycle, car, or large RV.* Photo courtesy of Alaska Marine Highway System.

Princess Cruises' Crown Princess *glides to a stop opposite Margerie Glacier in Glacier Bay, Alaska. Insert shows one of the line's veteran skippers, Augusto Lagomarsini.* Photo courtesy of Princess Cruises.

Luxury cruise liners one might have seen on the Alaskan waterways during past cruising seasons. Top, left to right: Star Princess, 63,500 tons with Princess Cruises; artist's rendition of a Carnival Cruises' vessel; and the unique Celebrity Cruises 47,000 ton Horizon. On second row is the World Explorer's venerable Universe and Royal Cruise Line's Royal Odyssey. Third row, Holland America's Rotterdam and Princess Cruises' Crown Princess. Fourth row, the 77,000 ton Sun Princess and Holland America's Nieuw Amsterdam. Fifth row, Cunard Line's Sea Goddess and Princess Cruises' Golden Princess. New, transferred, and replacement ships give the Alaskan waterways a continuous parade of cruiseliners each season.

In the 1996 cruise season, World Explorer Cruises along with its SS Enchanted Seas, *renamed* Universe Explorer, *offered unique 14 day cruises from Vancouver, B.C., to numerous Alaska ports. It marked the line's 19th year of service to many world destinations. The modernized* Universe Explorer *carries 739 passengers and 330 crew.* Photo courtesy of Dennis Myrick, V.P. World Explorer Cruises.

Pictured around the center picture of the retired sternwheeler Klondike, *a tourist attraction at Whitehorse emblematic of the gold rush days are several smaller sightseeing craft that operate in Alaskan waters. Top left, Sternwheeler* Discovery *operating out of Fairbanks; MV* Glacier Queen *off Columbia Glacier; at bottom from left, the MV* Fairweather *on Lynn Canal and the* Ptarmigan *cruising on Portage Lake. Photos courtesy of* Holland America Westours.

Royal Caribbean Cruises Ltd., headquartered in Miami, is sending its finest ships into Alaskan waters including the fabulous Legend of the Seas, *pictured here gliding gracefully in northern waters. Photo courtesy RCCL.*

Holland America Line's 50,000 ton Statendam, *popular 720 foot Alaska cruiseliner under Bahamas registry. She was named "1995 Ship of the Year" by national cruise magazines. Passenger capacity is 1,266 passengers. Photo courtesy of Holland America Westours.*

A sight to behold—the cruiseliner Legend of the Seas, *one of the newest and largest ships of the RCCL fleet moves through the waters of the Inside Passage as low clouds hover over the shoreline. Photo courtesy of Royal Caribbean Cruise Line.*

Artist's rendition of one of the Norwegian Cruise Line ships serving the ports of Alaska.

In 1963-64, the SS Princess Patricia of Canadian Pacific was converted from a day liner to an Alaska cruise ship at a cost of $1 million to accommodate 374 first class passengers. She is seen here in 1979 at a small Alaska port in her new color scheme. Since then the Alaska cruise business has accelerated to new heights.

Denali National Park in Alaska, one of the nation's largest and most pristine, is crowned by the mighty Mount McKinley, the highest peak in North America at 20,320 feet above a veritable paradise for wildlife. Photo courtesy of Princess Cruises.

The sleek Star Princess is pictured in Glacier Bay, Alaska, the sea flecked with ice dropping from the mighty glaciers. She was dropped from Alaska cruising in 1997 to become P & O Line's Arcadia. Photo courtesy of Princess Cruises.

To give one an idea of the huge amount of food that must be carried aboard the giant cruiseliners sailing Alaskan waters, an example is given here. For instance, the 63,000 ton Star Princess of Princess Cruises carried the following on a typical 12 day cruise for 1,500 passengers and 600 crew members. Fresh fruit, 44,000 pounds; fish, 25,000 pounds; fresh vegetables, 60,000 pounds; fresh milk, 1,300 gallons; poultry, 16,000 pounds; pasta, 5,000 pounds; eggs, 70,000; and meat 32,000 pounds. From the top chef to the dishwashers including food and beverage manager, the employees number about 95.

Like a wraith coming out of the sea mist, the Alaska State ferry Malaspina is seen in the waters of southeastern Alaska. Photo courtesy of D. Murrell for Alaska Highway System.

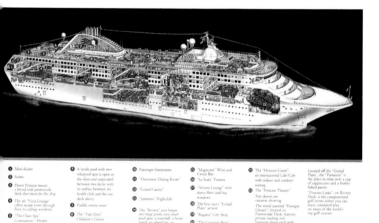

The latest entry in the Alaska cruise ship business made her debut about the time this book was published. She is the glamorous Dawn Princess of Princess Cruises (owned by P &O), sistership to the Sun Princess introduced in 1995. These 1,950 passenger vessels stand 14 decks high, offering the ultimate with state of the art showrooms; aft Vista Lounge and forward Princess Theatre. Other choices include the computerized golf center, children's fun zone, casino, library, nightclub, gyms, and swimming pools. A cutaway ship depiction show the inner workings of these 77,000 ton vessels. Photo courtesy of Princess Cruises.

Getting ready to test the waters of Alaska, the sleek new cruiseliner Century of Celebrity Cruises makes her debut.

Graceful as a swan, the cruise ship Westerdam *of Holland America Line is no stranger to the Alaska sealanes.* Photo courtesy of Holland America.

Off Juneau, Alaska, the elegant cruiseliner Noordam *is always a sight to behold.* Photo courtesy of Holland America Line.

Almost as if she was a permanent part of the seascape, the 53,872 ton, 1,494 passenger Westerdam *is pictured at the port of Juneau. This gorgeous Holland America superliner features all the amenities and more. Among other things, the 798 foot ship has a huge sliding glass roof over one of its swimming pools for times when the sun fails to shine.* Photo courtesy of Holland America Line, Westours Inc.

MS Nieuw Amsterdam, *sistership to the* Noordam, *is pictured here berthed at Ketchikan in 1993. The 704 foot vessel carries a proud name.* Photo courtesy of Holland America by G. Brimacombe.

Adjectives can't describe the beauty of a megaliner pictured adjacent the blue-white glaciers in Alaska's Glacier Bay. Pictured here is Holland America's 50,000 ton Maasdam. *Holland America Line is one of the oldest continually operating steamship lines in the world.* Photo courtesy of Holland America Line.

Grand dame of the sea, the 790 foot roll-on, roll-off vessel Westward
Venture *of the Totem Ocean Trailer fleet.* Photo courtesy of TOTE.

TOTE carriers, Northern Lights *(top) and* Great Land *on their regular
run between Tacoma and Anchorage.* Photo courtesy of TOTE.

The huge cruiseliner Sun Princess *in Alaskan waters. In 1995, she
held the record as the world's largest cruise ship, but has since been
superseded by a 105,000 ton Princess Cruises ship, the* Grand
Princess. *Photo courtesy of Princess Cruises.*

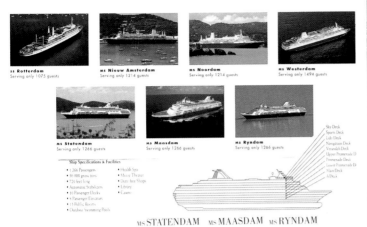

The majestic fleet of Holland America Line cruise ships which ply many world routes including Alaska. The line has gained top popularity with Alaska cruise tourists. Photo courtesy of Holland America Line.

Heavenly paradise—With Mt. Edgecumbe rising above Sitka, the trim MS Noordam of Holland America Line glides into focus. Photo courtesy of Holland America Line.

Greek reefer ship Milos Reefer was caught at anchor at the extreme northern tip of St. Matthew Island in the Bering Sea by miserable weather and heavy seas. While attempting to maneuver out of her anchorage, the vessel was driven aground on an uncharted reef. The Fred Devine company was contracted to remove the bunkers that remained trapped in the vessel's double bottom tanks and engine room, plus other pollutants, in an important fishing and wildlife area of Alaska. The vessel was wrecked in that Bering Sea outpost on November 15, 1989. When the Devine crew boarded the wreck they noted that vandals had stripped her of most of her fittings. Some 139,000 gallons of fuel were pumped from the wreck. Photo courtesy of Reino Mattila, Jr.

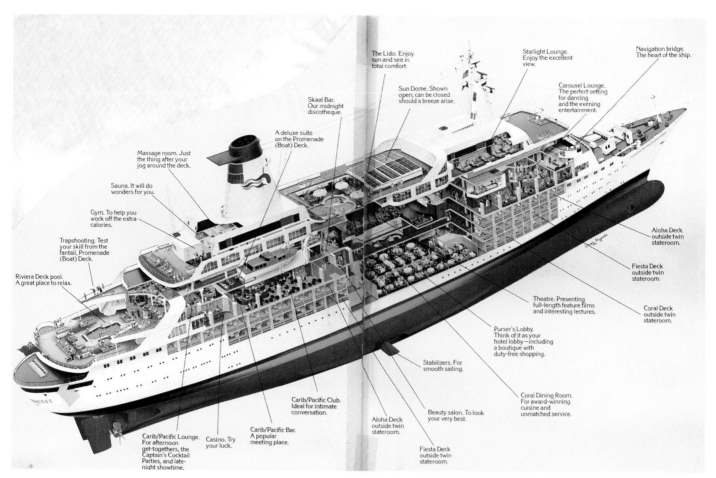

Massage room. Just the thing after your jog around the deck.

Sauna. It will do wonders for you.

Gym. To help you work off the extra calories.

Trapshooting. Test your skill from the fantail, Promenade (Boat) Deck.

Riviera Deck pool. A great place to relax.

Skaal Bar. Our midnight discotheque.

A deluxe suite on the Promenade (Boat) Deck.

The Lido. Enjoy sun and sea in total comfort.

Sun Dome. Shown open; can be closed should a breeze arise.

Starlight Lounge. Enjoy the excellent view.

Carousel Lounge. The perfect setting for dancing and the evening entertainment.

Navigation bridge. The heart of the ship.

Aloha Deck outside twin stateroom.

Fiesta Deck outside twin stateroom.

Coral Deck outside twin stateroom.

Theatre. Presenting full-length feature films and interesting lectures.

Purser's Lobby. Think of it as your hotel lobby—including a boutique with duty-free shopping.

Stabilizers. For smooth sailing.

Coral Dining Room. For award-winning cuisine and unmatched service.

Carib/Pacific Lounge. For afternoon get-togethers, the Captain's Cocktail Parties, and late-night showtime.

Casino. Try your luck.

Carib/Pacific Bar. A popular meeting place.

Carib/Pacific Club. Ideal for intimate conversation.

Aloha Deck outside twin stateroom.

Beauty salon. To look your very best.

Fiesta Deck outside twin stateroom.

Cutaway interior of the original "Love Boats" of the TV series, the Princess Cruises' Pacific Princess *and* Island Princess, *both of which have seen service in Alaskan waters. The program did much to promote cruising, but where these twin vessels seemed huge at one time, they are considerably smaller than the latest entrants into the Alaska cruise business. Though still operating in diverse cruising areas they may eventually be replaced by newer ships. Artist Shusei Nogaska made this drawing for Princess Cruises in 1976 for use in its travel folders.*

Below The Waterline

Ⓐ Rudder Ⓓ Draft Marks Ⓗ Plimsoll Marks
Ⓑ Propeller Ⓔ Stabilizer Ⓘ Bow Thrusters
Ⓒ Shaft Ⓕ Blue Boot-Topping Ⓙ Bulbous Bow
Ⓖ Keel

Crystal Cruises beautiful cruiseliner Crystal Harmony which, along with her sistership Crystal Symphony is seen here in a cutaway plan of her interior. The 49,000 ton, 787 foot super ships both cruise Alaska's waterways offering the ultimate in cruise travel. Photo courtesy of Cruise Travel Magazine and Crystal cruises.

Above, left and below: *Typical of the patrol craft that monitor the waters of Alaska is the USCGC* Liberty *pictured here.* Photo courtesy of U.S. Coast Guard 17th District.

tivities. The big breakthrough came in 1927 when the *Northland* replaced the aging *Bear*. Cutters with greater ice-breaking capabilities were necessary. Hi-tech evolution in sophisticated cutters with powerful engines and reinforced bow sections were forthcoming. In 1957, the icebreaker *Storis* along with the buoy tenders *Spar* and *Bramble* became the first deep-draft U.S. vessels to transit the Northwest Passage. When the tanker *Manhattan* made her epic voyage she was assisted by the Coast Guard icebreakers *Northwind* and *Staten Island*, but those icebreakers became obsolete alongside the newest innovations such as the $52 million, 12,000 ton, 400 foot *Polar Star* and *Polar Sea*, built by the Lockheed yard in Seattle in 1973-74. They became the most powerful in the world, able to go through thick ice like a knife through butter. If they couldn't cut through the packs they planed up on top and crushed it.

Bigger and better icebreakers will continue to play a role in the ice regions of Alaska, but now that man has solved a way of throttling Mother Nature's frozen wastes with surface craft, aircraft, and nuclear submarines, much of the drama and heroism of old is a near forgotten entity.

Scores of dramatic incidents occurred in the marine annals of Alaska's northland before the modern days of quick communication and response. Back in 1892, in the Bering Sea when the whaling vessel *Helen Mar* lay in the ice cutting up a whale, the nearby steam whaler *Jessie H. Freeman* harpooned a leviathan which in a wounded frenzy dove under the ice. In turn, the *Freeman* started ramming the floes tracing the whale by its trail of blood. Suddenly, a heavy fog closed in and the two vessels were lost from each other's view. By the time the shroud lifted the *Helen Mar* had vanished. The *Freeman* searched for hours and finally found one frantic crewman on the ice. Forty-eight hours later, the steam whaler *Orca* found four more battered survivors shivering on an ice floe, but they were the only ones who escaped from the *Helen Mar*. Of the four rescued by the *Orca*, two died from the effects of the exposure, and the total of dead came to 30.

The ill-fated whaleship evidently got pinched between two ice bergs and was crushed before boats could be lowered. The men saved themselves by clinging to the mainmast which had been thrown over the ice. Some speculated that the crazed whale might have rammed the vessel and split her planking.

There were so many grizzly episodes in the sea disasters of Alaska that the accounts could fill volumes. The whaler *Ohio* was also crushed in the northern ice, and 20 crewmen perished, and then there were other strange events that occurred among the rugged crews of the whaling fleet. For instance, at Kotzebue in the early days of the gold rush era, the *Northern Light* was the scene of a mutiny. The crew wanted to break their articles of shipping, and the ship's captain refused their request. In anger, six of the protestors bored holes in the hull near the keel so the vessel would sink and free them from the contract. Scuttlebutt apprised the skipper of the devious plot. He discovered the holes and put the pumps in action. The openings were then plugged and the ship saved. The culprits paid a heavy price for their failed shenanigans.

Speaking of mutinies, the name of the infamous Captain Bligh, before the *Bounty* incident, was listed among the officers on Captain Cook's *Endeavor* in his search for the elusive Northwest Passage. Cook reached Icy Cape, that bleak promontory, treeless and isolated, and there dropped the ship's anchor. Bligh, excellent navigator that he was, probed Cook Inlet for an opening. Both he and Cook determined there was no Northwest Passage at either Icy Cape or Cook Inlet. Cook was later killed by the Hawaiians in the Sandwich Islands, and Bligh, after his reprimand at the famous mutiny trial later commanded a ship-of-the-line, under Nelson. He last became an admiral and commandant of His Majesty's Dockyard.

Other incidents of interest involving Alaska's northern icy climes were among the records of Dr. Call, who we were earlier introduced to as a surgeon on the *Bear*. He had praise for some of the whale ship captains and their crude but effective doctoring practices when no help was available from the outside.

The whaling vessel *Mary D. Hume* was wintering off Herschel Island when a crew member suffered a badly injured foot where gan-

grene had set in. That was in March 1891. The vessel's skipper bossed the operation as the patient, put under chloroform, was placed on the mess table. With a butcher knife and hacksaw the foot was removed. The man survived. On March 9, 1894, both feet had to be amputated from a crew member of the whaler *Narwhal*. The flesh was peeled back, the bones cut off, and the flap of skin moved back over the opening. He too recovered.

Numerous other such amputations took place among those ailing in the whaling fleet. Surgeons were used when available but the crudest methods were often employed when no other choice existed. Though some of these slipshod measures ended in death, it was remarkable how many victims survived.

Though the government vessels saved many imperiled seafarers and their ships, occasionally the shoe was on the other foot. In 1910, the cutter *Perry* was checking out the activities of both Japanese and American sealing vessels hovering outside the three-mile limit off the Pribilofs. As usual, boardings and searches took place in accordance with the law.

One morning when pea soup fog blanketed the area, the *Perry* lost her bearings and ran aground. A frantic effort was made to refloat the vessel. Yards were sent down, topmasts struck and anything movable jettisoned, but the vessel stuck like glue. Radio distress calls were dispatched, but the cutters *Manning* and *Tahoma* were nowhere near the area. The crew took to the boats. Their experiences are told elsewhere in this chapter. The wreck remained for the whims of nature to turn it to a heap of rusted metal. Within a decade only her boilers, red with rust, marked the spot where the *Perry* met her demise.

One of the strangest of all the epics in Alaskan maritime history was the fantastic drift of the little steamer *Dora*, which later gained the moniker of the "Bull Terrier of the Pacific." On a routine voyage to Western Alaska and the Aleutian ports with cargo and passengers, the *Dora* departed Valdez on November 27, 1905. Dogged by severe weather and tumultuous seas, she sought shelter at Cold Bay. Then an attempt was made to put into Chignik Bay, but the persistent gale made it impossible to dock there, so she came about and put back to sea. Rolling and pitching violently, the struggling steamer made little headway when suddenly with a loud bang the main steam pipe between the engine and the boiler burst open and the *Dora* sat dead in the pulsating billows. Alone and helpless, left to the mercy of the sea, it was the beginning of a 63 day drift that carried her all around the North Pacific like a piece of driftwood. Her master, Captain Zimro Moore and chief engineer C. Moon looked at every alternative but there appeared nothing that offered help, nor could first officer P. H. Karbbe come up with a solution. Winds and currents became the erratic pilot for the *Dora* as her course became a crossword puzzle. All through the Gulf of Alaska she drifted, one time as low as the latitude of the Columbia River, but never was a search or rescue vessel sighted. Week after week passed, provisions ran extremely low and water was carefully doled out to passengers and crew. Rain was caught in the canvas covering the lifeboats. Boredom and fear set in. Mail pouches were opened for reading material. Fortunately there were only three passengers aboard, a blessing considering the worsening conditions. All the time, distress flags fluttered in the breeze and the American flag was flown upside down in the hope of assistance. Talk of starvation ran its course. Inasmuch as the *Dora* had no wireless equipment she could not make contact with either another ship or shore station. The situation grew desperate. Already the press had listed the *Dora* lost at sea with all hands, and the insurers, Lloyds of London, contemplated payment to the Northwestern Steamship Company, owner of the *Dora*.

In the interim, a search was conducted for any sign of the missing vessel or possible survivors. Among ships involved in the search were the Revenue cutter *Rush*, and the SS *Santa Ana*, skippered by Captain Frank Moore, brother to the *Dora*'s master. Aboard the missing steamer were 15 crewmen in addition to the three passengers, two of whom were boys, 11 and 17 respectively, being sent back to the States in care of the ship's officers. The other passenger was N. H. Moses, a fur buyer. It was not the time of year when passenger bookings were full, the Gulf of Alaska being one of the roughest wa-

USS Boxer, *an auxiliary steam-powered brigantine used for training naval personnel, was an Alaska visitor in bygone years.*

Ghost ship of the North was the label stamped on the SS Baychimo of the Hudson's Bay Company. She gained world-wide fame for the legendary drift in the early 1930s after being abandoned by her crew, amidst the ice floes. As the months faded into years the mysterious vessel appeared and disappeared in the frozen Arctic refusing to succumb to the pressure of the ice despite her damaged hull.

Aground in Alaskan waters on a murky day is the motor vessel North Star *of the U.S. Bureau of Indian Affairs which for many years went to Alaska's far north to supply the needs of the Alaska natives. She was born out of the Depression years when built at Seattle in 1932, and loaded to her capacity, made her annual pilgrimages northward. She was freed from her awkward position in this photo. The* North Star *saw Navy duty during World War II, and also served as a flagship for the Admiral Byrd Antarctic Expedition.*

Sophie Christenson. *She started out as a lumber carrier and ended up as an Alaska codfishing schooner, a sturdy vessel that was built at Port Blakely on Puget Sound, in 1901. Perhaps the king of the codfishers, the four-master, was operated for years by the salty Captain J.E. Shields. Other well known Alaska codfishing schooners were the* C.A. Thayer *and* John A. *of the Pacific Coast Codfishing Company; The* Wawona *and* Azalea *of Robinson Fisheries Company;* Louise *of the Union Fish Company;* Fanny Dutard, *owned by J.A. Matheson and earlier by Westward Packing Company, in addition to the* Sophie Christenson *and her running mate, the schooner* Charles R. Wilson. *Inset shows Captain J.E. Shields, who fought a one-man battle over fishing rights against the opposing Japanese in Alaskan waters (see story in text). The* Sophie *carried up to 45 men of which 22 were fishermen. Others formed the "dress gang" who dressed, cleaned, salted fish with rock salt, and cooked the meals.*

Owned by the Swenson Fur Trading Company, the schooner Nanuk *made Alaska history. In 1927 she was the sole commercial link between Alaska and Siberia, under command of Captain R.H. Weeding. She carried essential cargo to Habarovsk, Siberia, and returned with furs. In 1929, the vessel was locked in the Arctic ice near North Cape and held prisoner for eight months until the ice broke up in August. Two pilots attempting to fly the cargo of furs from the ship lost their lives when their plane crashed. The* Nanuk *is best known for her role in the famed far north movie drama,* The Eskimo, *filmed by MGM. She was also used in the movie* Treasure Island. *When the ship was trapped in the ice in 1929, she had been trying to reach the frozen-in company trader* Elisif.

ters in the world in the off season. The *Dora's* zigzag course continued and the souls aboard were wondering if they would eventually vanish into infinity unseen like occupants of the proverbial *Flying Dutchman*.

Came the last resort. The desperate officers and crewmen went to work. Out of pieces of canvas, including those covering the lifeboats, the men fashioned an unorthodox mainsail, foresail, and stay sail and hung it like garments on a clothes line from the *Dora's* two masts. Low and behold, the unorthodox rig was able to gather wind. With the gusts in her makeshift sails, under a slow gait she eventually reached the entrance to the Strait of Juan de Fuca, and on February 23, 1906, was assisted into Port Angeles.

The nation was enthralled with the tale of the missing ship that had mysteriously reappeared. One of the first to receive the good news via telephone was John Trowbridge, general manager of Northwestern Steamship Company in Seattle. The *Dora* would soon be back home and accordingly receive a tumultuous welcome. Captain Moore was held up as a celebrity, an iron man of the sea who brought the Bull Terrier of the Pacific to safe haven. The *Dora* was given an overhaul and returned to service. Unfortunately, the celebrated captain lost his life on August 26, 1914, when he went down with his ship, the passenger liner SS *Admiral Sampson*, which sank quickly after colliding with the Canadian Pacific liner *Princess Victoria* off Point No Point on Puget Sound. Despite a wide search, his body was never recovered.

And as for the rugged little 320 ton *Dora*, she stranded on a reef off Noble Island, December 20, 1920. By the time she was pulled free

and beached at Alert Bay in sinking condition, she was left to die on a lonely Alaska beach. She began her days when built at San Francisco in 1880, and served 40 years of hard usage.

Another vessel that was virtually resurrected from the dead was the SS *Curacao*. She was wrecked at Warm Chuck, Alaska, on June 21, 1913, and at low tide was down in 78 feet of water reportedly with no chance of redemption. In her holds were 800 tons of coal and 750 tons of cannery supplies. Insured for $110,000, the difficult location prompted the Pacific Steamship Company to abandon her to the underwriters. In turn, 60 days later, the sunken wreck and her cargo were purchased by farsighted salvagers from the Vancouver Dredging and Salvage Company for only $4,000. The Canadian firm worked in tune with Captain Harry W. Crosby of Seattle in a joint effort to raise the steamship. Crosby furnished scows and tugs and the salvage company equipment and divers.

After the general cargo was removed, including the coal, a channel was dredged out for a distance of 110 feet. Next, the sea bottom was scoured out beneath the ship's keel. Slings were then passed under the hull and a cofferdam fashioned. Some 600 empty gas drums, with a total lifting weight of 270 tons were placed in No. 2 hold and scows were placed on either side of the ship, equipped with winches, including six and a half inch cables and powerful pumps.

The novel salvage effort paid off as the 1,503 ton vessel was lifted from the sea bottom and dragged forward through the newly created channel to shallow water where necessary temporary patchwork could be accomplished before escorting her to a stateside drydock. It was one of the most successful efforts of its kind in Pacific annals. Said Crosby in his hour of triumph:

"We salvaged the cargo in the fall and returned the following June to continue the work of raising the vessel. It required another two months to complete the job working on three tides. The *Curacao* had been in a sunken or partially sunken predicament for one year and eight months."

Now, she was again afloat and would go on to a successful career after almost being given up as a total loss. Ironically, the former owners purchased her back from the salvagers for $90,000 and then gave her a complete overhaul and returned her to the tradelanes. After 45 years of service with Pacific Steam and the Alaska Steamship Company, the vessel was sold to Greek interests operating tramp ships out of Shanghai. Renamed *Hellenic Skipper*, outbound on her initial voyage for the new owners she suffered a major explosion on July 10, 1940 which sent her to the bottom of the sea in deep water 125 miles off Grays Harbor, Washington. This time there was no attempt at salvage.

During World War II, the Army Transport *Clevedon* was a victim of fire and explosion, the details hushed up by wartime censorship. The vessel was tied up at the Yakutat dock, and among her cargo were several drums of gasoline. With a blast and resultant fire, the locals and the military thought the Japanese were attacking, or that a saboteur had torched the ship. There was complete confusion. The flames

The motor vessel Expansion, *typical of the many smaller vessels used for years in Alaska hauling freight and mail between smaller Alaskan port settlements.*

The renowned four-masted schooner C.S. Holmes *made her annual trading voyages to the Arctic from 1914 until the beginning of World War II, first under the capable hands of Captain John Backland and later under his son Captain John Backland Jr. The schooner replaced the* Transit, *which was lost in the Arctic ice in 1913. Both vessels homeported in Seattle and voyaged under sail as far as Point Barrow. The elder Captain Backland became ill in the late 1950s and turned command of the vessel over to his son who had previously served as mate. The senior skipper was a deep-seeded spiritual Christian who held Bible reading and prayer meetings aboard ship during the rigid voyages, and frequently did goodwill work among the natives of the far north. His son, who gained a great knowledge under his father, took over all the Backland enterprises, and during World War II was inducted by the Navy as an ice pilot with the rank of commander. The senior Captain Backland, born in 1870 in Sweden, first came to the Northwest in 1906 as master of the bark* Kelburn. *Inset of Captain Backland, top left, and his son top right.*

threatened the entire waterfront, and a desperate battle to control the flames from spreading appeared to be a losing cause. Another Army transport in the harbor was engaged to tow the burning vessel away from the dock. With great effort, a hawser was attached and the *Clevedon* pulled out into the bay still burning like a Roman Candle. Amid minor explosions, she was shoved ashore on the other side of the harbor away from the town. With a rising tide, however, she floated free again and began drifting. Further explosions followed, and the red hot hull finally succumbed and down went the ship beyond recovery.

The initial explosion occurred at midnight. In Captain Emil Jackson's own words, he described the conflagration:

"I was in my cabin when it started. I had just taken my coat off and stretched out on my bunk or I wouldn't have these clothes now. The first officer came in and said we were on fire and then the gongs began to ring all over the ship. I went to the engine room. The crew was already beginning to fight the fire. There had been an explosion not loud enough for me to hear in my cabin—and by the time I got there, the flames were all over the engine room. We fought them with a gas extinguisher and then with foam extinguishers that soldiers brought down from the Army barracks. But there was nothing we could do. The fire was blazing too high. One man got burned around the hands and face getting out of the engine room, but the rest escaped without injury through the shaft alley."

Jackson then ordered everyone off the ship but the first, second, and third officers, plus the quartermaster. Captain Jackson continued:

"I stayed aft. The other transport came alongside with her bow even with us amidships so she could shove our bow on the beach without grounding herself. I made her lines fast and chopped our stern lines with an axe. The flames were beginning to get into the upper structure and she was afire amidships by the time they got us beached."

"I was dancing around back there trying to keep my feet from burning on the decks," recalled Jackson. "The four men up forward got their boat away and rowed back to the wharf. The lines from the other vessel broke under the impact of the grounding and as we beached, the *Clevedon* broke free. However, the other ship nosed her bow against our stern for a moment and I got off by jumping over the deck."

Captain Jackson went on to explain, "After about half an hour, the incoming tide carried the *Clevedon* off the beach and she drifted into the harbor with flames climbing to the tops of her masts. The fire lighted up the bay and was reflected in a weird color on the water. Flames roared from the open hatches as the cargo burned. Suddenly there was a series of loud explosions which hurled flaming debris high in the air, and the doomed *Clevedon* sank to the depths of the harbor."

Captain Jackson vividly recalled that it was a night of terror with officers and crew standing helplessly by in the glow of the raging inferno. The ill-fated *Clevedon* was originally the Italian freighter *Feltre* which sank in the Columbia River after colliding with the SS *Edward Luckenbach*, February 19, 1937. Purchased by Pacific American Fisheries, she was overhauled after being raised from the river muck. Pressed into the Alaska packing trade she was latched on to by the government for Army service during the war.

Epic stories of Alaska would not be complete without mentioning the crusty, codfishing schooner master, Captain J. E. Shields and his one-man war against Japanese intruders.

Alaska was one of the world's last strongholds for commercial sailing vessels idled in other world trades. The square-riggers of the Alaska Packers Association ended their days as cannery ships, and most of the old lumber schooners that once plied the Pacific Coast and offshore trades under sail ended up in the Alaska codfishing business. Perhaps the best known in the latter category was the staunch four-masted schooner *Sophie Christenson*. Captain J. E. Shields, shipowner and master mariner operated his schooner under the Pacific Coast Codfish Company banner. With nets spread across the sealanes followed by migrating salmon, Japanese fishermen had become a threat to the lucrative Bristol Bay salmon packing industry, and were further a barrier to the codfishing schooners operating out of Puget Sound ports. Shield's protests to the government had fallen on deaf ears so while in Alaska he dispatched a wireless message in the 1938 season requesting that a dozen rifles and plenty of ammunition be sent to his schooner, the *Sophie Christenson*, and also the *Charles R. Wilson*, skippered by Captain Knute Pearson.

The dispatch got front page news inasmuch that there had long been friction between the United States and Japan over fishing rights off Alaska. Word of the dispatch was sent around the world and appeared in many foreign newspapers. It also reached the captains of the Japanese vessels which Shields claimed were illegally fishing the Bristol Bay and Bering Sea waters. His one-man war bore immediate

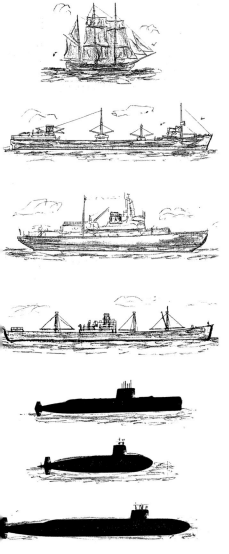

Types of vessels that have been seen on or under Alaskan waters down through the years, mostly in the ice-wracked seas of the far north. From top to bottom: American whaling vessel in the 1870s; Japanese factory whaling vessel; Russian icebreaker of the Lenin type; Standard Liberty ship of WWII, some of which became units of the Alaska Steamship Company following the conflict; first nuclear U.S. Navy submarine Nautilus *which navigated under the pole ice; nuclear submarine of the Skipjack class and the sophisticated Lafayette class nuclear sub precursor of the missile carrying variety. Adopting modern design from the whale, modern submersibles are capable of remarkable speed while submerged.*

Seaman Russ Hofvendahl, at the wheel of the four-masted codfishing schooner William H. Smith *outbound for the Bering Sea in 1937. The vessel homeported in San Francisco. Hofvendahl in later years became a prominent attorney in Santa Clara County, California, and authored the book* Hard On The Wind, *an account of his seafaring experiences.*

results as his second dispatch pointed out:

"Hurrah! Hurrah! All Japanese boats out of the Bering Sea. Rifles no longer needed."

Then came the U.S. Coast Guard, which had not previously been informed of Shield's hostile intentions. A ranking officer informed the man that "If there is going to be any shooting in the Bering Sea, the Coast Guard will do it."

That Shields had won his one-man war without firing a shot brought jubilation among the Alaskan fishing industry, but the American government was concerned about repercussions. (Pearl Harbor was yet more than three years away). That the Japanese had fled those rich Alaska red salmon waters without formal protest even surprised Shields. His two ships returned to Poulsbo headquarters after the 1938 season with healthy catches of cod and a great sense of accomplish-

ment in driving out the Japanese. Poulsbo had been a codfishing center for four decades, and Shields was hailed on his return to the mostly Scandanavian town on Puget Sound. In the holds of his four-masted schooner were 385,000 codfish, and a good catch was registered by the schooner *Wilson* as well.

Shields was not bashful about his victory, and freely gave forth with details. He told of one Nipponese fishing vessel he encountered that had three 90 foot motorized scows laying crab gear, while eleven more 50 foot craft were used to gather the catch in the rich Bering Sea waters. He also mentioned the Japanese vessels that were taking huge numbers of salmon which he felt were rightfully a bonanza that belonged to the Americans.

One night the *Sophie Christenson* drifted about in a persistent fog bank in Bristol Bay, so Shields ordered the hand pumped foghorn activated around the clock. He in turn climbed to the crosstrees, 85 feet above the deck and rigged up an automobile spotlight hooked up to a six volt battery in an effort to recover one of the missing dories manned by two of his men. He spent three hours up there alone in the cold, but his efforts paid off when the dorymen saw the beam in the murk and heard the foghorn. Soon after they were brought aboard with grateful thanks for their skipper's efforts.

During that 1938 season, one fisherman with a five pound sinker and two hooks landed up to a thousand fish in one day, and a total catch of 21,155 cod, the best of the *Sophie's* fishermen. His name was Ray Press. The routine day started at 4 AM with a hardy breakfast after which the dories would fan out to sea, with halibut for bait, over five miles from the mother ship which would remain at anchor until the dories returned after long hours on the banks.

Shields was master of many causes on his annual junkets to the northland. He was skipper, doctor, pharmacist, dentist, fish tallier, and judge of all disputes. His company for several years was the only one on the Pacific Coast to both produce and market codfish. Shield's son Ed became plant manager. He was also a captain and made his first voyage to the Bering Sea in 1934, becoming skipper of the schooner *C.A. Thayer*, which is presently a museum

SS Cordova *of the Alaska Steamship Company which made an epic run to assist in the rescue of the crew of the USRC* Tahoma *in 1914, after the cutter became impaled on an Aleutian reef. The* Cordova, *a 2,089 ton cargo-passenger vessel was built at Wilmington, Delaware, in 1912 and carried a crew of 30. She served the Alaska Line for many years until finally sold to Chinese buyers in 1947 and renamed* Lee King. *Sketch courtesy Win Stites.*

ship in San Francisco. Former codfishing schooners employed by other firms in the Alaska fishery were the *Wawona*, *John A.*, *Azalea*, *Fanny Dutard*, *William H. Smith*, and several others, all originally built for the lumber trades in the 1880s and 1890s. The *Wawona* is now a museum ship in Seattle.

There were also vessels like the four-masted schooner *C. S. Holmes* which for several years made annual pilgrimages with supplies for the Eskimos and other northern residents of the Arctic, under command of Captain John Backland, dean of all the Arctic traders. He had high principles and refused to carry any liquor or tobacco north to the natives. His son John carried on in his father's footsteps right up until World War II, and was then conscripted by the Navy as an Arctic pilot.

For more than three decades, each spring the *Holmes* would be loaded with a variety of supplies voyaging from Seattle to Point Barrow under sail. In 1926, when the *Holmes* returned to Seattle, aboard was a young Norwegian gentleman who had boarded at Teller. He was the photographer who had taken the initial photos of the dirigible *Norge* when explorer Roald Amundsen made his history making flight over the North Pole. Those photos first appeared in the *Seattle Times*, alerting the world of the epic flight, the first of its kind.

It might be well in this chapter to take a final look at the Alaska Steamship Company which was Alaska's bread basket and supply line for more than five decades. As mentioned earlier, it was the only company under the American flag of some 100 that survived long after the gold rush era came to an end. Started in 1897, Alaska Steam was merged in 1908 with the Northwestern Steamship Company. The new operation was headed by Charles E. Peabody. As earlier mentioned, the original ships of the fleet were small compared to some of the competitors. The first was the *Willapa*, which began her career as a bar tug. Next came the *Rosalie*, *Farallon*, and *Dirigo* and then the *Dophin*. Most famous of all the Alaska Line ships was the SS *Victoria*, which began her career at Dunbarton, Scotland, in 1870 as the *Parthia* of the Cunard Line, a sleek Atlantic passenger vessel. In her later years, the iron-hulled vessel came to the Pacific and was eventually sold to the Alaska Steamship Company. She was one of the favorite carriers during the gold rush years and before her days were ended, when sent to Japan to be scrapped, she had logged more than 80 years of service, most of it on the Alaska run. Renamed *Victoria* in 1891, her logs were filled with adventurous voyages to Nome and to other sectors of Alaska. Every citizen of Alaska had a warm place in their hearts for the "Ol Vic."

Originally a coal burner, she was converted to burn oil in 1910 when she was getting an overhaul. At that date her original bell, weighing nearly 250 pounds, was removed and E. T. Stanard, former president of the Company, became its owner. As an executive of the Kennecott Copper Company, in later years he was killed in a plane crash, and the estate presented the bell to the Cunard Line to be fitted on the new liner *Parthia*, namesake of the pioneer vessel.

The *Victoria* originally carried 793 passengers and a crew of 135. Her reputation was established as being the first merchant ship to break through the ice each year in reaching the Nome Roadstead. Her rugged iron hull made her the ideal carrier. Further, it was not uncommon for the ship to bring back as much as $2 million worth of gold on her return to Seattle from Alaskan ports. Bricks of gold were shipped in canvas bags each worth about $20,000, and when a safe was not aboard, gold often sat on the floor in the purser's quarters.

During a great part of her Alaska service the *Victoria* was commanded by the famous Captain 'Dynamite Johnny' O'Brien, an Irishman who established a brilliant seagoing career of nearly a half century, starting on square-riggers. He was loved in the same way as his ship and became close friends of famous authors such as Jack London and Rex Beach who once booked passage on the *Victoria*.

A race at sea was conjured up in 1908 when the respective skippers of the *Victoria* and her competitor the SS *Ohio* wagered on which ship could first make it back to Seattle from Nome. Passengers on both vessels were excited about the contest and bets were made by both crew and passengers. The respective vessels steamed out of the Nome Roadstead puffing black smoke. Though the *Ohio* hung in with her rival during the first part of the race she soon fell into the *Victoria's* wake, arriving at Seattle nine hours after the other. The *Victoria*, doing a good 14 knots, came breezing into Puget Sound with the traditional broom hung on her foremast, designating a clean sweep.

In 1905, the Guggenheim interests opened what would become the Kennecott Copper Company and also purchased some cannery operations. Three years later, when Peabody and Guggenheim got their heads together, the respective interests were merged, Alaska Steamship Company, which was serving many Alaska ports now was involved with copper ore shipments. In 1909, routing was shifted. The larger ships of the Alaska Line had been operating on the outside route between Seattle and Prince William Sound, but Peabody in that year sent all company vessels, except those on the Nome route, north through the Inside Passage, Cross Sound and the Gulf of Alaska. Later the company acquired faster ships like the passenger steamers *Alameda* and *Mariposa* from Oceanic Steamship Company, and cut the running time between Seattle and Ketchikan to 41 hours and 15 minutes in August 1911. The *Mariposa* bested the *Alameda's* fast run by 12 minutes, four years later. In February 1917, the SS *Alaska* cut the *Mariposa's* record over the same course to 40 hours and 28 minutes. Alaska Steam's largest passenger liner was acquired from the Panama Railroad Steamship Company in 1926. The SS *Panama* underwent extensive remodeling and emerged as the *Aleutian*, but her years were shortened on striking a rock in Uyak Bay, Kodiak Island, May 26, 1929, irretrievably lost.

A new and even larger passenger ship was then purchased, the Ward liner *Mexico*. She underwent a $1 million overhaul and was introduced as the new *Aleutian*, the largest and most luxurious of the fleet. She entered service in the spring of 1930, and became the flagship, offering among others, deluxe accommodations for 300 first class passengers.

During World War II, the entire Alaska fleet was taken over by the War Shipping Administration and assigned to the company under the general agency agreement. More than 80 ships, including its own, were operated by Alaska Steamship for the U.S. government, not only in Alaska, but worldwide as well. In 1944, ownership of Alaska Steamship Company passed from the Kennecott Copper Corporation of New York to the Skinner & Eddy Corporation of Seattle, and G. W. Skinner became president of the line. His son D. E. Skinner later acquired that post. The fleet consisted of 21 ships in 1951, but before the end of that decade, Alaska Steam threw in the towel, and alternate cargo shipping operations provided for Alaska's needs.

One of the most interesting epics in the history of the company involved the cargo-passenger steamer *Cordova*. The reader will recall earlier the wreck of the USRC *Tahoma* in the western Aleutians. Well, the *Cordova* played a big role in the rescue of her crew. It was rather ironic that a merchant ship would be the means of picking up castaways from a government patrol and rescue ship.

Captain Thomas Moore, master of the *Cordova*, was at Nome when news of the wreck of the *Tahoma* reached his ears on September 20, 1914. He steamed out of Nome at midnight bound for Unimak Pass. On September 22, he received word from the Unalga Radio Station that no rescue ships were in the vicinity and that the *Cordova* should immediately speed to the scene. Now the *Cordova* was not what one would call a fast ship but she gave it her best. Course was set for Kiska Island, 610 miles distance. Finding no trace of the wreck, the ship cruised offshore around the island, and on September 26, sighted a dim light from a small boat jockeying about in the swells. Aboard were 11 men including the *Tahoma's* commander, Richard Crisp. Taken aboard the *Cordova*, Crisp revealed they had been at sea for five days and nights, miserable from the exposure and virtually out of provisions. The survivors had been unable to make headway in the ship's boat in the irascible seas and had drifted about with a sea anchor out.

The hunt continued for other boats from the *Tahoma*. Heading for Aggatu Island, another craft with eleven survivors was located and the grateful men assisted aboard the *Cordova*. Several hours later another with 14 was found. On September 26, a fourth boat was located off the Simichi Islands with 26 souls aboard, including one Alaskan native woman and three native children.

Next the rescue steamer proceeded to Attu Island where a boat was sent ashore to see if any survivors were there. No luck. Steaming southward, the *Cordova* spoke to the survey vessel *Patterson*, also searching for survivors. Two days later a wireless message from the other ship revealed she had rescued the balance of the cutter's crew, numbering 29.

For 36 days the *Cordova* was on her rescue mission, fuel and supplies running dangerously low. The nearest source of fuel was at Akutan, 900 miles away. When one looks at a map of Alaska you can realize the great distances involved. In days past, especially on the 'outside' routes it was a long way between ports, and the sparse population made communication and supply difficult.

The *Cordova* finally reached Akutan on October 4, with her fuel tanks almost empty. Arriving later at Dutch Harbor, she released the shipwrecked sailors. At Latouche and Ellemar she loaded copper concentrates for the Tacoma smelter and then picked up canned salmon in southeastern Alaska ports before departing for Puget Sound. Finally reaching Seattle, she had steamed almost 8,000 miles in 59 days, one hour and thirty-eight minutes, according to Captain Moore's calculations. The cargo vessel turned rescue ship accomplished its mercy mission with no thought of expenses or loss of revenue, but affording only the traditional mercy accorded to those who meet with peril at sea.

There was another case of a near tragedy for the crew of the 2,696 ton Alaska cargo ship *Edith*. In 1915, the copper mines at Latouche were sending liquid concentrates back to Tacoma, rather than crude ore. Early shipments, yet to be perfected, were like mud, a difficult and runny material to handle. When the *Edith* took on an initial cargo of the 'muck' in the summer of 1915, she handled it well in her hold as long as the sea was smooth in Prince William Sound. Shortly after passing the Cape Hinchinbrook Lighthouse the seas began to build and the steamer which in the past had had trouble with shifting cargoes, was now having major problems. A huge swell hit her broadside and she heeled over on her beam ends as the liquid cargo shifted. Despite a desperate effort to right the ship she refused to respond. Captain C. B. McMullen ordered an immediate abandonment with all boats away. Shortly after, the 37 man crew was rescued by the SS *Mariposa* which tried to tow the derelict. It was useless, however, for the hawser parted and the *Edith* plunged to her grave in a moment of unendurable anguish. It all happened so suddenly, the vessel slipping under in a whirlpool of seething water, and the momentary cavity in the sea quickly sealed over its victim.

In all the epic stories in the maritime business of Alaska probably none stands out as vividly as the ton of gold landed by the SS *Portland*. It caused the spark to finally bring "Seward's folly" into the light of victory. Though her arrival is mentioned in another chapter, it is of interest that when she docked amid fanfare at the Schwabacher pier in Seattle in 1897, the captain's cabin contained three boxes and a large safe containing $700,000 worth of gold, plus an undetermined amount in the pokes of the returning miners, which would have doubtless brought the total to $1 million. On today's market the Portland's gold would be valued at $28 million, according to estimates.

Though the *Portland*, operating under the North American Transportation and Trading Company banner, became the ship of the hour as the famous ton of gold news story spread around the world, another gold ship, the SS *Excelsior* arrived at San Francisco with a treasure in gold, four hours earlier than the *Portland*, and received virtually no attention from the press or anyone else. It only goes to show what featured publicity can do.

The *Portland* fame overshadowed some of her unsavory past. She once was caught as an opium runner and as a smuggler, bringing illegal Chinese immigrants to America. Throughout her history she afforded northwest newspapers with more startling items than any other ship in the north Pacific. To fend off any piratical responsibility, the operators of the *Portland* dispatched a 37 mm rapid fire gun which was installed on the ship's forward deck before her epic treasure laden

voyage from Alaska. However, in 1898, the *Portland's* owner, Louis Rosenfeld of San Francisco, repossessed the vessel when her charter ran out and the fate of the cannon is unknown.

Built at Bath, Maine, in 1885, as the *Haytian Republic*, the 299 foot vessel was driven by a compound steam engine. Her eventual demise, near Katalla on November 12, 1910, is well documented, but the vessel was almost lost in December 1905 on a reef off Spire Island, nine miles from Ketchikan. First news of the wreck of the Alaska Commercial Company vessel was reported by the SS *Jefferson*. When the Canadian steamer *Amur* reached the location, her captain reported the ship full of holes and undoubtedly a total loss. On December 27, the SS *Santa Clara* removed eight crew members from the wreck, only Captain Lindquist and four crewmen remaining.

Next, it was reported the vessel was hogged and breaking up amidships, listing to starboard, and at high tide filled with water to her passenger deck. The steamer originally had aboard 58 passengers, but Captain Lindquist had earlier evacuated them and sent them off to Ketchikan along with 20 crew members and all the mail pouches.

Was the story blown out of proportion in writing the ship off as a total loss? Well, let's go to Captain Charles Lindquist's testimony before the Steamship Inspection Board at Seattle on January 25, 1906. Under oath he said:

"The *Portland* left Juneau at 4:34 A.M. on December 19 (1905), Cargo consisted of 620 tons of copper ore and about 50 tons of halibut, in addition to miscellaneous items of freight. At 6 P.M. on December 20 we were approaching Tongass Narrows. The night was dark, with generally easterly winds and rain squalls. Steering the usual compass course we passed the narrows without accident, and at 9:16 passed the Ketchikan wharf. Next we logged Battle Reef buoy and at 9:49 P.M. Mountain Point was on the port beam. It took about 15 minutes to run from there to Spire Island Reef, and at 10 P.M. we could barely see Spire Island Buoy off the starboard bow. Looking for the Spire Island buoy, I walked over to the starboard side of the bridge and was about to ring up slow (on the ship's telegraph) when I glimpsed at what appeared a tiderip dead ahead. It was not a tide rip but water washing over the rocks. I yelled hard astarboard to the helmsman but a moment later felt the ship rising beneath my feet. The ascent to the rock was so gentle, the second officer was not even aware of it. He was still trying to change course, and reported the ship would not answer her helm. I then called for the engines to be stopped, and immediately had the bilges sounded. The water was 23 inches deep in the forward bilge, and 18 inches aft. This did not seem excessive, so I called for full speed astern, and ran in reverse for two minutes without moving. (The tide had been receding for an hour when the vessel struck.) The engineer John Urbanek, reported that water in the ship was rising rapidly. He was ordered to start the pump, but said that water was coming in so fast that no pumps could do any good. The engines had been stopped, and I ordered the engineer to let the oil tanks drain into the engine room."

By 11 PM the ship was still drinking up water and began to heel over to starboard but held her composure on a 12 degree list according to the clinometer. The starboard boat was then swung out but the sea was too rough, and Lindquist would not risk sending his passengers to Ketchikan. By 2 AM the sea calmed somewhat and second mate E. D. Hichman and four seamen were sent to Ketchikan for assistance. A barge was then dispatched to the scene to remove the anxious passengers. Captain Lindquist could not understand what caused his ship to get 100 yards inside the buoy, as he claimed he was running the same course he had always followed previously. He was questioned about the possibility of the copper ore shipment having an effect on the ship's compass but didn't believe that to be so, thinking it more probable that the tides and currents were responsible.

Meanwhile, Captain Emile Genereaux and Captain S. B. Gibbs, representing the Marine Board of Underwriters (San Francisco) accompanied Captain Omar Humphrey on the SS *Cottage City* for passage north to inspect the *Portland*. They agreed there was a possibility of refloating the steamer but that the expense would be enormous. Ironically, the underwriters decided to purchase the wreck. They did finally raise her and sell her back to Alaska Commercial Company.

Genereaux headed the salvage work, and in turn chartered the freighter *Samson* to bring salvage materials to the wreck scene. At first the work was hampered by ice and snow, it still being January. Divers did succeed in patching the holes in the hull after which the copper ore was removed. A heavy canvas was then slipped beneath the vessel and at high tide she floated off.

The Revenue cutter *Rush* stood by to escort the *Portland* to Ketchikan. Next the tug *Pioneer* was engaged to tow the vessel back to Puget Sound where she went into a Seattle drydock and had a complete overhaul and refitting. After all that effort and expense she went to her final resting place near Katalla just five years later, and this time there was no salvation for the ship.

In March 1897, Seattle logged 18 ship arrivals and departures to Alaska. Within the year, that number jumped to 173 and climbing. Among them of course was the *Portland*. But the variety of the fleet engaged in the bonanza was almost humorous. For instance, take the 180 foot steam launch *Cutch*, built to the specifications of the Maharajah of Cutch (India). Vessels came from every direction and were of all descriptions. The aging sidewheel steamer *Eliza Anderson* which spent most of her years on inland rivers took off for Nome crowded with gold seekers, and she didn't even have a compass aboard. The voyage was sheer misery. She ended her days a wreck after gaining her destination, her miserable passengers praising God for their survival.

Then there was the SS *Willamette*, loaded to the gunwhales with 800 passengers and 300 horses, and a dining saloon designed to seat 75. The much smaller SS *Al-Ki* took on about 150 passengers who shared deck space with 900 sheep, 65 head of cattle, and 30 horses.

Several ships of the gold rush era had been pulled out of backwater moorages following dead-end careers, only to become big money makers in the mad rush north. Better ships like the *North Pacific*, *Idaho*, *George E. Starr*, *Victorian*, and *City of Seattle* were household names, followed by larger and more seaworthy vessels. The *City of Seattle* two years after her initial voyage to Skagway in 1898 returned to Puget Sound with three tons of Klondike gold, part of the bonanza offloaded at Seattle by 45 other steamers, including those returning from Nome with beach gold, that same year. There was also a fleet of river steamers, some new, some old, that were sent to Alaska for operation on the Yukon, Kuskokwim, and allied river systems. Such memories of course always hearken back to the earlier mentioned Robert Service.

He got his inspiration, as earlier mentioned, for his writing of the *Cremation of Sam McGee* from the sternwheeler *Alice May* frozen in Lake Leberge in 1900. It served as an improvised crematorium when the freeze-up made land burials impossible. An inspired Whitehorse bank clerk, Service became the bard of the northland.

The sternwheeler *Leah*, on her maiden trip upriver to Dawson City regained the cost of her construction ($41,000) when she transported a full load of gold seekers and a barge laden with their gear to the bustling river port.

Robert Moran, Seattle shipbuilder constructed and sent a fleet of 12,176 foot Yukon type sternwheelers north. All but one, sailing from Roche Harbor, Washington, survived the rugged voyage, arriving slightly battered at St. Michael. One, named the *Western Star*, was wrecked in Shelikof Straits, but her crew survived. Most of these river boats made big money for their owners. The 400 ton craft were each fitted with 24 staterooms for the more affluent, and spaces for 200 others in addition to freight.

The shipwreck and loss of life on the poorly protected Alaska waterways, plus the lack of inspection that allowed many unseaworthy ships to voyage northward, got a caustic criticism from the *Seattle Times* publisher Alden Blethen. He charged the federal steamboat inspectors with dereliction of duties. Said he: "Those fellows should be arrested and given a fair trial—and decorate the end of an elevated rope."

Though the big gold era got most of the publicity in days of yore, the fish canning industry carried on, not with a spurt but at a slow and steady pace. But the industry kept suffering losses among the ships that were affiliated with the business. We've already reviewed the tragic loss of the square-rigger *Star of Bengal*, but there were a number of other sailing ships on the cannery run to Alaska that also had unfortunate endings. There were three in 1917, all well known sailing vessels, rounding out their years in the sunset era of the commercial sailing ship. Sometimes their crews were not exactly the best, as steam had taken over for the most part, and many of the old shellbacks had retired and left the sea altogether.

It was said in San Francisco from where most of the cannery ships wintered, that come spring the police judges used to line up the bums, drunks, and derelicts before them and say, "Okay boys. Six months in the county jail, or ship to Alaska, What'll it be?" Surprisingly, some would choose to go to jail, as life before the mast in aging commercial sailing vessels was never a picnic, and working a cannery job was not easy either.

The annual salmon season lasted a little over four months. Those felons who opted to go north were loaded on launches and taken, under guard, to the various ships in the bay. Howard "Cooky" Cookson recalled shipping on the three-masted barkentine *Standard* in 1917. Counting crew and cannery hands there were nearly 300 souls packed aboard, including one female, the cannery superintendent's wife. The aging vessel, dating from 1878, was a product of Maine. Cookson was taking passage to operate the cannery radio station at Nushagak.

It took 36 days to cover about 2,000 miles to the Nushagak River on Bristol Bay. As wind filled the sails the aging *Standard* struggled with the elements to reach her destination. When almost there, on a pitch dark night, the unthinkable happened on May 14 when the barkentine piled up on Cape Constantine. A heavy sea was running and the wooden hull grinding on the rocky outcrops soon yielded and split asunder.

Distress rockets or light signals were useless in that unpopulated sector, and with no radio or wireless on the vessel the situation was just short of desperate. It was up to Cookson to make some kind of contact to gain assistance. He had earlier played around with a spark coil with vibrator among discarded junk in one of the cabins. He also had a few extra dry cell batteries which he rigged up as a power supply. Finally he was rewarded by a heartwarming buzz from the vibrator. From each secondary post of the coil he ran a wire, making a gap of about an inch for the spark. For an antenna switch he simply took the antenna lead wire and clipped it to the receiver if he wanted to receive, or to one side of the spark gap if he wanted to transmit.

As Cookson put his transmitter together, the *Standard* was pounding herself to pieces on the rocks. Crewmen and cannery workers were running about in every direction looking to the captain for an answer to their dilemma. The pumps had become useless and the ship was breaking apart. Able to bring in the Kvichak wireless station on his makeshift contraption, Cookson took heart that he could send out an SOS. Sitting astride an upended apple cart, his initial tries failed. Then finally on the third try his message got through.

At that juncture, the order to abandon ship was given and boats were put over the side filled with the large complement that had peopled the *Standard*'s decks. The survivors would have to spend the next four days in the open boats tossed about violently, existing on a ration of one sardine a day coupled with a few crackers and a swig of whisky. That combination didn't do much for those prone to *mal de mer*. Cookson recalled that until his dying day (1975) the memory of that unpleasant interlude lingered in his mind.

Vessels were sent out from the nearest shore station to rescue the survivors, and miraculously all made it through the ordeal. The SS *City of Topeka* picked up two of the *Standard*'s boats containing 45 persons and the steamer *North Star* picked up others. As for the *Standard*, she breathed her last, rolled over and became a total loss.

That same season, another fine old Downeaster finished out her days as a cannery ship. She was the *St. Francis*, owned by Libby, McNeill and Libby. Her destination was Koggiung on Bristol Bay. While winging her way in the difficult latitudes of Unimak Pass under shortened sail in a cantankerous sea, she was driven up on the rocky shores near lonely Cape Sarichef. Despite every effort to wear the ship around she struck the barrier broadside. Heavy seas cascaded over her decks, water quickly crawling up to the 'tween decks. Near panic broke out among the 281 crew and cannery workers on that fateful day of May 10, 1917.

The Pacific American Fisheries steamer *Norwood* after discharging her cargo at Port Moller cannery on the north side of the Aleutian Peninsula was heading west toward Unimak Pass when shortly after midnight an urgent SOS message was received from the *St. Francis*. "Full speed ahead!" was the command of the *Norwood*'s skipper. There was never hesitation when lives were in peril. The steamer pitched forward in the maelstrom, green water coming over her bow as she plunged head on into the billows.

Arriving at 9 AM at the wreck scene, mighty seas were still running, completely inundating the *St. Francis*. Most of her people had climbed into the rigging hanging there like bugs in a series of spider webs. Wireless operators on the respective ships kept up a dialogue but outright rescue was out of the question. The operator on the *St. Francis* informed the *Norwood* that the survivors would attempt to gain the beach through the water on the lee side of the wreck. It was requested that the boats from the *Norwood* pick up survivors from the beach. Despite the great gamble, all evacuated the wreck and made it to shore without loss of life. There were also few injuries which was a near miracle. Nor was it any less of a miracle that the *Norwood*'s lifeboats were able to negotiate the heavy surf without serious accident. All 281 persons from the *St. Francis* were rescued, the last boatload casting off from the beach as night fell over the dismal spectacle. So crowded was the *Norwood* that she immediately weighed anchor and steamed to Dutch Harbor where the survivors were placed under government supervision until arrangement could be made to book them back home. What might have been a terrible tragedy had a happy ending, if it is possible to associate a happy ending with a shipwreck.

A third sailing ship met her demise in 1917. She was the Maine-built *St. Katherine*, skippered by Captain Peter "Iron" Larson, and owned by Red Salmon Packing Company. Her end was not as dramatic as that of the *Standard* and *St. Francis*. She grounded in the Ugashik River and broke her back, and even though filling with mud, she was later refloated and saw a few years of limited service thereafter.

It was not a good year for the "Saints," all Bath built sailing vessels. A fourth member of the clan, the 1,576 ton *St. David* (of 1877) had been cut down to an ore barge from a full-rigged ship by owner Captain James Griffiths. While under tow of the tug *Commodore* on a voyage from Valdez to Anyox, B. C., the tug became disabled. Along came the cannery tender *Andrew Kelly*, which took the *St. David* to an anchorage at Yakutat, and then towed the *Commodore* to Ketchikan. The tug *Daniel Kern* was then dispatched to Yakutat to take the *St. David* under tow, but the old sailing vessel parted her towline and drifted ashore on Khantag Island on October 31. There, seas boiling in from the Gulf of Alaska pounded the vessel to pieces, and another well known veteran sailing vessel, once a proud unit of Flint and Company's fleet, passed into oblivion.

On and on the saga of lost ships continued on Alaska's sea routes. Still, much of the misery and shipwreck revolves around the gold stampede days. The Inside Passage is strewn with wrecks when ships steamed out for Skagway and Dyea, ports spawned on mudflats, from where the death type trails snaked their way to the treacherous Yukon River toward Dawson City, or the alternative sea route to St. Michael, frozen for the better part of the year, a sea lane that claimed several more ships and lives. Those who disembarked there had a rough river junket, by guess and by golly, 1,800 miles on the frigid Yukon, Dawson bound. Many didn't make it after hastily constructed river craft were dashed to pieces in the river rapids.

For 'He' commandeth, and raiseth the stormy wind, which lifteth up the wave thereof.
They mount up to the heaven, they go down again to the depths: their soul is melted because of trouble.
They reel to and fro, and stagger like a drunken man, and are at their wit's end.
Then they cry unto the Lord in their trouble, and he bringeth them out of their distresses.
The Holy Bible, Psalms 107

Doughty gold miners worked the Alaska gold field several years after the big boom. This photo was taken north of Fairbanks about 1915.

Numerous stories revolved around the famous Pullen House from the days of the gold stampede. Located at Skagway, numerous personalities of fame were guests at the establishment. This is the way the structure appeared in 1915. President Harding once stayed at the hotel, and it was nearby that the infamous Soapy Smith and Frank Reid had a shoot-out. Other famous Skagway personalities were Robert Service, Tex Rickard, and Alex Pantages.

Below: *The steamer* Starr *as she appeared in 1928, acting as the mail boat for Bering Sea and northern Alaskan ports. At that juncture the rugged little vessel was owned by the San Juan Fishing and Packing Company. Collection from Earl Korf.*

CHAPTER NINE

The Cruise Industry and Modern Cargo Transport

*Ships that pass in the night
and speak each other in passing;
Only a signal shown and a
distant voice in the darkness.
—Longfellow*

"It's like Utopia on water!" exclaimed one enthusiastic cruise passenger.

Millions have thrilled to the picturesque photos and eloquent words that appear in cruise line travel folders involving Alaska's waterways and scenic wonders. Though likened to Norway's sealanes and fjords, Alaska has a personality all its own, and it would be difficult to find one who has cruised its inland and coastal waters that wouldn't render its praises.

Alaska cruising is at its apex in our day and has become one of the very top priorities for cruise travelers the world over. Unfortunately the cruise season is limited to about five months a year when the weather and sea conditions are most favorable, but during that annual season Alaskan ports become lively meccas for the cruise ship passengers whether coming by luxury liners, mini-cruise ships, or by the ferries of the Alaska Marine Highway System, the only one that offers service the year-round. Operating out of Bellingham, Washington, the ferries serve southeast Alaska ports. All are splendid, modern car and passenger vessels.

Major cruise lines like Princess Cruises, Holland America Line, Cunard Line, Royal Caribbean Cruise Line, Carnival Cruise Line, Royal Cruise Line, Norwegian Cruise Line, Radisson Seven Seas Cruises, World Explorer Cruises, Celebrity Cruises, Crystal Cruises, Seabourn Cruise Line, and others were all serving Alaska cruise schedules at this writing, and calling at all the major ports along the shores of the Great Land. In addition, mini-cruise ships of the Alaska Sightseeing Cruise West Line and other local companies, provide informal cruises to many places the bigger ships can't go.

To say the least, it's a colorful parade of 'happy ships' cruising the inside and outside waters of Alaska during the cruise season. No doubt about it, the romance of the sea is legendary. In Alaska it weaves a magic spell for those standing at the railings or sitting in a comfortable ship's lounge watching the myriad of green isles, glaciers, waterfalls, villages, totem poles, and countless other attractions, especially along the Inside Passage where one feels he can almost reach out and touch the beautiful attractions before his eyes. It seems almost like it must have been in the beginning when God created his wonderland.

Whether it's a walk around the deck, dancing under the stars, gazing at a sunrise or sunset, over indulging on gourmet food, or sitting in the solitude of one's cabin, it is an experience once done, never forgotten. And what a contrast the luxury of cruise travel is today compared to the trying conditions suffered on the overcrowded, sometimes unsafe ships in Alaska's earlier times.

The expansion of the cruise industry has continued unabated with dazzling new, larger, or renovated luxury ships, quite different from the more utilitarian passenger liners that served Alaska faithfully but adequately for many years. The future at this time looks bright for the industry but gradually the bigger cruise lines merge, and sometimes the smaller firms find it more difficult to compete. In some ways it was like the aftermath of the gold rush era where only a few major lines survived after the big rush to Skagway and Nome subsided.

Today the scene is entirely different, for the great jet passenger planes of Alaska Airlines and other companies can carry passengers to Anchorage and other Alaska destinations in record time compared to sea travel. Instead of the old berthline ship services of yesteryear which was the only way of accommodating passengers, today most go by air for general purposes with the exception of the Alaska State ferries. On the other hand, cruise passengers go only for fine dining, fun, relaxation, and sightseeing.

The question is often asked why the huge cruiseliners of our day are always flying the flags of foreign maritime nations such as Liberia, Panama, Bahamas, Cyprus, etc.? It is also asked why so few of the larger cruise vessels fly the American flag. Higher wages, greater restrictions, and the cost of building ships in America are all reasons why the American merchant passenger fleet has been restricted to smaller vessels. American Hawaii Cruises is one of the only American flag operations that still plies the high seas with large passenger ships.

Our nation has also lost billions of dollars in revenue because of legislation which prevents foreign flag vessels from going between two American ports without touching at a foreign port between. The reason was to keep out cheaper foreign competition. However, in this writer's opinion that service should be offered if no American line is affording such a service.

Because of the U.S. laws, Vancouver B.C., has become the major embarkation point for the huge fleet of mega cruise ships servicing Alaska annually. Pacific Coast ports of the U.S. have lost large amounts of money in tourism, supply, publicity, etc., by restrictions on foreign flag vessels. Vancouver, on the other hand, has afforded first-class berthing facilities for passenger carrying cruiseliners and has made great financial gains by supplying the big ships with all the necessities of which food is a major factor, affording numerous shore side employment benefits.

The modern concept in shipping cargo to Alaska. The 790 foot long Westward Venture, one of a trio of modern Totem Ocean Trailer Express, Inc. vessels, features the latest in container transport and roll-on roll-off service to Alaska. TOTE is a privately-owned Alaska corporation offering service to Alaska between the ports of Anchorage and Tacoma, in addition to providing for overland highway and rail interconnections throughout greater Alaska, the lower 48 states, and Canada. Photo courtesy of Alan Stark, TOTE.

This vintage photo shows the sidewheel steamer Ancon, *which established regular service between San Francisco, Columbia River, Puget Sound, and Alaska in 1886. She was rebuilt from a coal hulk at San Francisco in 1873 for the Pacific Coast Steamship Company. The 266 foot liner, valued at $100,000 was wrecked at Loring, Alaska, when leaving that port on August 28, 1889, under command of Captain D. Wallace.*

Oddly enough, Liberia has the largest merchant fleet in the world, but for the most part, hardly any ships flying its flag have ever been to Monrovia, Liberia's port where the ships are registered. The country offers a flag of convenience—cheap registry with few requirements, monetarily or otherwise. Its the same story with other countries that offer flags of convenience. Most of the real owners of convenience flag tonnage are anything but citizens under the flag their ships fly. Some exceptions are Norway and the Netherlands Antilles.

Where freight is concerned, modern, fast container liners of Sea-Land Services, Inc., and Totem Ocean Trailer Express (TOTE) with roll-on, roll-off capability, offer year round service. In addition, a large number of tug and barge operations are serving the ports of Alaska-Crowley Maritime Corp., Foss Maritime Co., Alaska Transportation Co., Alaska Marine Lines, Alaska Marine Charters, and several others. It is a constant supply line from the North Slope south to Ketchikan, and from Kodiak to Juneau.

Notably missing in our day are firms like Alaska Steamship Company, Northland Transportation Company, the former Alaska Transportation Company, and others with passenger lines that served up until the 1950s. Times have changed, and Alaska rolls right along with the times to a greater degree than it ever has before.

With the individual cost of brand new mega-ships reaching and passing the $300 million plus category, Alaskan cruise enthusiasts are

being offered luxury never before known to sea travelers. Many of the newest and finest of the mega-ships are assigned to Alaska's seaways annually, and just how long this evolution in luxury cruising will last nobody can tell.

One sad note on the cruise ship scene came in 1981, when Canadian Pacific ended an 80 year old tradition announcing its farewell to the Alaska cruise business. The popular SS *Princess Patricia* was retired and offered for sale much to the chagrin of its supporters. For years she had sailed out of Vancouver, B.C., becoming one of the most popular ships serving southeastern Alaska ports. As competition entered the market, the small size of the *Patricia* and her limited capacity perhaps showed the handwriting on the wall. Canadian Pacific cited, "adverse market projections and high interest rates, steadily increasing operating costs and industry-wide market softening."

How wrong their projections proved to be, as the present market is the most lucrative ever. Though Canadian Pacific continues as a major factor in Canadian transportation—air, rail, truck and allied sea transport—its days as an Alaska cruise line have ended. After 18 seasons, 325 voyages, and 90,000 tourists, the 33 year old *Princess Patricia* brought an era to a close. It all began in 1901, when the Canadian Pacific Railway, today known as CP Rail, acquired Canadian Pacific Navigation Company. The historic lifeline to northern British Columbia and Alaska first attracted tourists in 1890, when Canadian Pacific Navigation ran a 12 day September cruise with the SS *Islander*, a unit of the fleet which later was placed under the CPR houseflag. (As earlier mentioned, the *Islander* went to her doom in 1901.)

For eight decades thereafter, Canadian Pacific operated its Alaska service, building a reputation for quality and service that continually attracted repeat passengers. Through the years, popular new ships were added, vessels like the *Princess Charlotte*, *Princess Adelaide*, *Princess Kathleen*, *Princess Marguerite*, *Princess Alice*, *Princess Louise*, and numerous others. In fact, the *Louise* put in 42 consecutive years of serving Alaska until her retirement in 1962. She had numerous admirers. The *Princess Patricia* was built at Govan, Scotland in 1948, and christened by Lady Patricia Ramsay, the former Princess Patricia and daughter of the Duke of Connaught. A former Canadian Pacific sistership to the *Princess Patricia*, the *Princess Marguerite* meanwhile passed to the British Columbia Steamship Company. Both ships were 374 feet long, considerably smaller than today's luxury cruise ships running to Alaska. With a capacity for 2,000 passengers and 60 automobiles, the 6,000 ton *Patricia* went into service on June 16, 1949, as a day ship on the Vancouver, Victoria, Seattle run, and in 1962 was converted for overnight cruises with accommodations for 320 passengers in 152 staterooms. After her $1 million overhaul, she began cruising to Alaska in May of 1963, replacing the retired *Princess Louise*. For the slack sea-

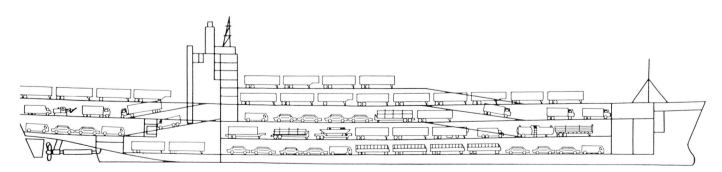

Length: 791 ft.   Width: 105 ft.   Height (from Sea Level): 110 ft.   Draft: 30 ft.   Speed: 24 knots.   Capacity: 410 40-ft EQ's

Wow! Would Noah ever have loved to charter this ship, at 791 feet in length and 105 feet of beam. This diagram is a cutaway of the interior of a Totem Ocean Trailer Express ship or RO-RO type vessel engaged in regular Alaska service from Tacoma, Washington. It is 340 feet longer than the ark of Noah's day and carefully designed to carry all types of vehicles that roll on and off the vessel with ease. Just think of the animals Noah could have accommodated aboard this mammoth ship. TOTE diagram.

The SS Humboldt, *once a popular passenger liner in Alaskan waters would appear like a midget alongside the mammoth cruiseliners of our day. She was built at Eureka, California, in 1897 as a steam schooner, but with the discovery of gold in Alaska she was quickly converted to a passenger vessel. For most of her career she was commanded by the legendary Captain Elijah Baughman, her skipper from 1900 until 1933 when the ship was retired and placed in the San Francisco boneyard. Ironically, the night that Captain Baughman died, the* Humboldt *broke loose from her moorings with nobody aboard and began drifting out to sea.*

sons she was chartered by Princess Cruises on the Los Angeles-Acapulco run. On the Alaska run, despite growing competition, many travelers preferred her low key, relaxing, and somewhat informal atmosphere compared to the more deluxe carriers. One Oregon judge had a love affair with the ship, logging some 37 voyages. The *Patricia's* officers and crew complied with the man's wishes. When he died he wanted his ashes brought aboard and scattered over the waters of the Inside Passage of Alaska, and his wish was carried out.

It was a nostalgic voyage when the steamer 'revved' up her 6,000 horsepower turbo electric engines on her last cruise from Alaska in 1981, saluting Wrangell, Glacier Bay, Tracy Arm, Ketchikan, and Prince Rupert on return to Vancouver and lay up.

Equally popular with Alaska cruise travelers was the classic three-stack liner SS *Princess Kathleen.* Her chronicle, however, ended in tragedy in 1952. It was September 7 of that year, the ship on her final cruise of the season. Proceeding northward in freshening winds and a heavy rain squall, it was early morning and a course had been set for Skagway from Juneau. Somehow the fickle winds and strong tides in Lynn Canal hampered movement on the prescribed course, as the rain beat fiercely against the wheelhouse windows.

Chief officer C. W. Savage, who had the duty on the bridge ordered a change of course to starboard, picked up his binoculars, and stepped out on the bridge wing, the rain beating in his face. He searched through the murk for a navigation aid or a landmark. About the same time, the forward lookout shouted, "Land ahead!" The warning was given over the intercom system and partly faded amidst the static. Savage hurried to find out what the lookout had sighted. Meanwhile the helmsmen (quartermaster) maintained the course. The first

One of the most elegant and graceful cruiseliners frequenting the Alaskan waterways is the Crystal Symphony, *pictured here and her sistership, the* Crystal Harmony. *Appearing like a gigantic luxury yacht, they feature many cabins with private verandas.* Photo courtesy of Crystal Cruises.

officer then saw the reported land but thought it sufficiently far away, reasoning with more starboard rudder the ship would clear the point. He finally gave the order, but within a few seconds, the *Kathleen* crashed into the rocks off Lena Point with a jarring impact. It was only a few miles south of Vanderbilt Reef where 33 years earlier the Canadian Pacific liner *Princess Sophia* had gone down with all hands, Alaska's worst sea tragedy.

The *Princess Kathleen* was a mile and a half off course when she piled up, and had many more passengers aboard than the ill-fated *Sophia.* Thus, there was great concern for the safety of the 450 passengers and crew.

Captain Graham O. Hughes was immediately aroused. He ordered the after tanks emptied and readied the boats. Distress messages were sent over the radio after which Coast Guard and commercial vessels altered course pronto and headed for the wreck. Despite every effort, the liner held fast to her perch. Any hope of her floating off was a pipe dream. Her hull had been badly ruptured, even more so than Captain Graham realized. Boats were put over the side and passengers evacuated with help from the Coast Guard. The seas were such on the lee side of the wreck that every passenger made it to shore without mishap. That in itself was a giant relief for the ship's captain and certainly for Canadian Pacific principals.

Just three hours after the last passenger was rescued the crippled vessel settled with the receding tide and developed a 19 degree list to port and ten degrees fore and aft, a highly dangerous position. In spite of a series of pumps in continual usage, water gained steadily in the hull as if the vessel was trying to drain the channel. By 11:45 AM it was obvious she was doomed, and all the officers and crew were forced to abandon ship. The timing was right, for within two hours she slipped off the rocky cradle and went down in about 150 feet of water.

Gone was one splendid vessel, a 1925 product of a Scottish shipyard. She had been commandeered during World War II as a wartime troopship and performed to perfection in the heat of war zones. Returned to Canadian Pacific after the conflict, she underwent a $1.5 million overhaul. Her demise was only partly covered by insurance, she being abandoned as a total loss. Salvage was considered impractical and the vessel languishes in her grave where a few amateur divers alone have dared examine her remains. Her interior decor with beautiful hardwood panelling made her one of the finest passenger carriers ever to ply Alaskan waters.

Another Canadian company that played a role in the passenger ship business to Alaska was Canadian National Railway, formerly the Grand Trunk Pacific. C.N.R. suffered a major loss on September 22, 1945, when its fast luxury liner *Prince George* was engulfed in flames when a fuel tank exploded after the steamer stranded in a fog off Ketchikan. As the flames shot skyward, the Coast Guard was able to attach a line and shove her on the beach at Ravina Island to prevent the fire from spreading to the Ketchikan waterfront.

Passengers remained calm during their evacuation, and the crew fought the fire valiantly until ordered to abandon. One of their number, a seaman named Verdun McDaniel, perished when trapped in the engine room by a backfire of the center stoker, but all others got off without serious injury. The ship burned for days becoming a gutted hulk. Eventually she was pulled off the beach and towed to Seattle for scrapping.

By and large, the modern day cruise ships have established an enviable safety record, and strandings have been much less frequent. Qualified pilots, alert captains and officers, better aids to navigation, both on the ship's bridge and radio room and along the shore, plus an alert Coast Guard presence have all teamed up to safeguard Alaska's waterways.

Still, occasional mishaps do occur among cruise ships. On October 11, 1980, Holland America's *Prinzendam* burned and sank in the Gulf of Alaska. Her 500 passengers and crew were safely removed. A Canadian tug was nearby but the Coast Guard would not allow the burning ship to be brought closer than 50 miles from shore. The *Salvage Chief* set out from Astoria, but the cruise liner went down in deep water the morning the salvage tug arrived and all hope of recovery vanished. The Dutch registered 8,566 ton *Prizendam*, skippered by Captain Cornelius Wabeke, was only seven years old when she went to her grave 79 miles west of Sitka. The tanker *Williamsburg* and tug *Commodore Straits* first came to her aid.

The Seattle-based Alaska cruise ship *Sundancer* ran aground off the north end of Vancouver Island in July of 1984 tearing a 30 foot hole in her hull. The stranding was close to the entrance of Seymour Narrows. Sundance Cruises representatives ordered the captain to evacuate the 501 passengers and the 289 crew members after which a skeleton crew sailed the stricken vessel to Duncan Bay while on a 30 degree list. There, at the paper dock, she sank to the bottom taking half the dock with her.

Chances of survival in mishaps are greatly improved at sea today, and usually the suffering of survivors is greatly lessened. Typical of Alaskan shipwreck of earlier times involved the earlier mentioned SS *Aleutian*, not the later passenger ship of the same name, but the first passenger ship of the Alaska Steamship Company bearing that name.

M. J. "Bill" Wilcox was purser on that vessel, and in his latter years recalled the events. It was in August 1928, that the *Aleutian* sailed north from Seattle carrying among the passengers several teachers and students on their way back to school in Alaska. On that voyage, the *Aleutian* ran aground in Seymour Narrows, just north of Maud Island Light. Fortunately, the swelling tide refloated her and with minor damage she returned to Seattle. The following year, however, was not so fortunate for the ship. On a regular schedule on May 29, she called at Uyak Bay on Kodiak Island. Picking up passengers, the steamer took aboard a young lady who was a Kennecott employee at Latouche. In addition to first class passengers there were 30 cannery workers in steerage who were to be delivered to a cannery ship. When the steamer, in command of Captain J. G. Nord, was searching for the other vessel she ran aground on Amook Island striking what is now Aleutian Rock on the charts. Pivoting on the rocky barrier the ship gutted herself, rapidly sinking by the bow until her stern was 50 feet in the air, according to Bill's account.

It took only ten minutes for her to go under. A hasty evacuation by lifeboat saved many lives. Wilcox remembered going back to his purser's quarters to open the ship's safe. When he was informed the ship was about to go down, he reluctantly bowed to prudence, and was yanked away by chief officer Tom Healy.

The almost forgotten Kennecott woman passenger who was still aboard sleeping at the advent of the sinking suddenly burst from her stateroom clad only in a skimpy nightgown. She promptly jumped into the frigid water. Cold and nearly panic stricken she was dragged into one of the lifeboats.

The *Aleutian* then slipped beneath the sea in 300 feet of water. Wilcox never forgot about that safe. Though he wondered if it was ever found by divers, he knew that much of the $5,000 cash therein had earlier been paid to the crew, but there was also gold and jewels hidden in its confines.

One crew member went down with the ship when he went searching for a lucky emblem, but the other 169 persons aboard escaped in the steamer's seven lifeboats. They landed on Amook Island and were later picked up by the cannery ship the *Aleutian* had been searching for. The survivors were then taken to Larsen Bay from where

a survey vessel awaited to transport them to Seward and onto the SS *Admiral Evans* for return to Seattle. It was no fun either for the earlier mentioned survivors of the SS *Mount McKinley* of Alaska Steamship Company. She stranded in a snowstorm near Scotch Cape on Unimak Island March 11, 1942, under command of Captain Arthur Ryning. All the passengers and crew were safely removed but had a cold wait before help came. Salvage of the ship was considered, but dismissed, and the 360 foot liner was left to turn red with rust, its skeletal remains marking her grave.

From the yellowed papers of one of the personnel who served on the Lighthouse tender *Fern* in the 1930s, we're told of the wreck of the steamer *Oaxaca*. It appears she was owned by a Hancock oil executive who fancied himself as being as knowledgable as any Alaska pilot. On attempting to take his vessel through Wrangell Narrows he got hung up on the wrong side of Burnt Island light. Hard and fast aground at high water, the steamer was high and dry on the ebb.

The *Fern* was laying idle at Petersburg with most of the crew ashore when a distress message was received. Finally, 19 of her crew were rounded up, and the *Fern* put out into the narrows on a miserable rainy night. By the time the tender reached the locale of the wreck the tide was out so far that only slimy green rocks lay where water had been. The whaleboat could not get near the *Oaxaca*, so the passengers aboard had to be helped over the obstacle course to where the whaleboat waited. Some 30 persons were removed along with their luggage. It wasn't suitcases or seabags but trunks, hat boxes, cosmetic cases, and similar beauty items of the affluent, all of it handled as the rain pelted down in sheets. Only the crew remained on the Panamanian-registered vessel.

Now the reader might ask what this incident has to do with cruise ships? Well, Mr. Hancock had gotten his hands on the vessel which during World War I had served as a "mystery ship," one that posed as an innocent merchantman, but in reality was equipped with an assortment of heavy weapons for use in destroying unsuspecting enemy vessels. She was earlier classified as a Royal Canadian sloop. Hancock purchased her for a song, and after some refurbishing, including deluxe accommodations, turned his creation into a steam yacht to impress the VIPs. He operated the vessel like an early day cruise ship, yacht-style. And he liked women.

Aboard was a well stocked bar with every kind of alcoholic drink. Being under Panamanian registry, his ship was immune to the rules and regulations of the United States government, which gave him a free hand. The *Oaxaca* was what one might call a free-wheeling pleasure ship. Despite working hard to rescue the passengers and their gear from the ill-fated vessel, Mr. Hancock didn't invite the rescuers aboard to sample the resources of his alcoholic stash. He was perhaps worrying about his 'dream boat' ending her days atop a relentless unyielding barrier. So much for a private cruise ship.

Earlier, before the wreck, the vessel served briefly as a passenger-freight carrier for the American Mexican Steamship Company between Los Angeles, San Diego, and west coast Mexico ports which obviously was a short-lived operation. She then passed to Captain Ray Sterling and again to Captain J. W. Hobbs, well-known Canadian rum runner. The rest of the story has already been told. Her chronicle ended in Alaska, much to Hancock's sorrow.

Most of the devil-to-pay shipwreck dramas of the yesteryears where passengers were endangered are pretty much relegated to the past. Cruise tourists today have a confident air that modern technology has solved many of the problems faced by passenger ships before the advent of sophisticated ship and shore computerized and electronic wonders. Still, precautions must never be neglected, as human error is still possible. Failure to properly read images on a radar screen, an immobilized aid to navigation, poorly rehearsed evacuation plans, or the excessive use of alcohol or drugs are all possibilities. Present rules and regulations authorized by the government and carried out by the Coast Guard have done much to assure safety at sea.

Where Alaskan passenger-carrying ships for many decades were utilitarian for the most part, they were essential to those who depended solely on them for transportation. Some units were in the favorite category while others were sometimes shunned, but all served a purpose in their time. However, even the top of the line Alaska liners of the past were nothing compared to the "floating fun islands" cruising our waterways today. Such huge vessels are fabulous, in some cases featuring decor that would make the old ship interiors look totally inferior.

In fact, as this book is written, Princess Cruises has introduced the largest passenger cruise liner in the world on the seasonal run to Alaska, the *Sun Princess*. (second of the name). Cleverly and meticulously designed to give a feeling of intimacy, she offers such amenities as five dining options, two main showrooms, two atriums, a 24 hour international food court, and a pizza parlor. As large as she is, at 77,000 tons, she held her record for less than a year as both Princess and Carnival introduced mega liners of over 100,000 tons—the *Grand Princess* and the Carnival *Destiny* respectively—while the competitors also introduce ships, just as luxurious, but in the 38,000 to 85,000 ton category. Many of the huge cruise ships planned for the future will be assigned on summer cruises to Alaska, which obviously is one of the most lucrative and desirable places in the world to cruise.

Ships like the 105,000 ton *Grand Princess* was designed to carry 2,600 passengers, plus a huge crew, and her cost, $400 million. How large will cruise liners get? It would seem that competition as to who can build the largest liners must soon reach its apex, as port facilities in many cases cannot keep pace, and costs of operation of such behemoths must be based on what the individual companies feel renders a proper return on their investment.

While some cruise firms keep building bigger ships with more and more accommodations, other lines cater to the wealthy class only, with ultra service in a yacht-like atmosphere. Still others facilitate the less affluent tourists and offer all the amenities with refurbished older ships, or the informal but friendly mini-cruise vessels. In order to avoid taxation, high crew salaries, and certain rules and regulations, most of the larger ships serving the Alaska cruise traffic are registered under foreign flags, although U.S. currency is heavily involved in many of the foreign operations.

Carnival Cruise line's two new 100,000 ton giants have accommodations for 3,350 passengers, the largest ever for passenger vessels, and second only to the overcrowded and ridiculously squeezed in service men who were given passage on troop transports during two World Wars. Practicability and cost ratio may throttle the pace to build ships much over the 100,000 ton category just as the competitive oil companies in recent decades ceased building the world's largest supertankers. There comes a limit to such monsters, and as earlier mentioned, many of the world's largest oil tankers eventually spent much of their time in idleness after reaching the 550,000 deadweight ton category, with lengths to 1,500 feet, equivalent to about five football fields.

Most of the larger new mega-cruise ships are not longer than 900 feet in length but have huge bulk above the waterline. The *Norway*, ex-*France*, at 1,035 feet is longer, but not as heavy. At 76,000 tons, she has a passenger carrying capacity of 2,044. She long held the distinction as the largest in all dimensions, but has now been superseded by the newest mega-liners both from tonnage and passenger-carrying capacity. The *Norway*, of Norwegian Cruise Line, was always considered impractical for the Alaska run, but that is not necessarily so for the latest mega-liners.

It never came to fruition, but the so-called World City Line had considered building a passenger cruise ship, named the *Phoenix*, with 5,000 berths, which if ever constructed would have eclipsed any peacetime passenger carrying ship ever imagined. Noah's Ark was only 450 feet long, the size of a World War II Liberty ship.

The expansion of the cruise industry continues unabated with dazzling new ships appearing almost every month. But for the first time in many years, the number of passengers may not be keeping up with the burgeoning number of berths. The reaction of most lines, is to offer better discounts in the hope of filling cabins, and in maintaining the all important market share which tends to make competition ever keener. Every passenger is a source of revenue in the shops, casinos, bars, and on shore excursions, while affording a portion of the crews' salary in gratuities.

If a cruise line is unable to charge what it needs to gain a reasonable return on its investment, costs of operation have to be trimmed. The weaker lines may disappear or be merged, and individual ships not turning a profit are sold. As of the present, the game goes on, and cruise travel has captured the hearts of millions of Americans and foreigners as well.

Where food is concerned, the giant cruise ships have hired world renowned chefs and gourmet cooks, which is a feature attraction for cruise passengers. It has often been stated that on a cruiseliner people never eat to live, they just live to eat. The ability to stock and manage food for what is tantamount to serving a small city is nothing short of remarkable on the big ships, not to mention the alcohol beverages in the bars and the specialty items in food and drink to accommodate those with health problems. Cruise lines are becoming overly creative, almost supernormal with some of the innovations being introduced to consumers. On one cruise ship, a McDonalds golden arch was raised for hamburger lovers. On another, Hollywood became an interior decor theme. Then there was a unique biodegradable golf

Without doubt, the most durable and popular passenger vessel to ever sail the seas of Alaska was the SS Victoria. *Built as the Cunard Line's* Parthia *in 1870, she came to the Pacific a few years later and eventually became a unit of the Alaska Steamship Company. From the gold rush days until the latter days, "Ol Vic", as she was affectionately labeled, spent years carrying thousands of passengers to and from Alaskan ports, and was often the first to break through the ice of the Bering Sea to reach Nome annually. She is pictured here in the ice-rimmed Bering Sea in the upper photo, and in the lower, packed with a capacity load of passengers. Photo courtesy of Puget Sound Maritime Historical Society.*

After World War II, the SS Victoria *was converted to a freighter for the Alaska Steamship Company, replaced in the passenger sector by more modern liners. Finally in 1956, her hull was purchased by Japanese interests. The Canadian tug* Sudbury *towed her across the Pacific to a scrap yard in Japan where her iron hull was cut up, bearing a final name of* Straits Maru. Photo courtesy of Puget Sound Maritime Historical Society.*

ball to placate environmentalists who objected to millions of the 'real' golf balls being driven into the sea and polluting the oceans.

Pizza parlors, fully equipped gyms, saunas, pools, hot tubs, music, class act entertainers, and every other kind of pleasurable activity has or is being introduced to attract the traveler including basketball and volleyball courts. The cruise industry agrees that though fares may seem high that it's the best vacation value, as the price is generally all inclusive.

As for Alaska, no matter how the ball bounces, God's remaining natural wonders will continue to increase tourism to the Great Land, which has no parallel. And what God has put together let no man tear asunder, even though situations like the caribou mixing with the storage tanks and pipelines at Prudoe Bay exist. Other land uses are constantly debated, but the future appears mostly bright for Alaska now that environmental and proper zoning laws have been implemented. Cruise passengers are often overwhelmed by the beauty of Alaska, and Robert Service certainly described it well in his poem "The Call of the Wild":

Have you gazed on naked grandeur
Where there's nothing else to gaze on,
Set pieces and drop-curtain scenes galore
Big mountains heaved to heaven…

One who booked passage on Royal Caribbean Cruise Lines' luxurious 69,000 ton *Legend of the Seas* (Captain Michael Lachlaridis) noted on approaching a glacier, the 24 knot speed that got the ship there, more than 1,000 miles in 48 hours—Vancouver, B.C. to the most spectacular 'stop' on a seven day cruise through southeast Alaska. What a contrast to the old passenger liners to Alaska many of which could barely move at half that speed.

In older times, by ship from Vancouver to Juneau required three to four days along the islanded shores of the Inland Passage, past lush green timber and along the 800 plus miles with virtually no scars along the forested shores, hardly the site of a campfire, no belching smoke, population congestion, or noisy vehicles. There were places that nary the human foot had ever trod.

That's the way it was and that's the way it still is. Time has stood still along much of the Inland Passage and in other sectors of Alaska as well. Before one reaches Ketchikan, the first port on the Inside Passage northbound in Alaska, the cruise passenger today may still see the rusted remains of the once popular SS *North Sea*, a passenger vessel that was a unit of the Northland Transportation Company. She ran aground in 1947 and refused all efforts to be refloated. She lies on the eastern shore near the Indian village of Bella Bella, B.C. Though passengers and crew escaped the wreck she remained a grim reminder of what can happen when a ship gets off course.

Another reminder is at the museum in Juneau where two yellowed liferings from the ill-starred SS *Princess Sophia* hang, harking back to that terrible sea tragedy of 1918 on Vanderbilt Reef. When one looks at the pilot house of the newest cruise liners to Alaska with endless panels of computerized innovations, navigation and safety factors, it would be difficult to see how any ship could get hung up on a reef or collide with another vessel.

Every warning device is there. Southeastern and southwestern Alaska are the desired cruising areas, but it's doubtless that cruise ships will ever haunt the remote Bering and Arctic Sea portals. That is unless the owners of the Explorer Cruise Line ever elect to put together such a cruise. Anything is possible in the future, if the demands and the profit returns are there for the cruise industry.

As this book went to press a super new 380 foot Alaska State Ferry was under construction by the Halter Marine Company of Gulfport, Mississippi. Delivery was set for 1998. The vessel will feature roll-on roll-off design, capable of handling 120 vehicles and accommodations for 500 to 750 passengers depending on the route. The ship will have a vehicle elevator, side doors, and a stern ramp. A helicopter pad will support emergency response requirements allowing the vessel to be used as an emergency command post should such an occasion arise. The ocean-going ferry is the newest addition to the Alaska Marine Highway System since the *Aurora* was placed in service in 1977, and it shows the increasing interest in marine travel to the 49th state, at an affordable price. The yet unnamed vessel is being built on a bid price of $80,476,854.

Said Commissioner Joe Perkins, "Alaska's Marine Highway System is an important part of the National Highway System. Upgrading national highways in Alaska is an important part of Governor Tony Knowles' transportation initiative."

The governor had earlier pledged to invest $120 million a year over 12 years to upgrade national highways in Alaska, and of course the marine segment is an important part of the overall effort. The new ferry was designed with the help of residents of coastal communities from Ketchikan to Unalaska to better meet their needs, and will become a vital part of the system's fleet of eight ships.

Faded newspaper picture of the first recognized cruise ship to Alaska, Pacific Coast Steamships' SS Idaho. *She brought the first large excursion party to Alaska in 1881. The picture depicts her in 1890, moored by anchor, as an excursion party comes ashore by lifeboat to get a closer look at scenic attractions. What a contrast to the fabulous Alaska cruise ships of our day.*

Long associated with the northland was the auxiliary schooner Maid of Orleans. *The notorious craft had tested many waters and many trades. She served as a lumber carrier, a copra trader, a rum runner, black-birder, codfishing schooner, and Arctic fur trader. The sailing vessel had an auxiliary engine installed in 1934 and was equipped by the Alaska Trading Company as a trader among the Aleutians under Captain H.E. Harris. Alaska-bound in February 1936, she was wrecked in a snowstorm on Sarah Island in northern British Columbia. The Coast Guard cutter* Haida *rescued part of her crew and the others finally made it to Boat Bluff Lighthouse.*

Claimed to be one of Alaska's best kept secrets, many of the state's unique and historical towns and cities are connected only by water or air. The Alaska Marine Highway System offers a flexible and affordable alternative to packaged tour and cruise travel. One can put their car or RV on one of the system's ferries and sail to Alaska year round from Bellingham, Washington, or Prince Rupert, B.C. During the summer one can drive to the twin cities of Stewart, B.C. and Hyder, Alaska, then put his car on the ferry to discover other Alaska cities, or board as a walk-on passenger and return by either domestic or international airline. Such a mode of travel permits a more leisurely and thorough exploration of the 32 scheduled ports served along the southeastern and southwestern Alaska sea routes, where scenic beauty abounds. Cultural entertainment is provided for passenger pleasure and knowledge.

Ports of call in addition to the non-Alaska ports of Bellingham and Prince Rupert are Hyder, Ketchikan, Prince of Wales Island, Wrangell, Petersburg, Sitka, Juneau, Haines, Skagway, Angoon, Kake, Hoonah, Metlakatla, Pelican, and Tenakee, all of which are on the Inside Passage in southeastern Alaska. Ports served in central Alaska are Cordova, Valdez, Whittier, Seward, Homer, and Seldovia. Southwestern Alaska ports of call include Kodiak, Port Lions, Chignik, Sand Point, King Cove, Cold Bay, False Pass, Akutan, and Unalaska/Dutch Harbor.

No other state is provided with such an unusual and effective marine passenger and freight operation as Alaska. To better understand the marine segment of the novel highway system let us review a bit of history. It all began with a relatively small ferry named *Chilkat*, a motor vessel that connected Juneau and Haines. By 1963, three additional vessels were added, the blue-painted *Matanuska*, *Malaspina* and *Taku*, originally operating from northern terminals at Skagway and Haines to a southern terminus at Prince Rupert, B.C.

Within a year the MV *Tustumena* expanded service to distant Kodiak, and Alaskans were thrilled with the welcome connections by sea. In its first full year, the AMHS transported more than 83,000 passengers and 16,000 vehicles. By 1967, additional ports of call were added and the route expanded to a new southern terminus at Seattle.

As the ferry system grew, a remarkably good safety record was established. Highly qualified ship's officers and crew, excellent man-

agement, and fulfillment of all safety regulations made the blue, gold, and white fleet a cut above. What a difference from the old days when Alaskan shipwreck was almost a weekly occurrence. It wasn't that many of the older seafaring men weren't qualified, but that modern electronic innovations and safety guides have vastly improved over the decades, as well as equipment inspection and air and surface rescue and emergency capability.

The system's pioneer ferry, the *Chilkat*, made her final voyage in 1988 with no small amount of nostalgia. Retired after banner service, she was sold in 1990, and in her wake came a trio of "glacier" ships. The *Columbia*, *LaConte*, and *Aurora*, all named for massive Alaska glaciers, added a new era to Alaska sea transport.

In 1989, the Port of Bellinghan captured a nice piece of the action when they replaced Seattle as the system's southerly terminus, providing modern facilities and community cooperation. In addition, it shortened the sea route to southeastern Alaska. It further opened the door wider to the two non-connecting routes, enabling passengers to travel through the scenic Inside Passage or via Prince William Sound to Southwest Alaska and the Aleutians. Several of the units of the eight ship fleet offer stateroom accommodations. Food and beverage service is available on all the vessels, and from the informal aspect passengers can opt to sleep on the deck.

Tourism has become one of Alaska's most important industries, accounting for ten percent of the total, and growing at the rate of five percent annually. The Alaska Marine Highway plays a large role in that increase. The 1993-94 season hosted a million visitors. In fact, in fiscal 1994, more than 400,000 passengers and 108,000 vehicles were transported on the system's ferries, not to mention the great tonnage in freight. Jobs are generated for 860 Alaskans who earn $35 million in annual payroll and $10 million in benefits. During the busy summer season, seagoing vessels of the B.C. Ferries fleet also serve Alaska's Inside Passage, offering vehicle and passenger service from Prince

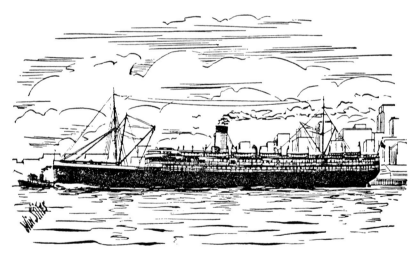

SS Aleutian, *largest and most palatial passenger ship that was owned and operated by the Alaska Steamship Company. She was acquired in 1929, after the former* Aleutian *was wrecked at Uyak Bay, Alaska, that same year. The new* Aleutian, *built in 1906, was purchased from the Ward Line, which had operated her as the* Mexico. *The ill-fated* Aleutian, *built in 1898, was the former* Havana *and had also carried the name* Panama *during her years of service on the Atlantic seaboard. The* Aleutian *pictured in this sketch by Win Stites was a vessel of 6,207 tons, twin screw, steel hull, and excellently appointed. She had a close call in February of 1945 when stranding in Wrangell Narrows. The Coast Guard cutters* Citrus *and* Aurora *pulled her free. As the Alaska Line's passenger service drew to a close, an attempt was made to put the* Aleutian *on the California-Hawaii run but the Hawaiian Pacific Line folded. The steamer then became the* Tradewinds *of the Caribbean Atlantic Cruise Line in 1955. Her tenure, however, was short and she soon went to the ship breakers.*

A rainy day at Dutch Harbor, Alaska, the big Sea-Land D-7 class container ship, Sea-Land Tacoma, is pictured at dockside. Lower left, one of the former Sea-Land container ships, the SS Seattle is pictured berthed at Kodiak in July 1964. A C-4 type vessel is much smaller than the diesel powered D-7 carriers presently in service. Lower right, the MV Sea-Land Kodiak is shown at her namesake port in December 1987. She is 710 feet in length, as are her sisterships, Sea-Land Tacoma and Sea-Land Anchorage.

Rupert and Port Hardy, offering a 15 hour daylight cruise aboard the seagoing ferry liner *Queen of the North* to Southeastern Alaska. In 1995, B.C. Ferries marked its 35th anniversary featuring the largest ferry fleet on North America's Pacific Coast, a fleet totalling 40 vessels, the largest ranging up to 550 feet in length. All B.C. ports are served the year-round.

Returning to the Alaska Marine Highway System, we find that all of its vessels offer elevator access except the smaller MV *Bartlett* which has a stair climber lift. Passengers without staterooms on all vessels are offered a limited number of recliner chairs, and even places to roll out sleeping bags. Such arrangements have made it possible for low income individuals to enjoy all of the grandeur of Alaskan waterways at a very affordable fee. The Inside Passage stretches 1,080 miles from Bellingham through British Columbia to Skagway, the world's longest marine highway. Passengers thrill at passing more than 1,000 islands, 10,000 miles of shoreline, and 50 major glaciers in and around the two main Alaska marine sea routes. One man described the Alaska ferries as the "poor man's 'Love Boats' ", and that man was Captain Dale Julian, a veteran skipper of the fleet. He enjoys seeing numerous happy campers cruising through Alaska's marine fairy land.

The Alaska Ferry System has had a very commendable safety record with but few accidents. Probably the only one of consequence was when the MV *Taku*, (Captain Jim Sande) with 324 passengers aboard ran aground on West Kinahan Island, near Prince Rupert, B.C., July 29, 1970. Steaming at 17 knots, the vessel struck at midnight and held fast. All passengers were safely evacuated with only four minor injuries. The 352 foot vessel was eventually pulled free and towed to Seattle for costly bottom repairs.

Some love to roam, o're the dark seas foam,
Where the shrill winds whistle free.
—Chas. Mackay

DISTANCES AND TIMES BETWEEN SOUTHEAST ALASKA MARINE HIGHWAY PORTS

Port	Travel Time	Travel Miles
Port Bellingham to Skagway	67 hrs.	949
Bellingham to Skagway via Sitka	82 hrs.	1116
Bellingham to Ketchikan	37.5 hrs.	595
Prince Rupert to Skagway	33.25 hrs.	430
Prince Rupert to Skagway via Sitka	47.25 hrs.	584
Prince Rupert to Ketchikan	6 hrs.	91
Hyder to Ketchikan	9.75 hrs.	143
Ketchikan to Wrangell	6 hrs.	89
Wrangell to Petersburg	3 hrs.	41
Petersburg to Juneau/Auke Bay	7.75 hrs.	123
Haines to Skagway	1 hr.	13
Juneau/Auke Bay to Haines	4.5 hrs.	68
Juneau /Auke Bay to Pelican	6.5 hrs.	91
Sitka to Juneau/Auke Bay	8.75 hrs.	132
Petersburg to Sitka	10 hrs.	156

DISTANCES AND TIMES BETWEEN SOUTHCENTRAL/SOUTHWEST MARINE HIGHWAY PORTS

Port	Travel Time	Travel Miles
Whittier to Valdez	6.75 hrs.	78
Valdez to Cordova	5.5 hrs.	74
Cordova to Whittier	7 hrs.	97
Cordova to Seward	11 hrs.	144
Valdez to Seward	11 hrs.	144
Homer to Seldovia	1.5 hrs.	17
Homer to Kodiak	12 hrs.	136
Homer to Port Lions	9.75 hrs.	184
Seward to Kodiak	13.25 hrs.	185
Kodiak to Port Lions	2 hrs.	48
Kodiak to Chignik	19 hrs.	249
Chignik to Sand Point	9.25 hrs.	138
Sand Point to King Cove	6.75 hrs.	98
King Cove to Cold Bay	1.75 hrs.	25
Cold Bay to Dutch Harbor	14.25 hrs.	210

HIGHWAY MILEAGE

Haines to Valdez	approx. 14 hrs.	702
Haines to Fairbanks	approx. 13.5 hrs.	662
Haines to Anchorage	approx. 16 hrs.	785
Skagway to Valdez	approx. 16 hrs.	761
Skagway to Fairbanks	approx. 14 hrs.	710
Skagway to Anchorage	approx. 17 hrs.	832
Skagway to Whitehorse	approx. 2 hrs.	108

—Courtesy Alaska Marine Highway System

during each voyage. TOTE (Totem Ocean Trailer Express), however, boasts a 96 per cent on-time arrival record over the prior two years before the penning of this book, a remarkable achievement. Dockside, radical changes in the mooring level of a ship calls for specialized ramp equipment.

Economic growth slowed in Alaska in 1986, when, concurrent with plummeting oil revenues, Alaska entered a recession lasting almost four years. Since then the market has rebounded receiving a jump start from the *Exxon Valdez* oil spill cleanup, and bolstered by more oil exploration, development of other resource industries such as seafood, coal, and timber, plus growth in the service sector in tourism and international trade.

In 1996, the shipping industry was elated to learn that a rocky shoal rising from the floor of Cook Inlet, known as Knik Arm, was to be blasted away at long last. For decades it had prevented ships from entering and departing the Port of Anchorage at low tide. It had not only hampered commercial vessels, but had prevented Navy and Coast Guard ships from homeporting at Anchorage. Cruise liners also frequently skipped Anchorage.

One side of the shoal was to be shaved off by the Army Corps of Engineers and readied in 1997.

A rundown of modern cargo transport to Alaskan ports includes the following. The two principal carriers, as earlier mentioned, are Totem Ocean Trailer Express and Sea-Land Service. Both operate super modern deep sea vessels. TOTE with its trio of roll-on, roll-off vessels is unique in every way. Competitor, Sea Land Service, operates three large capacity ships in the Alaska trade, each capable of 700 forty foot equivalents (containers).

Tug and barge contract services by major operators such as Foss and Crowley during peak shipping months varies from ten days to twice a month to Anchorage, Kenai Peninsula, and Whittier. Smaller barge lines, specializing primarily in regional service to the Southeast, the Aleutian Chain, or the North Slope offer seasonal connections drawing upon a combined fleet of more than ten barges and 20 allied vessels.

(FERRIES) SHIPS SERVING THE ALASKA MARINE HIGHWAY SYSTEM, AS OF 1997 (ALASKA STATE FERRIES)

Ship	Speed	Tonnage	Length	Date Completed	Vehicles	Passengers
Columbia	17.3	3946	418	1974	158	625
Matanuska	16.5	3029	408	1963	108	500
Malaspina	16.5	2928	408	1963	107	500
Taku	16.5	2624	352	1963	83	475
Aurora	14.5	1280	235	1977	44	250
Leconte	14.5	1328	235	1974	44	250
Tustumena	13.3	2174	296	1964	42	210
Bartlett	12.0	933	193	1969	41	190

★ Speed indicated is in knots. Tonnage is gross measurement. Fleet is subject to change with new ferries contracted for at this writing. Courtesy Alaska Marine Highway System

Where cargo is concerned there are three major challenges for ships in the Alaska trade. First, the route on the Outside Passage (Tacoma to Anchorage) is a rigorous 1,450 nautical miles, with seas sometimes surging to 60 feet and winds gusting to more than 100 mph during the winter season.

Cook Inlet can be ice-filled for more than 100 miles, five months of the year. Tidal variances of up to 35 feet and surging at six to seven knots twice a day pose a navigational challenge in crossing a shoal

Firms such as TOTE in its southbound operations facilitates transfer of seafood exports to carriers destined for international markets, tramp ships from Japan, Russia, and Korea offering what is often a more direct, low cost albeit lower quality transoceanic service for shipping cod, salmon, and herring.

Overland shipments provided by trucking companies and vehicle shippers, transiting via the ALCAN Highway offer little or no improvement over water carrier service and is a more expensive op-

One of the most popular passenger steamships ever to serve Alaska was the SS Alaska *of the Alaska Steamship Company. Built at Tacoma, Washington, in 1923, she was an advanced twin screw turbo electric vessel with excellent accommodations. She was sold in 1955 and became the cruise ship* Mazatlan *on the Mexican run. Her stint as a cruise ship was short, and the vessel was eventually scrapped.*

tion. At least four major airlines provide time sensitive cargo service at a premium price and competes with the services offered by the major shipping lines on certain types of freight.

Talk about innovative, Totem Ocean Trailer Express offers a novel twist. Drive north to Canada and Alaska in your RV, then enjoy a relaxing flight or sea cruise back, while TOTE safely returns your vehicle by cargo ship. The plan offers an opportunity for one to extend their vacation time in the northland and not have to worry about the long trip back on the ALCAN Highway. TOTE's roll-on roll-off ships sailing two to three times a week between Anchorage (Ak) and Tacoma (Wa) transit time is a mere 66 hours (no passengers).

One brings his RV to the terminal where it is immediately assigned to a limited access area for inspection and condition recording, not to be moved again until the vessel loads. No need to containerize the RV. It is driven aboard ship to a protected stow position and professionally secured. Ample space is allocated fore, aft, and on each side. On arrival at Tacoma it is driven off to a receiving area in the yard and held for pickup.

The trailership is particularly beneficial to the shipper of high value goods, from consumer products (including automobiles) to sophisticated electronic and industrial components. Temperature sensitive freight such as liquids, farm produce, and dairy foods are protected in refrigerated or insulated trailers that are plugged into the ship's electrical system.

As earlier mentioned, TOTE's trio of trailerships, the *Westward Venture*, *Great Land*, and *Northern Lights* have speeds of 24 knots, most unusual for cargo vessels, which from a distance have the appearance of aircraft carriers. Founded in 1975, TOTE is a privately-owned Alaskan Corporation, headquartered in Seattle. It began as a subsidiary of the Philadelphia based Sun Company, whose financial resources and impetus effectively launched TOTE's venture into the Alaska trade. In 1982, the firm was purchased by a group of its own officers and Northwest businessmen who formed Totem Resources Corporation.

TOTE's initial vessel *Great Land*, came on line in September 1975, followed by the *Westward Venture* in 1977 and the *Northern Lights* in 1993. Nearly 30 percent of the company's personnel have been with TOTE since its inauguration, and 74 percent have been with the operation for five years or more. They work as a close knit team and are customer friendly. By applying state of the art technology and proven methodology, the firm offers a viable, preferred carrier service, playing a prominent role in Alaska's future. TOTE has one of the most modern computerized tracking and G billing systems in the shipping industry. It monitors cargo throughout the transit and provides customers with timely accurate documentation.

Company ships carry one pilot, nine officers, and 20 crewmen. They offer 12,000 ton cargo capacity (410, 40 foot equivalents), and fast port turnaround of ten to fifteen hours. In addition to the huge ships, the land-based fleet consists of 312 insulated trailers; 343 reefer trailers; 670 dry vans; 154 flatbeds; six expandable flatbeds; four open tops; six tankers and two lowboys (subject to change).

Compare the 30,000 horsepowered steam turbines in each TOTE vessel with the standard Liberty cargo vessel of World War II which developed only 2,500 horsepower offering less than half the speed of the present cargo carriers.

The lot of a seafarer today is highly pleasant compared to those of yesteryear who sailed before the mast. That hard, demanding lifestyle of old created the far out story telling ability during long days at sea—thus the birth of the yarn and the chantey. One such poetic yarn that has endured is titled, "Wish I Could Tell a Lie".

I stood one day on a breezy bay, watching the ships go by,
When an old tar said, with the shake of his head,
I wish I could tell a lie.
I have seen sights what would jigger your lights as they jiggered mine for sooth,
But I ain't worth a darn at telling a yarn, when it wanders away from the truth. I was on a bark, called the Nancy Stark, a league
and a half at sea,
When Captain Snook with a troubled look, he came to me and said,
Now bos'n Smith, make haste, forewith, and hemstitch the foremain sail,
Accordian pleat the spanker sheet, for she's gonna blow a gale.
I straightaway did as the captain bid, and no sooner the job was through,
When a north wind crack, set us dead aback and murdering lights how she blew.
She blew the tars right off of the spars, and the spars right off of the masts;
Anchors and sails, and kegs of nails, went by on the wings of the blast.
The galley shook when it blew the cook right out through the starboard grim;
Pots and pans, kettles and cans went clattering after him,
It blew the fire right out of the stove and the coal right out of the bin,
And we cried alack when it blew the beard right off of the captain's chin.
Then the old man said, with the shake of his head, and the words they blew out of his mouth;
We are lost I fear, if the wind don't veer and blow awhile from the south.
When the wind hauled around with a hurricane sound and blew straight in from the south.
It blew the tars back onto the spars and the spars back onto the masts,
Anchors and sails and kegs of nails onto the ship stuck fast.
The galley shook when it blew the cook right back on the starboard poop;
Pots and pans and kettles and cans, without even spilling the soup.
It blew the fire back into the stove and the coal back into the bin.
And we cried hurrah! When it blew the beard right back on the skipper's chin.
There's more to my tale, and the sailor hale, that would jiggle your lights for sooth;
But I ain't worth a darn, at telling a yarn, when it wanders away from the truth.
—By an unknown skipper of a square-rigger

For cruise passengers, Alaska is indeed America's last true wilderness—a playground of nature without comparison. Bountiful wildlife on sea and land is everywhere. A bald eagle might be seen in the sky above, harbor seals frolicking with their pups riding an ice floe, a whale making a thunderous breach right along side one's ship, and magnificent sunrises and sunsets with vivid coloration reflecting in the water. Today, comforts on Alaskan waters aboard a vessel, be it large or small, is in steep contrast to the often rigorous and difficult sea experience in days of yore. No yarn needed here, it's all reality.

For a chronology of the shipping picture in Alaska over the past decades let us review the following:

In all the history of Alaskan sea transportation no company equalled the long duration of serving Alaska, hauling cargo and passengers, than did Alaska Steamship Company, which as earlier alluded to, logged more than 75 years of service starting in 1895 when Charles E. Peabody and associates placed the little wooden steamer *Willapa* in service to combat the monopoly by the Pacific Coast Steamship Company. When the *Willapa* struck Regatta Reef near Bella Bella, B.C., on March 19, 1897, it placed a major hardship on the owners' but tenaciously they struggled against the competition with lower rates and small vessels until 1908 when a merger between Peabody and the Northwestern Steamship Company eventually boosted the fleet to 15 vessels.

In 1915, the Alaska Line was sold to Kennecott Copper Company and the ship's holds were often filled with copper concentrates from the big mine near Cordova. When that booming item declined in the late 1930s, the mine deteriorated and Kennecott sold the steamship line to its final owner, the Skinner and Eddy Corporation of Seattle. In 1944, Gilbert Skinner purchased the Alaska Line and merged it with Northland Transportation Company, a two-ship operation Skinner had earlier acquired. A joint passenger and freight operation continued to grow into one of the larger American steamship operations. After several successful years, competition from the government subsidized air transport and the Alaskan highway, which, combined with rising operation and labor costs, caused the abandonment of passenger service in 1954.

Following that sad chapter in company history, Alaska Steamship modernized its cargo fleet and kept pace with the latest advancements. It was the first carrier to use radar to aid navigation in the difficult Alaskan passages, wreck-strewn in earlier times.

Along with Alaska Freight Lines, it pioneered the concept of containerized cargo in Alaska. While Malcolm McLean and Milton Odom were working out the details of Sea Land's purchase of Alaska Freight Lines in 1963, Alaska Steamship was converting its Liberty freighters *Nadina* and *Tonsina* into semi-container vessels. Those ships' deckhouses were elevated, booms and cargo handling gear updated and other innovations augmented. As a result, cargo to Alaska entered a new phase. Perhaps the best known of the Alaska Lines cargo ships of the Liberty class was the SS *Chena* which gained the label of "Tidal Wave Ship". She miraculously escaped the 1964 Good Friday earthquake at Valdez with no major damage. Challenging the resultant tsunami, the tough old war-built ship was hammered by giant seas that rolled her a good 50 degrees as she was discharging her cargo at a Valdez dock. In the deep trough she struck bottom with a grinding crunch and was then lifted over the dock wreckage. Still, she survived, as did her crew.

Alaska Steamship, during its final years served up to 48 Alaska ports. The line was the lifeline of Alaska, but there were the usual slowdowns in an area that boomed or slept with the seasonal changes, and the problem of serving both the small ports as well as the more productive larger ports. The task was great, especially with competitors barking at its heels with more innovative cargo methods. Competitors scraped off the cream by serving only the major Alaskan ports, and the end grew near for the historical Alaska Steamship Company.

By the mid 1960s, fierce competition from tug and barge operations caused a decline in Alaska Steamship revenues and the final spike in the coffin was Sea-Land's entry into the Alaska service, zeroing in on the Anchorage market where Sea-Land became the first carrier to provide year-round service.

Seeing the handwriting on the wall in the light of rising fuel, wage, and insurance costs, Alaska Steamship executives reasoned they could no longer retain their market share in the light of competition; and the Skinner Corporation threw in the towel in 1971. The Alaska Steamship Company became a page of past history. The firm sold its southeastern Alaska service to Foss Launch & Tug Company and liquidated its fleet of semicontainer and breakbulk cargo ships.

Like hungry wolves on the horizon, shipping executives considered the spoils and planned even greater things for the future of growing Alaska. In 1948, Al Ghezzi formed the Alaska Freight Line Service, setting up a sea service to Valdez with a connecting inland route to Fairbanks. Two years later, the ownership of Alaska Freight Lines changed hands after its founder faced severe financial setback from the DEW-Line Project (Crowley Red Stack). Lloyd Burgess of Alaska gained controlling interest in Alaska Freight Lines.

In the interim, Pan Atlantic sailed the SS *Ideal X*, the carrier's first containerized transport ship from Port Newark to Houston in 1956, and four years later its chief executive Malcolm McLean would create the birth of what would become one of the world's largest containerized sea transport operations in the world, one segment dedicated to Alaska. McLean changed his Pan Atlantic Steamship Corporation to Sea-Land Service Inc., and the fleet grew.

A year later (1961) back in Seattle, Alaska Freight Lines changed ownership for the third time, Milton Odom gaining control. Then in 1963, Odom signed an agreement with Sea-Land, whereby the latter would handle Alaska Freight Lines. In 1964, Sea-Land took over Ames Terminal in Seattle and set up a fast Seattle-Anchorage direct service. A new era had dawned for Alaska with sophisticated container ships. Sea-Land placed two C-4 class vessels, the *New Orleans* and *Mobile* in the Alaska service, each carrying 166, 35 foot containers.

Widespread damage in Alaska with the 8.7 magnitude earthquake on Good Friday, May 1, 1964, played havoc for a period with Alaska shipping, but Sea-Land did not send its first ship in the new trade to Alaska until May 3, when the *New Orleans* did the inaugural, marking the first deep water containership service to Anchorage. By July 22, Sea-Land provided regular scheduled service from Seattle to both Anchorage and Kodiak. The burgeoning city of Anchorage was delighted, and in September, Sea-Land signed a 20 year agreement for terminal facilities at the Alaska port.

When Charles Hiltzheimer was appointed general manager of the Alaska operation by Sea-Land president Michael McEnvoy in the fall of the year, progress resumed, and the SS *Anchorage* made her historic Cook Inlet passage cracking through ice without an icebreaker or tug, proving that year-round service to Anchorage was achievable. By 1965, greater demand placed the SS *Summit* on the Anchorage run, and a few months later the container vessels SS *Anchorage* and SS *Seattle* were modified to increase van capacity from 178 to 292, 35 foot containers.

When Atlantic-Richfield discovered giant oil reserves at Prudoe Bay in 1968, Alaska took on a rosy complexion. The discovery had a domino effect for shipping lines. The following year, R. J. Reynolds Tobacco Company and McLean Industries, Sea-Land's parent company, announced merger plans and a few months later Sea-Land ordered eight SL-7 class vessels, the largest and fastest containerships in the world, capable of 33 knots.

As earlier mentioned, Alaska Steamship folded tent in 1971, and Sea-Land received a military contract to handle cargo to Adak and Kodiak, formerly served by Alaska Steamship. The following year Sea-Land took over the Aleutian route from Naval transport ships. More vessels were added with greater carrying capacity, and Cordova calls were included. In June 1974, construction began on the Alaskan pipeline and Sea-Land deployed a fifth vessel, the SS *Newark*, to the Alaska service. Three sailings per week were then possible from Seattle.

Sensing a growing market, the Totem Ocean Trailer Express, as earlier mentioned, launched its maiden entrance in the Alaska sea trade on September 10, 1975, with the RO-RO concept. That same year, Sea-Land upgraded its Alaska fleet to C-4X class vessels, each able to carry 360, 35 foot containers: the *Mobile, Galveston, Boston,* and *Philadelphia.*

Then sparks began to fly when TOTE filed a $5 million trade restraint suit against Sea-Land, a dispute that would last three years, after which TOTE relocated its terminal operations to the Port of Tacoma. With completion of the Alaska pipeline in 1977, both SeaLand and TOTE picked up steam. In March of 1979, Sea-Land began Alaska-Japan service with the chartered container ship *Strider Isis*, and American President Lines began an Alaska-Japan service from Dutch Harbor with huge "Pacesetter" class ships with a capacity of 1,484 TEUs.

In 1981, Sea-Land looking into the economy of operating its giant container ships worldwide, sold its largest ships, six SL-7 class vessels, to the U.S. Navy and used proceeds from the sale to purchase modern D-7 vessels for the Alaska trade, to be readied for operation by 1986-87. As 1982 rolled in, TOTE was purchased from its parent, Sun Oil Company, by Northwest investors headed by Robert McMillen. A year later, Sea-Land signed a 30 year terminal contract with the Port of Tacoma.

The new economical diesel-powered vessels were finally under construction in 1984. That same year, R. J. Reynolds Tobacco interests spun off ownership of Sea-Land Service Inc. to its shareholders, and S. L. emerged as an independent publicly held company with stock on the New York Stock Exchange. In 1985, Sea-Land moved its Alaska operation from Seattle to Tacoma, and more giant container cranes were installed dockside.

Several months earlier, another newcomer entered the Alaska sea trade, Seaway Express, introducing two giant 485 by 104 foot triple deck barges, each with a capacity of 320 FEUs. Its entry caused problems for small barge operators and some were forced out of business. Pacific Western Lines, a subsidiary of Sealaska Corporation, and Foss Alaska Lines, a 15 year old subsidiary of Foss Launch & Tug Company ended their scheduled tug and barge operations to Alaska.

On September 13, 1986, Seaway Express filed for chapter 11 bankruptcy after only two years of operation. Meanwhile, Alaska Barge Lines (TOTE owned operation) began Alaska service. Finally on August 18, 1987, the first of Sea-Land's new 710 foot diesel container ships, the D-7 MV Sea-Land *Anchorage*, entered the Alaska trade followed by her sisters, MV Sea-Land *Tacoma* in October, and the MV Sea-Land *Kodiak* in December.

Low cargo volume forced termination of TOTE's Alaska Barge Line that same year, and in 1988 other lows hampered all Alaska services. The price of oil dropped, a giant oil spill messed up Cook Inlet, and cargo demands fluctuated. TOTE's *Great Land* was out of service for 11 weeks at Tacoma when her engine room flooded. In 1992, things picked up, Sea-Land delivering its millionth container to Alaska, but

two years later the International Brotherhood of Teamsters strike against Trucking Management Inc., closed Sea-Land's West Coast operations, including the Port of Tacoma, for 23 days—a costly shutdown.

The Alaska scene in sea trade, rail, and trucking now appears bright, with most of the previous problems solved. It's full steam ahead for a promising future. Seafood exports to Asia continue to grow which brings more and more sophisticated fishing vessels to the Alaskan scene. Alaska lumber is also in demand. Sea-Land was among the firms that worked to overturn the ban on Alaska North Slope oil. The Alaska Department of Commerce and Economic Development estimated an incremental impact on state revenues of $40 to $100 million dollars per annum, a great boost to the economy. Alaska collects about 80 percent of state revenues from oil taxes and royalties.

SHIPS NOW SERVING
OR THAT HAVE SERVED
THE SEA-LAND CONTAINER FLEET
1964-1996

Name	Length	Speed	Year Built	Crew	Container Capacity
New Orleans	496	17	1944	39	166 (35 feet)
Mobile	496	17	1945	39	166 (35 feet)
Anchorage	496	17	1944	38	166 (35 feet)
Seattle	496	17	1945	38	166 (35 feet)
Summit	523	17	1943	39	226 (35 feet)
Aleutian Developer	—	16	1960	—	90 (35 feet) plus breakbulk
Mobile	523	17	1945	38	360 (35 feet)
Galveston	523	17	1945	38	360 (35 feet)
Boston	523	16	1945	38	360 (35 feet)
Philadelphia	523	16	1945	38	360 (35 feet)
Anchorage	710	20	1987	21	701 FEUs
Tacoma	710	20	1987	21	701 FEUs
Kodiak	710	20	1987	21	701 FEUs

★ Sources: Lloyd's Register and Sea-Land Service Inc.

CHAPTER TEN
Unusual Shipwrecks

A rotten carcass of a boat,
not rigged,
Nor tackle, sail nor mast;
the very rats
Instinctively have quit it.
—Shakespeare

Phantom ships have long captivated the imagination. From ancient times, seafaring men were highly superstitious and had strong feelings about the supernatural. The writer Ayres once wrote:

Tis' the phantom ship, that, in darkness and wrath,
Ploughs evermore the waste ocean path,
And the heart of the mariner trembles in dread,
When it crosses his vision like a ghost of the dead.

No nautical tale of old has so lingered as that of the *Flying Dutchman*. Many versions of the story exist depending on the salty ports of old that shellbacks hailed from. The American sailor chose the yarn of the Dutch trading vessel *Palatine*, which was wrecked on Block Island in 1752. High water reputedly lifted the wreck from the rocks, and wreckers are said to have touched the torch to her as she drifted away. There was one woman aboard who refused to leave the troubled vessel as it moved seaward under rags of canvas hanging from her yardarms. Another authority claimed the *Palatine* was not wrecked until 1784, but agreed she was burned by wreckers.

Whittier, the great poet alluded to

"The spectra-ship of Salem, with dead men in her shrouds,
Sailing sheer above the water, in the loom of morning
clouds."

Poets and novelists through the years have used both exotic words and imagination to describe such a phantom ship.

Longfellow embellished words to captivate the reader when he wrote the following:

"On she came, with a cloud of canvas,
Right against the wind that blew
Until the eye could distinguish
The faces of the crew."
"Then fell her straining topmasts
Hanging tangled in the shrouds,
And her sails were lowered and lifted
And blown away like clouds."
"And the masts with all their rigging,
Fell slowly, one by one,
And the hulk dilated and vanished
As a sea-mist in the sun."

Other writers claim the phantom ship was the *Carmilhan*, and another the ship *Rotterdam*, lost with all hands, which reappeared at times with her ghostly crew, always an omen of disaster to those who witnessed its presence. We could go on and on with such

tales, but what we are leading up to is the phantom ship of the north. The account of the *Baychimo* is true, not fiction, but her weird drift among the icefloes of the Arctic, without a human hand to guide her, had almost supernatural aspects.

The legendary steamer was a unit of the Hudson's Bay Company. In 1929, she played a major role in the first commercial use of the Northwest Passage. Sailing out of Vancouver, B.C. she steamed around Alaska as far north as Cambridge Bay which she reached on August 29 of that year. HBC's steamer *Fort James* started from the other side of the passage at Nova Scotia and Newfoundland the previous year and spent two winters near King William Island. Contact between the two vessels was then made by the auxiliary schooner *Fort McPherson* which had been maintained by Hudson's Bay within the Arctic Circle on permanent supply and exploration duties. She rendezvoused with the *Baychimo* at Cambridge Bay and then voyaged 250 miles to join the *Fort James*, the trio of vessels forming an unbroken chain of communication between west and east coast ports of Canada. The Hudson's Bay Company had accomplished a mark in history in completing the link for the first time in two and a half centuries of operation.

In the fall of 1931, we find the *Baychimo* in trouble in the ice of the Arctic. Calls for assistance brought a plane from Nome and most of the passengers and crew were transported to the safety of that town. The steamer's master, Captain Sydney A. Cornwall, and the remaining crew members established a shore camp near the icelocked *Baychimo* to keep guard over her during the harsh winter. Several weeks later something very strange occurred.

It was Christmas Day and the temperature stood at a frigid 60 degrees below zero. Suddenly, the thermometer did a complete turn around reaching to 10 degrees above zero in a matter of hours. The

Wreck of the cargo vessel Kennecott, *Captain Johnson, on Graham Island (B.C.) in the winter of 1923 while en route from Cordova to Tacoma with copper concentrates. Note the survivor coming ashore by breeches buoy. The* Kennecott, *built at the Todd yard in Tacoma, was reputedly the first all-steel ocean going motor ship built in the United States. The 469 foot vessel was only three years old when wrecked.*

phenomenon was accompanied by howling wind which reached its highest velocity the following day. As some of the ice broke up, the water level rose along the shore more than six feet. Not until the following day did the men risk leaving the shelter of their hut.

When they came out to check on the ship, all they found was a voluminous ridge of ice where the *Baychimo* had been frozen in. Despite the freakish weather, Cornwall and his men strapped packs on their backs and headed toward Point Barrow in search of the ship. On reaching their destination, they were informed that the vessel had been sighted and boarded, and with the assistance of the Eskimos, trader O. D. Morris had managed to retrieve the valuable cargo of furs. By the time Cornwall was able to reach the reported location the *Baychimo* had mysteriously disappeared again, a large hole in her hull from severe ice damage. It was generally assumed that the steamer had sunk, but then five months later she was sighted drifting with the ice floes, several hundred miles from Herschel Island, by trader Leslie Melvin.

No less mysterious than the proverbial *Flying Dutchman*, the *Baychimo* became Canada's modern version of the ghost ship under perplexing circumstances. Later in 1932 she was occasionally sighted by Eskimos in remote areas and was sometimes boarded at great risk. Still, she in latency moved northward. In August 1933 she was spotted by the schooner *Trader*. Some of her crew, accompanied by author Isobel W. Hutchinson, boarded the battered vessel with no small amount of trepidation. The experience gave inspiration to the lady author in writing the book *North to the Rime-rimmed Sun*.

With her phantom crew, the *Baychimo* continued her erratic drift and was sighted now and then after 52 months of defying the killer ice. How long her voyage to nowhere continued nobody knows, and like the *Flying Dutchman*, she may still be drifting. Though nobody has reported seeing her in recent years, neither were there witnesses to her possible demise.

The James Griffiths steamer *Anyox* was chartered by HBC for the 1933 Arctic supply and trading season and narrowly escaped a similar fate as that of the *Baychimo*. She was caught in a pincers of grinding ice floes and the seawater poured into her fractured hull. Only the quick thinking of Captain B.D.L. Johnson saved the vessel when the pumps could no longer keep up with the inflow. He rallied the crew to improvise a collision mat from spare canvas. Made fast with Manila rope, it was brought under the ship's keel and secured on the port and starboard sides. The crude remedy allowed the pumps to again become effective, controlling the in flow until the *Anyox* could later be beached for more permanent repairs.

During that same Arctic season the schooner *C. S. Holmes* also had a scare in the ice, 73 miles from Point Barrow. Had it not been for the quick response by the U.S. Bureau of Indian Affairs motor vessel *North Star* (Captain S.T.L. Whitlam) the *Holmes* might have been crushed like the many vessels before her. The *North Star* pulled her free and towed her to Barrow and safety.

A more recent wandering unmanned ship was the 8,905 ton Liberian-registered cargo vessel *Athena*. She had sailed from Pacific Coast ports in 1983 bound for mainland China, with general cargo when trouble occurred. Springing a leak in No. 5 hold in the north Pacific, the vessel was taking on water rapidly. The seas were gargantuan. The skipper attempted to set a course for Japan, but the ship's condition deteriorated, and an attempt was made to reach safe haven at Adak, less than 600 miles distant.

By June 10, the effort to save the vessel appeared hopeless and the captain the following day ordered abandonment in the ship's boats.

Probably no Alaska passenger liner suffered more mishaps than did the SS Northwestern. *She is seen here in just one of her many strandings, this one in Wrangell Narrows, Alaska, June 12, 1919. Built as the* Orizaba *in 1883, her rugged construction permitted her to hurt easy but heal fast. Seemingly indestructible, she became a victim of a Japanese bomb while serving as a barracks ship at Dutch Harbor during World War II. It was a direct hit and though she never went to sea again, her iron hull was still intact.* Photo courtesy of Winter & Pond.

With great difficulty they got away into the pulsating ocean. Fortunately their earlier distress signals had been received along with the correct longitude and latitude of their ship. After suffering from mild exposure they were rescued. Meanwhile, U.S. Coast Guard aircraft flew over the *Athena* and estimated that she would sink within ten hours. The following day a Coast Guard cutter searched for the derelict using both radar and sonar. On finding no trace of the vessel they assumed she had sunk. Her Greek owners, listed under the Mareduc Maritime Corp., of Monrovia, were informed, and inasmuch as the vessel was written off as a total loss, the insurance company planned to pay indemnity the following month.

But the *Athena* didn't sink. On July 10, a passing Japanese freighter reported sighting the *Athena* still afloat, partially submerged, and a major danger to navigation. She was 250 miles from her last reported position. Insurance payment was accordingly held up. The Astoria-based salvage tug *Salvage Chief* was immediately contacted by the powers to be to seek out the abandoned ship and take her in tow. On a Tuesday evening the *Salvage Chief* put out from Astoria headed for the Aleutians and hopefully a rich price of salvage money if the Greek-owned vessel could be brought in.

Fred Devine Diving & Salvage Company, owners of the *Salvage Chief*, had employed a Hercules C-130 aircraft to aid in the search for the elusive cargo ship. The plan was to tow her to Dutch Harbor where temporary repairs could be made. But first the ship must be found. In the days that followed, the plane and the tug fighting fog and inclement weather conditions covered a 400,000 square mile area but found no trace of the *Athena*. The exhausting search failed to produce any results and finally was abandoned by Devine salvage master Bob Belsher. Unlike the *Baychimo*, the *Athena* finally succumbed to the dastardly Pacific seas.

No salvage firm in the Pacific had more feathers in its cap than Fred Devine Diving & Salvage. The *Athena* case was one of the very few that failed to produce results, and that was certainly no fault of the company. Things turned out somewhat better in an earlier Alaska salvage it job of a very different nature. This one involved what had become a fixed monument of World War II.

She was the rusted 7,200 ton Japanese freighter *Nozima Maru*, bombed by American war planes while bringing in badly needed supplies for the Japanese troops that had invaded and fortified Kiska Island in the Aleutians. It was during the early years of the war. There was great concern on the part of the United States that Japan was pushing ever eastward along the Aleutian Chain.

Out of the sky, under heavy fire by the enemy, one of the U.S. bombers swooped down and scored a direct hit on the *Nozima Maru*, square in No. 2 hold, ripping out the starboard quarter of the vessel and badly damaging her bow section. The vessel sank in shallow water right opposite the shore. At low tide she sat upright as if trying to steam away. For nearly 15 years she just sat there immobile. That's when the Fred Devine Company decided to take a big gamble. They would invest more than $100,000 to refloat the vessel and tow her to Japan for scrap metal.

Many had claimed that the *Nozima Maru* was probably constructed from steel sent to Japan from Pacific Northwest ports prior to World War II. The writer recalls the huge amounts of scrap metal shipped to Japan from Seattle in the 1930s, despite protests from locals who often paraded at dockside with signs.

be made watertight, the holes patched, and water pumped out. Following that procedure the salvage vessel would then move in with heavy dredging equipment and pump sand away from under the stranded freighter.

Captain Reino Mattila, master of the *Salvage Chief*, reckoned the stranded ship would then be inched slowly away from her perch until she was freely afloat. The plan worked beautifully, and after the refloating, the salvage crew checked over all the repairs carefully making the hulk as seaworthy as possible. Then it was towed to sea stern first with help from the Canadian tug *Sudbury*. It was mid-October before they left Kiska.

Devine hoped to make the run in 21 days, but the going was rough, the *Nozima* occasionally popping a rivet. New leaks had to be sealed. The LCM *Dixie*, named for one of Devine's daughters, capsized and was lost off Adak, but the flotilla moved onward at 4.8 knots, pumps and compressors constantly in use. Broken cables reduced speed to two knots.

Only one day short of reaching the safety of the Japanese port of Hakodate, the *Nozima Maru* suddenly capsized and sank. All personnel aboard were rescued by the two tugs. The single item saved was the vessel's huge bronze propeller which had been stowed aboard the *Salvage Chief*. Though there was remorse and discouragement among

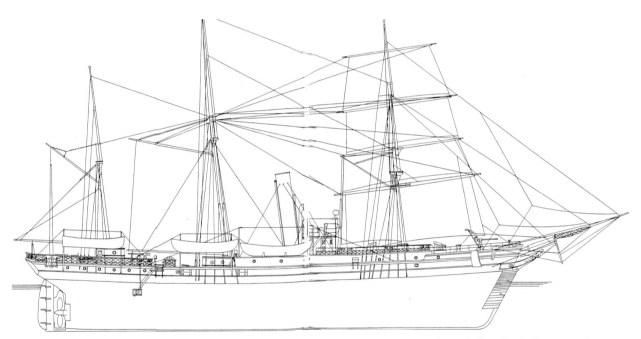

Outboard line drawing of the USRC Bear, *the law enforcer of Alaska's far north for several years both under the Revenue and Coast Guard services. The stout vessel, dating from 1874, was ice-strengthened and proved herself time and again. No government vessel played a greater more effective role in Alaska than did the* Bear.

Loaded down with salvage equipment and supplies, the *Salvage Chief* sailed on July 31, 1956, on what owner Fred Devine claimed was his biggest gamble at that period. Bristling with salvage gear on deck and below deck, the vessel sat low in the water. Some 20 truckloads of supplies had been taken aboard including 600 chickens and a variety of food supplies, not to mention the 55,000 gallons of oil pumped into the fuel tanks. Earlier, the *Chief* had installed at Swan Island in Portland a new 32 ton cargo boom designed specially for the salvage endeavor. Other equipment included a 50 foot LCM landing craft named *Dixie*, a motor lifeboat, six welding machines, a steam donkey engine, electric winches, air compressors, diesel generators, and more than five miles of cable.

The plan was to cut away the forward section of the vessel, salvage metal parts of the bow and stow them in the undamaged part of the hull as ballast for the tow to Japan. This done, the bulkheads would

the hard working salvage crew, they took the failed gamble in stride, sold the propeller to Japanese interests and used the funds for a party to drown their sorrows, following five months of dedicated labor.

Despite the regretful loss, the Devine firm continued to perfect a long series of highly successful salvage jobs throughout the Pacific, and is still active at this writing. In another rather unusual salvage job in Alaska, performed by the Devine firm, in January 1979, the purpose was to refloat a wreck and then sink her in deep water. Once again Captain Reino Mattila was in command of the *Salvage Chief*. He stated proudly, "It took six weeks to float her and four months to sink her again."

He was making reference to the retired Alaska cruise ship *Glacier Queen*, which sank in Seldovia Bay, November 9, 1978. Formerly a Royal Navy Corvette, the vessel was sold to C. B. West in 1958 for the Alaska Cruise Line. Built in Scotland in 1944, and commissioned

SS Dolphin, *one of the earliest ships annexed by the newly formed Alaska Steamship Company, was placed on the Alaska run in 1892. She is pictured aground off the Pearse Islands at an unknown date. Refloated, the vessel ended her days as a Chilean gunboat.*

by the Canadian Navy as the HMCS *Leaside*, she was used for escort duty, anti-submarine operations, and patrol work. After the war, she was converted to a 275 foot cruise ship and renamed *Coquitlam* prior to her later sale to West. Eventually replaced by larger cruise ships, the *Glacier Queen* was retired and at anchor in Seldovia Bay. Suddenly one day she sank at her mooring, and her leaking fuel tanks spread sticky oil all over the bay, endangering the fish life of the bountiful Seldovia area.

The *Salvage Chief* was finally summoned to raise the vessel and tow her oil-soaked hull to a spot where it could be disposed of in deep water. Those who had earlier purchased the vessel had done some piecemeal salvage work removing brass work and other fittings. They were undoubtedly responsible for her sinking, having removed portholes. Weight from the water entering the hull caused the ship to list and eventually fill. Down she went in 48 feet of water.

The Coast Guard's Pacific Strike Team was alerted due to the fact that the ship contained residual bunker oil that was seeping out, polluting the clam beds and salmon feeding grounds. The vessel was additionally a hazard to navigation.

It was shortly after mid-November when the *Salvage Chief* put out from the Columbia River with a crew of 20, and five professional divers. Arriving at Seldovia on November 22, the crew went to work on Thanksgiving Day. Four divers were down at a time installing 90 patches over the portholes and 200 other patches where water could seep in. The largest was 13 x 13 feet. Inasmuch as the water was frigid, it caused difficulty with the air lines freezing. When ice crystals began to form down a hose, the diver was forced to surface. Underwater work continued through the entire month of December while oil booms contained the spill. At long last, the *Glacier Queen* was sealed sufficiently that lifting her from the sea bottom could begin. As of January 9, the *Chief* began pumping out water and pumping in air. After 52 days the old cruise ship was slowly raised to the surface.

The Alaska newspapers labelled it "the most expensive ever in terms of cost per barrel recovered," referring to the cleanup of the oil mopped by a firm assisting the Devine operation. The U.S. government ordered the hull taken to deep water off Middleton Island, an area the National Marine Fisheries Service claimed was safe from adverse effects on the environment.

Several days were required to prepare the *Glacier Queen* for the tow. Meanwhile, the salvage vessel recovered the big anchors, put a towline on its charge and packed it with explosives. Due to adverse weather the tow didn't get underway until January 16. It would be the last hurrah for the ill-starred cruise ship which had been involved in two previous mishaps, one a collision in which three of her passengers were injured.

When the tow reached the vicinity of Cape St. Elias, in 2,000 fathoms (12,000 feet) Mattila put two of his men aboard the *Glacier Queen* to release the towline and then set things in order to detonate 175 pounds of shaped charges and dynamite which had a 30 minute fuse attached.

With a mighty blast, it took only four minutes to sink the 1,400 ton vessel. With a successful conclusion, the *Salvage Chief* returned to Astoria after two months away to await the next assignment. The total cost of the salvage job, disposal of the ship and oil cleanup came to $2.4 million.

It was the Coast Guard helicopters that played a major role in the rescue of the crew of the 126 foot tug *Mikimiki*. For 14 hours on January 6, 1989, the tug's crew had attempted to keep their vessel afloat in Cook Inlet. The veteran towing craft wallowed wildly in 25 foot seas and howling winds as the water was rising in her hull, the pumps unable to win the battle. Distress signals alerted the copters and even though the conditions were anything but favorable for the rescue mission, they responded.

ADI Richard Klinnert, 20 years in the Coast Guard, claimed it to be the greatest challenge he'd ever faced in a 30 minute effort to lift four men from the sinking vessel. Oscillating seas, and powerful winds that bested 70 mph on the Beaufort scale, were the menu of the day. Coast Guard whirley birds took turns trying to get the vessel in the best position to perfect the rescue. While the second copter was refueling at Homer, the tug's skipper reported that abandonment of his command was a necessity. Helicopter number one had spent precious minutes trying to hoist the four men skyward, to no avail.

A third chopper was then ordered out to assist from the Kodiak base, but the icing conditions and the murk made it difficult for the navigator ATI Daniel DeMarchis to find the *Mikimiki*. The icing had caused the navigational equipment to function improperly, giving out conflicting longitude information. Eventually DeMarchis spotted a flare from the troubled tug and then zeroed in on its location.

Steam schooner ashore near Valdez. She is the Excelsior, *the little vessel that arrived in port with gold from the Klondike ahead of the famous SS* Portland *in 1897. She was given no publicity, but the* Portland *went down in history. Built on Humboldt Bay in 1893, she was a familiar caller at Alaskan ports. She was pulled off the beach in this photo, date unknown.*

Klinnert, the flight mechanic, claimed he could only see a small portion of the tug's stern in the overcast. It was hard to tell the sky from the sea. Jockeyed about like a feather, the copter crew was finding it increasingly difficult to get the lowering basket in the proper position, sort of like trying to get a square block in a round hole. He feared the basket cable might get snagged when hitting the tug's superstructure. At times the *Mikimiki* would elevate upward to within 25 feet of the hovering aircraft and again plunge into a trough.

Nearly 20 attempts were made by Klinnert and DeMarchis before they were able to lift any of the apprehensive seamen. Several times the basket landed on the deck but had to be pulled up again before anyone could get in it. Klinnert said, "We had to have the boat just right. They couldn't let go the railings until the boat was flat. I could see them holding on, then they would dive for the basket."

The wind was blowing the basket 25 to 35 feet in a pendulum fashion and it made a dangerous situation for those trying to control it. DeMarchis even used his feet in an effort to stop the conveyance from swinging and spinning before it reached the copter.

"It was scary to see it go out of sight with a person in the basket the first time," continued Klinnert. "I was afraid he'd get slammed against the ship's rails."

When finally the four men were lifted, the helicopter was very low on fuel and set an immediate course for its Kodiak base leaving the sinking tug to the mercy of the sea. "I'm glad I don't have that kind of case every day," confessed Klinnert.

It was Coast Guard helicopters once again that performed a classic act of rescue early in January 1989. Two whirlybirds and a surface ship were required to save 54 Koreans from the wrecked 285 foot Korean Motor vessel No. Six *Chil Bo San* off Unalaska Island. It all began when the Coast Guard received a distress call that the *Chil Bo San* was dead in the water with a broken propeller shaft, drifting helplessly toward barren Unalaska Island, three miles away. The date was January 11, 1989, and to any who are familiar with the storm-plagued Aleutians in the winter time, the adverse circumstances are well understood.

A few hours after receiving the distress call, the Coast Guard already had an aircraft skyborne. By the time it arrived the Korean vessel had been driven onto the jagged rocks by strong northwesterly winds and 20 foot seas. She had lost all power and flashing hand-held lights were sending out signals in Morse Code to other fishboats in the area who in turn alerted the Coast Guard of the wreck's situation and location.

The Coast Guard radioed a broadcast for commercial aid and contacted all ports for help. A Coast Guard C-130 aircraft flew into the area to survey rescue possibilities. Findings indicated the wreck was probably beyond redemption but that the crew, if all else failed, could make an attempt to gain the rock-strewn beach. Meanwhile, the vessel was being slammed by exploding breakers and had taken a slight port list.

The following day, Coast Guard Station Kodiak dispatched two HH3F helicopters and another C-130 with relief crews for the copters, being that the locale was nearly 500 miles southwest of Kodiak Island. It required 21 hours for the C-130 flight. Meanwhile the Korean motor ship *Pung Yang Ho* was on the scene, and under difficult sea conditions sent in a lifeboat to rescue a large segment of the crew. Trying to maneuver the small craft alongside the *Chil Bo San* took some clever seamanship, and even then the motorized lifeboat broke her rudder rising on an elevator-type breaker and banging against the wreck.

Twelve men were left on the ship and the Coast Guard helicopters went to work hovering over the vessel and dropping a rescue basket to raised arms on the slanted deck. One by one the survivors were lifted to safety. The *Chil Bo San* was left to the mercy of the unkind seas. The cold but grateful dozen were flown to Dutch Harbor, and the other survivors were cared for aboard the *Pung Yang Ho*. Some 54 in all were rescued in a joint effort that was perfected under difficult circumstances without loss of life.

A letter of appreciation was sent to the Coast Guard's Admiral Nelson:

Please accept my deep appreciation for the rescue efforts the Coast Guard performed last week in saving the 54 crew members of the vessel Chil Bo San.
Thanks to the efforts and excellent training of the Coast Guard, what could have been a tragedy was avoided.
Again on behalf of the Korean government I wish to thank each and every member of the Coast Guard for their untiring rescue efforts.
Sincerely, Byung Sam Bae
acting Consul-General

It appeared that the year 1989 kept the Coast Guard on constant alert in western Alaska, especially where foreign fishing vessels were concerned. Among the series of distress calls was one from the Japanese-owned refrigerated cargo ship *Aoyagi Maru*. On this occasion the 290 foot vessel after losing power was hurled against a reef in Lost Harbor, 40 miles east of Dutch Harbor on December 10, during the transfer of frozen fish with the American fishing vessel *Bering Trader*.

There was concern for the 19 man crew and the danger of oil pollution. Diverted from her regular patrol, the Coast Guard cutter *Rush* was dispatched to the scene to rescue the crew. The assistance of a tugboat which happened to be in the vicinity was enlisted. The vessels and their crews performed admirably in plucking the survivors from the wounded ship.

Meanwhile, the *Aoyagi Maru* was written off as a total loss by its Japanese owners. That necessitated a second Coast Guard presence, this time from the Marine Safety Office in Anchorage, Marine Safety Detachment, Kodiak, and the Pacific Strike Team, in association with the Underwater Construction Company of Anchorage. Their purpose was to find the best way to dispose of the fuel oil from the ship to keep it from polluting the rich fishing and wildlife area. The team arrived February 21 and were greeted by the overpowering odor of 74,000 pounds of rotting cod that had gone bad when the refrigerated holds on the *Aoyagi Maru* no longer functioned. It was so bad that the men working in the ship's hold had to don oxygen masks and scuba dry suits.

Unalaska's mayor Paul Fuhs, part of the team, was an explosives expert and for 12 days he and the others prepared the vessel for detonation. Explosives were placed in three rows the entire length of the wreck. Then, diesel fuel was poured over the explosives. Charges were placed along the outside of the hull to counter the interior explosion and keep the hull intact. Cliff Center, project manager for underwater Construction handled that segment of the plan. The explosives were to ignite the fuel without rupturing the hull, and Lieutenant Jim Madden, on scene coordinator's representative saw to that.

At 9:30 PM on March 19, flames shot up from the bowels of the ship, followed by a muffled blast. There was no turning back for in 30 minutes, 1,200 pounds of high explosives ignited destroying what remained of 100,000 gallons of fuel in the tanks. There was a sigh of relief among the principals involved. So far so good. The experiment seemed to be a success. The proof came the next day when Coast Guard and Underwater personnel searched the area for signs of pollution. They found none.

Prior to the big blast, a representative of the U.S. Fish & Wildlife Service had been sent to Lost Harbor to clear the area of sea birds and other wildlife. Later inspection showed no dead or injured creatures. It was termed a perfect blast, the eleventh ship dynamited by Fuhs in his career.

On April 3, the Coast Guard team attempted to board the shattered vessel but was unable to do so because it was still red hot and smoldering. Later on, peering through holes in the hull there appeared no fuel remaining. It presented quite a contrast seeing the bloated wreck sitting on its Lost Harbor perch, bow into the snow-covered rocky ramparts of the island.

But the story did not end here, for Underwater Construction's two work boats *Krystal Sea* and *Bettye K.* were diverted to the side of the Japanese freezer ship MS *Swallow*, wrecked at Ulatka Head while awaiting a pilot to guide her into Dutch Harbor, February 27, 1989. Her cargo of rotting crab and leaking fuel needed emergency attention.

In wartime colors, the SS David W. Branch, *long in the service of Libby McNeill & Libby, is pictured aground in Alaskan waters during the war years while serving as a transport vessel. She was salvaged and repaired. After the war she was sold to Greeks and renamed* Luxor, *then to the Israelis, renamed* Negbah *as an emigration ship.*

Absorbent snares were placed on each side of the 280 foot vessel and containment booms placed to keep the oil from spreading. The stinking crab was transferred to the *Krystal Sea*, after being separated from containers, and then dumped into the sea in 300 feet of water, two miles from the wrecksite. Though much of the oil had escaped from the ruptured hull, cleanup crews recovered more than 3,000 pounds of the oily debris from both the water and the beaches.

Fuel transfer operations were completed on April 6. Twelve pumps, including two from the Coast Guard Strike Team were utilized to complete the job. So thick was the gooey stuff that heaters placed on the deck of the *Swallow* had little effect in cutting its constituency. While Unalaska mayor Paul Fuhs conferred with the Japanese consul and the owner's insurance company at Anchorage over deposition of the wreck, Lieutenant Matt Carr of the Marine Safety Office at Anchorage termed the *Swallow* incident as "the case of the doomed crab cargo."

The ironic part of the whole story was that earlier the American registered 324 foot crab processing vessel *Yardarm Knot* was laden with a $2.5 million cargo of Alaska snow crab bound for Japan when she was wrecked February 20, on a reef off St. Paul Island. In an effort to save the cargo, the *Swallow* had been diverted to the scene to offload the crab into her reefer compartments. Then, only seven days later the *Swallow* drifted bow first onto the beach at Ulatka Head as previously mentioned. Thus the valuable cargo was then re-loaded on the *Krystal Sea*, taken to deep water and dumped; $2.5 million down the drain.

Meanwhile, attempts to free the *Swallow* failed, and owners Hidaka Kaiun Company Ltd. of Japan wrote her off as a total loss. The 19 man crew had been safely removed earlier. Lt. Cmdr. Bill Hutmacher, the on-scene coordinator's representative from the Anchorage Marine Safety Office, earlier pointed out that the displaced crab had to be removed before it completely thawed as it could have released a toxic gas and posed a health danger.

In the interim, a C-130 Coast Guard plane brought in 2,000 feet of inflatable containment boom. Ten of the ship's 11 fuel tanks had been punctured. Nearly 89,000 gallons of No. 6 fuel and 30,000 gallons of diesel presented a dangerous potential to Dutch Harbor's four $1 million a day fish and crab processing facilities, in addition to the area's wildlife.

As in previous oil spill jobs, the Coast Guard worked in harmony with Underwater Construction employees, and the sticky mess was throttled in time to prevent major damage.

At this stage the reader might ask how there could be so much maritime fishing activity in such an isolated area as north and south of the Aleutians? Despite the often cantankerous seas and stormy weather, plus the sparse population and barren islands, what is probably the richest fishing grounds in the world exists there. Ships of many nations work its waters during the better season of the year and are willing to invest heavily due to good profits. It has been said that during the good months there is more population at sea than on land. The great distances between islands present a formidable challenge for the Coast Guard in responding to the many distress calls and other emergencies that are so frequent as can be seen from the episodes mentioned here during the 1989 season alone.

Oil escapement endangering the environmental qualities of Alaska has become a major headache for the Coast Guard, but each case has to be addressed with prompt response. On November 15, 1989, the 485 foot Greek motor ship *Milos Reefer* ran aground and impaled herself on a huge rock off forlorn St. Matthew Island. The ship's captain aware of his exposed position which offered little hope of salvage abandoned the vessel, he and his 27 man crew taking to the lifeboats. They were rescued a day later by a Polish processing vessel.

The ill-fated refrigerated cargo ship was mostly in ballast being readied to accept a cargo of fish from processing vessels when the stranding occurred. Some 237,343 gallons of fuel were on board, some of which had escaped, despite the ship's double bottom. Isolation, heavy seas, and powerful winds prevented any immediate chance of the Coast Guard removing fuel and lube oil. The temperature was in the low 20s and the wind blowing hard. The surf was unusually high.

Captain Richard Asaro, C.O. from the Anchorage Marine Safety Office, was the on-scene coordinator on the *Milos Reefer* cleanup. It was a challenge, as the wreck lay in an isolated position 400 miles southwest of Nome in the Bering Sea. Coast Guard vessels such as the 378 foot cutter *Midgett* was diverted to Kodiak to bring authorities, including Coast Guard personnel and a representative of the ship's owner to the wreck. The buoy tender *Firebush*, out of Kodiak, was loaded with 37 tons of cleanup equipment and sent to the isle.

A few boardings were made on the *Milos Reefer* to survey damage and check on the spilled oil. Much of the time boardings were impossible. A diver, J. Whitekettle, was contracted to survey the underwater damage and barely escaped with his life. While underneath the ship, surf and currents caused her to roll pinning him down. Emergency measures were taken fearing the worst. Five minutes later the vessel rolled back to its former position and the diver was able to extricate himself. A Coast Guardsman was also slightly injured during boat operations.

The executive officer of the Anchorage Marine Safety Office, Commander William Morani, Jr., gave a ghostly appraisal of the wreck. He said: "The *Milos Reefer* was like a ghost ship—no power, complete darkness, food still on the crewmen's plates in the galley, luggage lined up along the passageways in the deck house." The team found a note on the messdeck chalkboard that read, "Tues. (God Is Love) 11-14-89."

It was decided by the end of November that due to increasingly dangerous conditions that further removal of fuel would have to wait until the following spring. The decision left the fishing industry and environmentalists most unhappy. The *Firebush* had earlier been forced to change her anchorage from a sheltered location when the sea kicked up billows that caused her to roll 30 to 40 degrees. There were traces of oil on the beach and amid chunks of ice and snow. A beach report, however, showed only four oil-tainted dead birds and a lifeless walrus.

Fortunately the wreck weathered the bitter winter months. It was decided that the constant danger of major pollution would eventually occur unless immediate steps were taken. Thus it was that the Fred Devine Diving and Salvage team was hired to drain the ship of all remaining fuel. In late spring of 1990, the *Salvage Chief* was underway with a crew of 24. On reaching the wreck, the crew boarded the rusting ship and found that everything moveable had been stripped,

Down by the bow in Naket Inlet, the steam schooner Despatch stuck her nose into a place to be avoided in 1916. Refloated and repaired, she later became Pacific Steamship Company's Admiral Rodman. In this photo she was owned by the Border Line Transportation Company, and was typical of a large fleet of wooden steam schooners originally built for coastwise trade. She dated from 1899.

Pacific American Fisheries cannery steamer Pavlov was wrecked at Tugudak, Alaska, on February 17, 1916.

Barge Washington wrecked near the locale of the Cape St. Elias Lighthouse, October 10, 1915. She was one of a fleet of barges of the Alaska Barge Line of Tacoma which hauled coal, lumber, shingles, and piling to Alaska and returned with cement and general cargo. Note the timbers on deck.

Barge St. David broke loose from the tug Daniel Kern, and was wrecked on the beach near Yakutat in the fall of 1917. The St. David was formerly a full-rigged Downeast sailing vessel of the Flint fleet and later the California Shipping Company. Later yet she was cut down to a barge.

She beat the odds. The popular Alaska liner SS City of Seattle ran aground in Tongass Narrows, near Ketchikan, Alaska, on August 13, 1913, but was shortly after refloated. One of the liners that gained fame during the gold rush years, she earned the title of "Alaska Lightning Express" for her fast runs to the northland. In 1921, she was sold by Pacific Steamship Company to the Miami Steamship Company and finished out a successful career on the east coast.

evidently by daring individuals that had boarded her in the interim. The main purpose for the Devine crew was not salvage but removal of the oil. The project was undertaken in conjunction with London Offshore Consultants of Houston, Texas.

Divers from the *Salvage Chief* first entered the water-filled cargo tanks to gain access to the double bottom fuel tanks, then constructed cofferdams to pump the fuel out and transfer it to a supply ship. Custom designed steam heating equipment was used to ease the flow of the oil in the 35 degree water. An estimated 139,000 gallons of bunker fuel oil was removed in the 30 day operation. The danger of major contamination was over, and the miserable wreck was left in solitude for the rust and weather to do its dastardly deed of final destruction while the seabirds whitened her decks with their droppings.

Immediately after the *Milos Reefer* job, the *Salvage Chief* proceeded to Port Lions on Kodiak Island to refloat the sunken 180 foot fish processing vessel *Smokwa Shell* which was leaking oil. Damaged beyond feasible repair, the wreck, after being raised, was towed to the 1000 fathom curve and promptly scuttled.

There is always a risk for Coast Guard helicopter crews in that isolated part of Alaska. In 1990, one of the HH-3Fs had just concluded the rescue of six commercial fishermen from the American fishing vessel *American Star* which ran aground on Otter Island, south of St. Paul Island. The survivors were each lifted to the aircraft, when a call was received from the Korean fishing vessel *Cheong Yang Ho* to rescue a crew member who had suffered a crushed hip. The vessel was only a short distance by air. As copter pilot Dave Gunderson and his crew flew over the 300 foot Korean ship, she was pitching and rolling in near 20 foot seas. It presented a difficult challenge to hoist the man, according to Gunderson:

"It had two A-frames and a whole bunch of cables, so we couldn't hoist from the back. Then in the middle, by the wheel house, it had all antennas and the radar and we couldn't lift from there. The bow was clear accept for a flagpole stanchion in front."

Contact was made with the vessel to give the skipper steering instructions to assist the lift. "The boat was going the wrong way for the wind, without having to back up, so we told it to stop and it came dead in the water," Gunderson recalled.

The helo moved downward and dropped a trail line to a man waiting on deck. When the seaman grabbed the trail line, the pilot backed off, and crewmen Amatruda lowered the litter to the deck.

"We moved in. I was hoisting from about 100 feet. I had a good view of the boat, but I was so high I couldn't see where the patient was being treated," said Gunderson.

The injured man had been carried on deck and placed in the litter, but as the helicopter moved forward into hoisting position the trouble began. Somehow the cable got wrapped around a stanchion but was eventually cleared. Moving in a little closer, once again the cable wrapped around the stanchion. As the vessel pitched downward there was insufficient slack on the cable. The hoist was put down, but the boat plunged faster than the mechanical hoist could reel out the cable. It suddenly snapped like a rubber band and went up into the rotor system. Amatruda and Torgerson were in the side door, and for a moment it appeared the helo was in danger of crashing. Quick reaction from the flight crew, including co-pilot Bill Ryka and pilot Gunderson saved the machine.

A new cable had to be rigged and the rescue operation repeated. There were some mighty frightened individuals both on the helicopter and on the ship where the suffering man wondered if he'd ever be lifted skyward. With frantic effort on behalf of all involved, the caper finally proved successful and the chopper headed for base. They say it's all in a days work, but before the year 1990 had ended the Coast Guard found two bodies in the Gulf of Alaska after the tug *Stedfast* sank off Kayak Island, 60 miles S. E. Of Cordova, September 23.

The buoy tender *Ironwood* rescued eight crew members from the tug *Sea King* after the vessel suffered an engine room fire, 200 miles west of Dillingham in the Bering Sea, October 16. The following day, the *Ironwood's* crew rescued four crewmen from the sinking tug *Tiny* which had been dispatched to tow the *Sea King's* barge filled with 4.2 million gallons of petroleum products, destined for Nome. While at-

tempting to rig the tow, the *Tiny* (a Crowley tug), collided with the barge and went down. Another Crowley tug was sent to lasso the barge, and the *Ironwood* took the burned *Sea King* in tow for Dutch Harbor.

The buoy tender *Sweetbrier*, despite 70 knot winds and heavy seas, managed to take the broken down 172 foot processing ship *Alaskan Command* in tow on November 19, and turn her over to a towing craft two miles out of Seward. And on and on it goes, not only with search and rescue, but with constant seizure of vessels illegally fishing in Alaskan waters such as the Korean fish processor *Kyung Yang Ho* and *Gae Cheong Ho* which paid $305,000 in seizure costs to the United States. They were fishing in disputed waters of the Bering Sea. Both were released after the fine was paid.

THE MAJOR ROLE PLAYED BY THE 17TH COAST GUARD DISTRICT

The Seventeenth Coast Guard District encompasses the entire state of Alaska and 33,000 miles of coastline. Coast Guard forces are responsible for search and rescue over 3,853,500 square miles of water; more square miles than the continental United States covers. As the nation's smallest armed military service, the Coast Guard performs its missions in Alaska with slightly over 2,000 military and civilian members located at 39 units.

Their major responsibilities in Alaska include: search and rescue (SAR), maritime law enforcement, aids to navigation, military readiness, and marine safety. Alaska is home to two medium endurance cutters, seven buoy tenders, and five patrol boats.

There are Coast Guard air stations in Kodiak and Sitka. Kodiak houses four HH-60J helicopters, four HH-65A helicopters and six C-130 aircraft. Sitka houses three HH-60J helicopters. In the summer months, both Kodiak and Sitka supply helicopters and crew to an Aviation Support Facility in Cordova to provide search and rescue services in Prince William Sound and the northern Gulf of Alaska.

SAR and law enforcement remain the bread and butter missions of the Coast Guard in Alaska. Although helicopters and patrol boats respond to the majority of the SAR cases, any unit can be dispatched to these missions. Because of their long-range capabilities, C-130s are often launched to locate people in distress. The aircraft can drop life rafts, food, fresh water, communications gear, pumps, or other supplies to vessels or aircraft in trouble. The majority of the Coast Guard's law enforcement role in Alaska is enforcing the 200-mile Exclusive Economic Zone. Most of the fish caught in the zone are sold to foreign countries. The Coast Guard's law enforcement responsibilities extend over more than 950,000 square miles of sea. All vessels and aircraft in the district are used for fisheries patrols. In addition, medium and high endurance cutters from the West Coast and Hawaii assist in patrol efforts.

There are about 1,200 aids to navigation throughout Alaska. These include buoys and 12 lighthouses that are maintained by buoy tenders and an aids to navigation team. The buoy tenders include one 65-foot tender and six 180-foot tenders. These vessels are based around the Gulf of Alaska at Kodiak, Homer, Seward, Cordova, Sitka, Petersburg, and Ketchikan.

The Coast Guard's aids to navigation program also includes Loran C stations which provide long-range navigational radio signals to vessels and aircraft for position plotting purposes.

Alaska's worst shipwreck from the number of lives lost (*Princess Sophia*) has been reviewed in this book. Though it was both tragic and regretful, especially with not one survivor, it doesn't compare to the world's most regrettable ship disasters during this century, according to the Guinness Book of World Records.

History's worst marine disaster in war or peace occurred January 30, 1945, a little more than three months before the end of World War II in Europe. A Soviet submarine torpedoed the 25,000 ton German passenger ship *Wilhelm Gustoff*, loaded with refugees off Danzig,

Germany (now Gdansk, Poland). Some 7,700 persons lost their lives.

Other records this century where more than a thousand lives were lost:

February 26, 1916 - French cruiser *Provence* sank in the Mediterranean. Death toll, 3,100.

December 6, 1917 - French munitions ship *Mont Blanc* and Belgian steamer *Imo* collided at Halifax, Nova Scotia. Death toll, 1,600.

April 14-15, 1912 - British liner *Titanic* went down after striking an iceberg. Death toll 1,503.

May 7, 1915 - British liner *Lusitania* torpedoed by a German submarine off Ireland. Death toll 1,198.

December 26, 1954 - Japanese ferry *Toya Maru* sank in Tsugaru Strait, Japan. Death toll, 1,172.

December 3, 1948 - Chinese refugee ship *Kiangya* wrecked south of Shanghai. Death toll, 1,100.

The king of all salvage vessels in the Pacific is the *Salvage Chief* which we have already been introduced to. She and her crew have been involved with about 100 ship salvage jobs and with only a few exceptions most have been successful. Though the vessel has ranged far and wide, it is of interest here to mention a few more of her Alaska episodes.

In March and April of 1971, we find the 180 foot crab processing and freezer vessel *Theresa Lee* hard aground on outer Iliaski Island, Alaska. She plowed onto the outer barrier at full speed, laden with a cargo of frozen crab valued at half a million dollars.

As usual, the *Salvage Chief* got the call. A salvage master and diver were dispatched to the scene to evaluate the situation. The company agreed to undertake the operation on a no-pay no-cure contract. The *Chief* sailed out of Astoria and performed a yeoman job of not only refloating the *Theresa Lee* but saving the cargo. The vessel was towed back to Seattle and repaired.

Among the numerous large barges refloated by the Devine team in Alaska was the cargo barge *414*, severely damaged by ice. She sank north of Wainright in the Chukchi Sea. The barge was loaded with base camp and other equipment for Atlantic-Richfield, at Prudoe Bay. It was October 1975, after extensive diving operations that the barge was raised, pumped out, and towed to Escholtz Bay where the cargo was transferred to another barge, and the *414* towed back to Portland, held up by air. She was repaired and returned to service.

In December 1977, the *Salvage Chief* and her crew saved two barges near Cold Bay, Alaska. The barge *Norton Sound* was blown ashore inside a lagoon too shallow for the *Chief* to enter. It lay behind a sand bar, so kedging anchors and a helicopter had to be utilized. The salvage crew using a winch drum on one of the on-board cranes winched the barge out from the sand bar so a towline could be made fast to the salvage tug. The Bell 212 helicopter flew a total of 7,900 feet of messenger line to the barge and a similar amount of ten-inch nylon and 1 3/4 inch wire cable to make the connection. The *Norton Sound* was then winched to safe waters and saved.

Meanwhile, the deck cargo barge *Galena* was blown high and dry on Operl Island. Utilizing the full strength of her winching power, the *Salvage Chief* pulled her free after some sand was excavated around the hull using a dragline bucket and a crane aboard the *Galena*.

One of the saddest incidents involving the Devine firm was going to Dixon Entrance in December 1979 to take in tow the capsized iron ore carrier *Lee Wang Zin*. In a winter storm, the ship had flipped over, drowning her entire crew, with the ship floating upside down and leaving a trail of leaking oil. The *Salvage Chief* was called to take the derelict in tow. A helicopter put men on the hulk and they proceeded to cut clover leaf pattern holes in the bulbous bow so chain bridles could be locked in place. The vessel was then towed to deep water where she went to Davy Jones' Locker without further contaminating the waters.

In November of 1980, the *Salvage Chief* set some kind of a record by refloating the container barge *Tazlina*, aground near Cape Yakataga, in only two hours. She had earlier broken loose from her tug and was at first feared a total loss.

Left three photos: *Claimed as one of the most dramatic shipwrecks in Alaskan waters, the Canadian Pacific steamer* Princess May *had her stupendous pose in news sheets around the world when she ran aground August 5, 1910. She was southbound from Skagway under Captain McLeod with 100 passengers and 68 crew and officers, when fog closed down in Lynn Canal. Striking the barrier at high tide she sat up on a 23 degree angle on the ebb. A major salvage effort eventually freed the vessel and tugs ushered her off for bottom repairs. The American salvage steamer* Santa Cruz *and the Canadian counterpart* William Jolliffe *were utilized to free the* Princess May. *The survivors were temporarily cared for at the nearby Sentinel Island Light Station.* Upper photo courtesy of O.T. Frasch; lower photos courtesy of Winter & Pond.

The drama of Alaska's maritime chapters keep unfolding with each year. From the majesty of the great cruiseliners to the commercial fishing vessels the constant marine parade continues unabated.

The breaking waves dashed high
On a stern and rockbound coast,
And the woods against the sky,
Their giant branches toss'd.
—*Felicia Hemans*

"Would'st thou,"—so the helmsman answered,
"Learn the secret of the sea?
Only those who brave its dangers
comprehend its mystery!"
—*Henry Wadsworth Longfellow*

Though Alaska's sealanes are far safer than a few decades back, the dramatic horror of ship disaster continues. In our day perhaps the most endangered species are those sophisticated fishing vessels in Alaska that work the often frigid and ill-tempered waters of the Gulf and Bering Sea. Splendid fish factory vessels such as Pan-Pac's *Acona* and also the *Alaska Monarch* which went down in deep, dark waters in the early 1990s are prime examples. Despite every possible precaution, Mother Nature sometimes has the final word, which is why human vigilance must continue with a capital V.

And a word for supply barges and tugs which often operate under adverse conditions in angry seas such as those that long equipped the DEW Line operation in the far north. Losses are often unavoidable in other sectors of Alaska. For instance, in October of 1974, 70 miles south of Sitka, the 486 foot barge *Kenai* broke loose from the tug *Arapahoe*. The $10 million barge went down in deep water with 13,800 tons of anhydrous ammonia and urea valued at more than $2.5 million. The cargo was bound for Pasco, Washington farmers. Owned by Collier Carbon and Chemical Company, the *Kenai* was southbound on one of her fortnightly delivery missions when she foundered. Such losses are not uncommon, but are massive headaches for marine insurance companies as well as for owners and customers.

Above and right: *The steam schooner* Thomas L. Wand *got out of the sea channel in the fog and took up residence on the beach near Ketchikan on May 10, 1914. She was later freed without major damage and was finally totally wrecked south of Point Sur, California, on September 16, 1922.*

Two dramatic photos of the stalwart Alaska Steamship Company's SS Alaska aground on Elliott Island, B.C. Placed in service in 1925, she was a twin-screw, double-bottom vessel with collision bulkheads and automatic watertight doors. Thus she was able to survive her several strandings along the Inside Passage during her successful chronicle. She was built at the Todd yard in Tacoma expressly for the Alaska service. Yes, she survived the stranding as shown. Photos courtesy of Schallerers.

Far left, left and above: *Still in her wartime suit of gray, the popular SS* North Sea *of the Northland Transportation Company, southbound from southeastern Alaska, ran aground on a pinnacle rock near Bella Bella, B.C., on February 13, 1947. In command of Captain Charles Graham, she had aboard 150 passengers and crew who were all safely evacuated. Some of the crew remained aboard in the hopes of saving the vessel. The Canadian Salvage Company was called in, but they too failed to budge the ship. The cargo of canned salmon and general freight was removed and loose gear retrieved, but a later storm broke the vessel's back and she was left to die, some of her remains still visible at this writing. The* North Sea *was built in 1918, and bore the aliases* Plainfield, Mary Weems, *and* Admiral Peoples, *before being purchased by Northland Transportation.* Joe Williamson photos.

Left and below: *SS* Northern Voyager *aground near Juneau, Alaska, on July 15, 1946. She suffered minor damage despite being high and dry at low tide. Note the persons on the dry sand beach. The* Northern Voyager *was a unit of the Alaska Transportation Company.* Photos courtesy of Winter & Pond.

A scene of gloom, the veteran bark Colorado, *dating from 1864, sailed under canvas until 1898 when her tired hull was converted to a barge for Alaskan service. Two years later she broke loose from her towing vessel and went aground in Wrangell Narrows where her timbers were left to rot.*

Hopelessly aground on the outer fringes of lonely St. Matthew Island in Alaska, the Greek MV Milos Reefer *turns red with rust and snow whitens her hatches and decks. She was wrecked November 15, 1989, but the crew escaped.*

Alaska sternwheeler Northwestern, typical of many river steamers that served the Great Land's river system. She rests after sinking to the bottom of the Kuskokwim River near Bethel, Alaska, in the 1950 era. She was built at Portland, Oregon, in 1912 as the Grahamona.

From war vessel to freighter to luxury super yacht, the SS Oaxaca *ended her days on Burnt Island in Wrangell Narrows after her 30 pampered passengers were removed from the "fun ship" by the crew of the lighthouse tender* Fern *in the mid-1930s. Owned by a Hancock Oil executive, the vessel had somewhat of an unsavory past (see story in text).*

A nature-made drydock was the cradle of the SS Farallon *hard aground near Fort Wrangell on July 23, 1899. Salvaged, her troubled career continued, finally ending at Iliamna, Alaska, on January 5, 1910, when en route from Valdez to Dutch Harbor in command of Captain J.C. Hunter.*

Above, left and below: *Three ex-commercial sailing vessels that served their days in Alaska as cargo barges. Top, the* James Charger *was bound for Tacoma with 2,000 tons of Alaska gypsum when she parted from the tug* Tatoosh *and wrecked at Dall Patch Shoal on October 22, 1914. Center, the barge* James Drummond, *built as a four-masted schooner, was wrecked on Mary Island, Alaska, but was later refloated and during World War I changed back to a schooner. Bottom, the former square-rigger* Bangor, *dating from 1874, broke free from the tug* Tyee, *and in that October 1909 gale was swept ashore in Karta Bay, Alaska.*

The remains of the passenger liner Ohio as seen in 1947. She was wrecked in Heikish Narrows, August 24, 1909, a heavy loss for her owners. Her hull was valued at $175,000, cargo at $150,000. Joe Williamson photos.

The passenger liner SS Admiral Rogers of the Pacific Steamship Company aground while cruising the Inside Passage. She was the former SS Spokane, which after an overhaul in the early 1920s emerged as the Admiral Rogers. This photo shows just one of several minor strandings of the vessel during her career. She survived them all. The usual calm waters of the Inside Passage during the better months of the year made salvage a lucrative and profitable business.

Candidate for service in British Columbia and southeastern Alaska waterways, the Prince Albert was an early addition to the Grand Trunk Pacific fleet which later became Canadian National. She was first to claim the "Prince" moniker. Built at Hull, England, in 1892 as the Bruno, she is seen here wrecked on Butterworth Rocks in B.C. waters in 1914. Seriously damaged, she was later refloated, became a rumrunner, and ended her days as a large tug.

Amazingly, she lived after assuming this ungainly position. The SS Princess May cradled on Sentinel Reef, Alaska, in August of 1910. Her running mate, the SS Princess Sophia, had a similar experience on Vanderbilt Reef, just a few miles distant, eight years later. She, however, slipped off the reef and foundered with her entire company of 343 souls.

Above right, right and below: Three of the strandings suffered by the SS Northwestern of Alaska Steamship Company during her heyday. She held the record for the most strandings of any of the liners in the Alaska trade, but survived each incident. Upper photo shows her aground near Valdez. In the lower left picture, she's high and dry at Eagle River, and in the lower right, she became like a fish out of water in Wrangell Narrows, June 1, 1919.

The Japanese MV Aoyagi Maru, *a refrigerated cargo ship, is pictured in December 1988, at Lost Harbor, Alaska. Her crew was rescued by the U.S. Coast Guard cutter* Rush. *The Coast Guard contacted Paul Fuhs to detonate the remaining fuel to prevent pollution from the wreck. The vessel was wrecked 40 miles east of Dutch Harbor on December 10 with 74,000 pounds of fish in her reefer holds. When striking the reef her electrical system failed and the stinking fish could be smelled for miles downwind. The dynamited and burned vessel is pictured here on March 19 (see story in text).*
Photo courtesy of Coast Guard's Ed Moreth.

Too hot for roasting marshmallows. The Japanese reefer vessel glows in the night air burning furiously when the fuel on board the Aoyagi Maru was detonated to prevent spillage and contamination near Dutch Harbor after her stranding. Photo courtesy of Ed Moreth, USCG.

The three-stacked, trim passenger liner Prince George burns furiously in the bay at Ketchikan, Alaska, in 1945. Photo courtesy of Schallerer's Photo Shop.

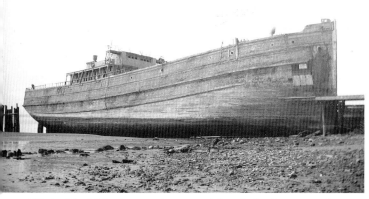

Wreck of the SS Bering, seen here grounded on the beach as a type of breakwater in Seattle-Ballard area. She was towed back to Seattle after being wrecked in southeastern Alaskan waters in 1942 shortly after America declared war on Japan. The wooden-hulled vessel was built on Humboldt Bay in 1918 as the Annette Rolph. She later became the Arthur J. Baldwin, operating between Puget Sound, the Bering Sea, and the Arctic for the Arctic Transport Company. (Lomen Commercial Company). She joined the Alaska Steamship Company as the Bering in 1936. When she was wrecked in Alaska operating for the War Shipping Administration by company agreement, Alaska Steam was reimbursed $100,000 for the vessel's loss. She was condemned after reaching Seattle, and purchased by the Tregoning Boat Company.

Opposite page, left: Coast Guard workers clean oil from their clothing after working aboard the Japanese MV Swallow, hard aground near Dutch Harbor. She was wrecked on February 27, 1989, and threatened the area with pollution. Photo courtesy of Chris Haley, USCG.

Opposite page, right: A Coast Guardsman checks the site of the grounded Japanese reefer vessel Swallow in February 1989. He appears like a midget alongside the bulbous bow of the stricken vessel. Before all cleanup work began, the Swallow's crew were safely evacuated, but the vessel was a loss. Photo courtesy of Ed Moreth, USCG.

An inglorious ending to a one-time popular passenger liner. She began her days as a trans-Atlantic liner and came out west for the gold rush days. The SS Ohio began her Alaska run under the Empire Line and then was owned by the White Star Line. She was almost lost in the Bering Sea bound for St. Michael from Nome when ice seriously damaged her hull in 1907. Two years later she was totally wrecked in Heikish Straits, Alaska, her remains sticking like glue for years thereafter. Photo taken by the late Joe Williamson in the 1950s.

Double shipwreck. This photo, copied from a long classified U.S. Navy photo, shows an aerial picture of the ill-fated Russian cargo vessel broken in two off Seal Cape, Alaska. She is the Turksib, *which was driven aground in adverse weather in 1943, laden with war cargo for Russia. To her assistance came the USS* Rescuer, *a salvage vessel, which was also driven aground. Both vessels were total losses (see dramatic story in the text).*

Teamwork both on air and sea. Out of Seward, Alaska, a Coast Guard 110 foot patrol boat and an HH type helicopter stand ready for action. Photo courtesy of U.S. Coast Guard.

Guarding the Alaskan Coast

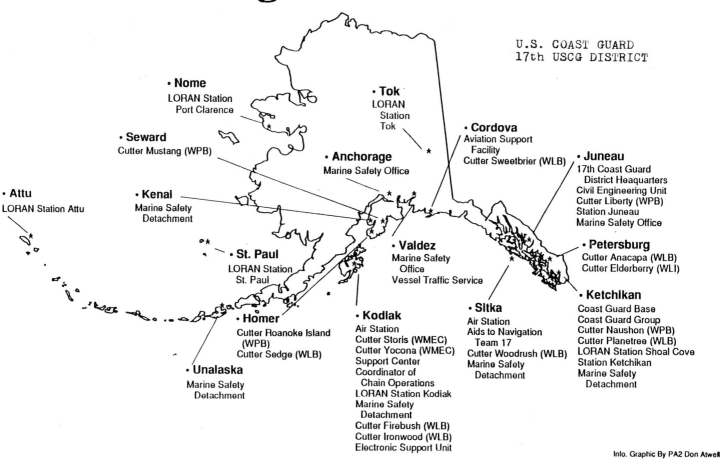

U.S. COAST GUARD
17th USCG DISTRICT

• Nome
LORAN Station
Port Clarence

• Tok
LORAN
Station
Tok

• Cordova
Aviation Support
Facility
Cutter Sweetbrier (WLB)

• Juneau
17th Coast Guard
District Heaquarters
Civil Engineering Unit
Cutter Liberty (WPB)
Station Juneau
Marine Safety Office

• Seward
Cutter Mustang (WPB)

• Anchorage
Marine Safety Office

• Attu
LORAN Station Attu

• Kenai
Marine Safety
Detachment

• Petersburg
Cutter Anacapa (WLB)
Cutter Elderberry (WLI)

• St. Paul
LORAN Station
St. Paul

• Valdez
Marine Safety
Office
Vessel Traffic Service

• Ketchikan
Coast Guard Base
Coast Guard Group
Cutter Naushon (WPB)
Cutter Planetree (WLB)
LORAN Station Shoal Cove
Station Ketchikan
Marine Safety
Detachment

• Homer
Cutter Roanoke Island
(WPB)
Cutter Sedge (WLB)

• Kodiak
Air Station
Cutter Storis (WMEC)
Cutter Yocona (WMEC)
Support Center
Coordinator of
Chain Operations
LORAN Station Kodiak
Marine Safety
Detachment
Cutter Firebush (WLB)
Cutter Ironwood (WLB)
Electronic Support Unit

• Sitka
Air Station
Aids to Navigation
Team 17
Cutter Woodrush (WLB)
Marine Safety
Detachment

• Unalaska
Marine Safety
Detachment

Info. Graphic By PA2 Don Atwell

Headquartered at Juneau, the 17th Coast Guard District has an immense responsibility overseeing the vast waterways of the 49th state.

One of the more dramatic rescue operations by the U.S. Coast Guard in Alaskan waters involved the King crabber Alaskan Monarch in the icy Bering Sea in the winter of 1990. The 96 foot vessel on her way to St. Paul Island to offload 100,000 pounds of crab entered a two-mile long field of crushed ice, 1,000 feet offshore. The ice snapped off the vessel's rudder and transducer and left her helpless. A Kodiak-based Coast Guard helicopter and the cutter Storis responded to the distress call. The copter managed to pluck four crewmen from the ill-fated vessel before a wall of ice and water washed the remaining two into the frigid waters where it appeared they would perish. Quick action by the helicopter managed to pluck them free, after the captain had been pinned under a block of ice. All hands were taken immediately to the St. Paul clinic, none with serious injuries. The badly holed Alaskan Monarch belched up her entire 7,125 gallons of fuel and was carried in the icefloe against the rocky outcrops of the island, a total loss on that dismal day in March 1990. Photo courtesy of 17th Coast Guard District.

Breakers pound the grounded Japanese reefer vessel MV
Swallow off snow-smattered Ulatka Head, Dutch Harbor,
Alaska, on February 27, 1989. The vessel was wrecked
while waiting for a pilot to take her into the harbor. The
crew of 19 were rescued, but the cargo of $2.5 million
worth of crab was lost. Ironically, the Swallow had earlier
taken on the crab cargo from the American processing vessel
Yardarm Knot which had been wrecked off St. Paul
Island, February 20. Photo courtesy of Coast Guard,
PA2 Chris Maley.

Like a wounded whale, the SS City of Seattle sits high
and dry as seen in these four pictures, as of August 13,
1912, near Ketchikan, Alaska. She was one of the lucky
ones that was eventually refloated.

Epilogue

To say the least, the citizens of Alaska have three basic qualities. They are tough, resourceful, and friendly. Not everybody would prefer the contrasting life of the northland, but those who have chosen that way of life are strong individualists and consider their native, or adopted homeland, as the case may be, the greatest place to live in the world.

Sometimes those hardy ones take a licking, but as the old watch commercial says, they always come back ticking, and usually kicking.

A massive land with a relatively sparse population, there are probably no pranks of nature that have failed to strike Alaska at one time or another. Even as this book is written, the Great Land was struck by two massive quakes registering more than seven on the Richter scale, and two devastating fires. Only a modicum of publicity told of the earthquakes beneath the surface off Adak Island. Though a tsunami warning was issued, the isolated area had only minor waves generated, and no center of population was near the epicenter. Alaskans take such quakes as a fact of life, for they are frequent.

The Big Lake fire, 60 miles north of Anchorage in June of 1996, destroyed about 350 homes and buildings and blackened 37,000 acres, computed into 56 square miles of valued forest land. About 1,000 people were driven from their homes as the flames sent billows of black smoke skyward. For days, local firemen and reinforcement fire fighters from the lower 48 states fought the blaze on land and from the air. In the interim, a second conflagration erupted on the Kenai Peninsula devouring another 23,000 acres of forest and brushland.

The fires were believed to be the work of arsonists who chose a time of a long lasting drought period to do their dastardly deed. Does such devastation daunt the spirit of Alaskans? By no means! For instance, Martin Buser, two-time winner of the Iditarod Trail sled dog race, whose home was at Big Lake, ferried as many as 80 dogs to the safety of an island in the middle of the lake, after which he returned to his mainland home to beat back the flames licking at his edifice. Most of the homes around him were destroyed but Buser stood fast suffering from the intense heat and ash. With axe, shovel, and hose he won his epic battle with fire just like winning the 1,000 mile dog sled races—a true Alaskan sourdough of modern times.

As the fire burned on, 74 inmates of the Point McKenzie minimum security work farm were evacuated. Meanwhile, Alaska Railroad trains southbound from Fairbanks had to be halted as flames leaped up to the railbed from the black spruce and brush forests.

What goes around comes around as the old saying goes; so it is with Alaska. As oil is constantly being pumped from the North Slope, new gold areas have once again come to light. Only recently the low-key gold production in the state underwent a remarkable change, bringing back memories of the rip-roaring gold stampede of 1897-98.

Gold miners have always been as much a part of Alaska as husky

The author's father, James A. Gibbs, lived among the gold fields of northern Alaska in the early part of the century. At the age of 12 he was delivering newspapers to the miners via dog sled.

dogs and bush pilots, but now gold is being extracted by the sophisticated equipment developed at this stage in history. The Fort Knox Gold Mine, the largest project to hit Fairbanks since construction of the trans-Alaska oil pipeline in the 1970s, opened in late 1996 to become America's largest gold producer. The mine area on Fairbanks' northeastern outskirts reputedly will produce 350,000 ounces of gold per annum. The project is nothing like the days when scruffy, greenhorn miners with primitive tools and pans waded in frigid streams thirsting for the shiny stuff.

Today, with hi-tech equipment and the encouragement of the state, gold mining is back with a capital "G". In fact, the enthusiasm has spurred other Alaska mining firms to get on the bandwagon. Ryan Lode Mines, Placer Dome, Silverado Mines, and others have geared up. Elsewhere in Alaska's interior, near the isolated village of McGrath, Nevada Consolidated Goldfields Inc., has opened the Nixon Fork Mine which plans to mine 60,000 ounces of brilliant ore each year.

The latter day "rush" got a shot-in-the-arm because of Alaska's new mining incentive law which allows companies to subtract up to $20 million in exploratory expenses from taxes or royalties owed to the state. Thus, 17 mining firms applied for such credits. Further, the legislature repealed work hour limitations for underground mines. As a result, mining claims doubled and mining exploration, development, and production increased by one-fourth.

There was basic jubilation in the Fairbanks area, but there was also opposition by citizens who liked it the way it was before. The Fort Knox mine is well out of the city limits, on state land, and to quell the protestors, plans were announced to turn the giant pit into a fish-stocked lake once the mother lode peters out.

Environmentalists keep a wary eye on the revived mining activities. Earlier they targeted the huge underground Alaska Juneau Mine which produced three million ounces of gold in the early part of the century. It was closed by World War II, but is now activated by Echo Bay Mines of Alberta, Canada. At least that has been the plan as they try to hash out environmental complaints. The citizens of Juneau have generally opposed the effort, fearing pollution due to the usage of cyanide for gold recovery. The firm earlier was forced to abandon plans for a huge tailings dam in the Juneau Valley. A final effort in 1996 to dump tailings underwater was discussed, although the practice has been outlawed in the United States for more than a decade. So at this writing, problems continued to dog Echo Bay Mines at Juneau, but it is full speed ahead up Fairbanks way and at McGrath.

Now, how do all these new developments concern the maritime trade of Alaska? Gold production always has a domino affect on the state's entire economy. It not only swells the population but also increases new business and manufacturing. More freight and supplies

The loading dock at Whittier, Alaska, during the harsh winter of 1950. Despite the deep snow the harbor remained free of ice.
Photo courtesy of Captain John D. Eicher, USNR, Ret.

are shipped by sea. Air travel as well as truck transport increases and so does tourism. Tug and barge operations increase and there is more diversified cargo for the roll-on roll-off ships and container carriers.

Despite the wintertime woes of Alaska, climate-wise, the spirit of the Great Land remains undaunted and life goes on with increasing verve and enthusiasm. The chaotic days that followed the purchase of Alaska in 1867 will never return, in fact, Alaska has come into its own as never before in its history. Where it used to be bumps and grinds, it is now a steady economy. One might title it the dramatic story of rags to riches, and the eight golden stars in the form of the dipper on the blue flag of the state of Alaska are shining brighter than ever before.

Through earthquakes, seismic tidal waves, howling blizzards, hurricanes, bitter cold, drenching rains, irascible seas, depression, isolation, fire, sea tragedy, and every other negative aspect, Alaskans have not only endured but have turned Seward's Folly into a land of tremendous wealth and great promise for the future. A salute to the 49th state is in order!

The basic importance of Alaska as a military outpost was well established in World War II and continues to be so in our present era. As a control center for sea and air activities, it is vital to the national defense, and the Aleutian chain brings it ever closer to Siberia and Asia. During World War II, the Alaska-Siberia air route opened in September of 1942. By the end of the fracas, Soviet flyers, courtesy of the U.S. Lend-Lease arrangement, had piloted 7,926 U.S. planes from Ladd Field, Alaska, to Siberia, yet ironically, the U.S.S.R. constantly balked at our nation's request to establish air bases in Siberia for attack on Japan during the conflict. Russia was also reluctant to return an armada of lend-lease American ships after the war ended.

As the Asian markets become among the world's most lucrative, Alaska continues to play an important role, especially with petroleum products and a variety of refrigerated sea food, plus timber products.

Be one Cheechaco or Sourdough, a newcomer or local, the spirit of Alaska once gained becomes ingrained. For the most part the demanding days of yesteryear are over in Alaska, even though a select few still desire the primitive lifestyle of old. Though such ways have been generally relegated to the past they still make interesting stories in our time. None reflected those otherwise forgotten tales of the northland better than poet laureate, Robert W. Service.

We landed in wind-swept Skagway. We joined the weltering mass.
Clamboring over their outfits, waiting to climb the pass.
We tightened our girths and our pack-straps;
We linked on a human chain,
Struggling up to the summit, where every step was a pain.

Gone was the joy of our faces, grim and haggard and pale;
The heedless mirth of the shipboard was changed to the care of the trail,
We flung ourselves in the struggle, packing our grub in relays,
Step by step to the summit in the bale of the winter days.

(from "The Trail of Ninety-Eight")

As we bring this story to a close let all be thankful that our good Lord turned back the ambitious plan of the Japanese military in World War II to invade Alaska step by step through the Aleutian chain of islands to the bulk of the land mass. American ingenuity was able to turn a desperate situation around in the face of negligent unpreparedness.

A good example was the military port of Whittier where a vast majority of military supplies for the armed forces was off-loaded from scores of supply vessels. The Johnny-come-lately port, created in 1939, is located at the west end extremity on the western arm of Prince William Sound, known as Passage Canal. It's an all year ice-free port, 62 miles from Anchorage. Little heed had been given to Whittier as a port until the clouds of war appeared in the European theater; not

U.S. Navy quarters at Whittier, Alaska, in the winter of 1951. Photo courtesy of Captain John D. Eicher, USNR, Ret.

even initially when the 468 mile Alaska Railroad was completed in 1923. When the port was fully operational it was linked by the Alaska Railroad following the completion of two massive tunnels in 1942. Despite the fact it is near the Chugach Mountain region, a breeding ground for glaciers, 20 within a ten mile radius, the average winter temperature is only 38.5 degrees. Some 180 inches of rain fall, and in addition, 181 inches of annual snowfall, but hardly ever is the port shut down where other important Alaska ports in Southwestern Alaska are hampered by ice during the winter months. The dock depth at low tide is 48 feet which gives an indication of the value to shipping in an area of extreme tidal fluctuations. The military supply line through the port contributed mightily to Alaska's valuable and successful role in winning the conflict with the Japanese.

As the port grew in importance, its deeply hidden secret was little known to Admiral Isoroko Tamamoto, commander of the Japanese combined fleet, who envisioned a pincer naval endeavor to control both the south Pacific and Alaska. On May 5, 1942, the Japanese Imperial headquarters called for "Invasion and occupation of the western Aleutians to prevent the enemy from attacking the Japanese homeland." Under command of Rear Admiral Kakuji Kekuda, planes were sent out from the carriers *Ryujo* and *Junyo* to bomb Dutch Harbor. That same night a Japanese attack on Adak was turned back by adverse weather. That invasion came on June 4, when 32 bombers and fighters wrought considerable damage, including the earlier mentioned bombing of the beached station ship *Northwestern*, where one report claimed four military men killed.

Aerial battles persisted, the Japanese losing ten planes and the Americans 14, mostly due to adverse weather. In all, 72 Americans lost their lives.

On June 5, the Nipponese landed 1,250 soldiers on Kiska and 1,200 on Attu the following day. On the latter, 39 Aleuts and a few whites were captured. Meanwhile the American military frantically built air fields at Cold Bay and another on Adak. At the latter facility an assorted armada of 250 tugs, barges, and scows landed men and cargo. Within three days some 43 planes took off, flying 250 miles to bomb Kiska. By the end of October, 72 American planes were reported lost compared to nine Japanese aircraft.

The battle continued, and on January 11, 1943, the U.S. landed troops on Amchitka and set up a post. Two months later, the major sea battle of the Alaska campaign ensued, the Battle of Komandorskis (Komandorskiye Islands) northwest of Attu. The Japanese pulled back after 3.5 hours of steady bombardment, ships and planes firing back and forth all the while.

In early May, 4,000 American troops invaded Attu, as the battleship *Nevada* lobbed salvos against the enemy. A continuing land battle with fierce consequences saw many killed and wounded on both sides, the Japanese in desparate attacks paying an awful price. Of the 2,400 Japanese military men on the isle, only 28 survived. Earlier, the *Nevada* got a bit of revenge because she was one of the few major fighting ships to get free during the Pearl Harbor raid of December 7, 1941. Attacked, damaged, and beached, she was hurriedly repaired after that dark day for the Hawaiian Islands.

After Attu fell, the Japanese secretly evacuated Kiska, unknown to the Americans and Canadians. Many had been removed from the island via Japanese submarines, 820 in all. Three of the submarines were reported later lost at sea claiming 250 lives. The other Japanese soldiers were evacuated by surface craft when three cruisers and 11 destroyers sneaked past American defenses. Unknown to the Allies who were prepared for a major battle, they were greeted by only a few hungry dogs. In their hasty evacuation, the Japanese had left numerous war supplies behind. Casualties occurred when a land mine was triggered accidentally, the invaders thinking it firing by the enemy. Mistakenly, the Americans and Canadians began shooting at each other point blank each thinking it was the enemy. As a result, 20 Americans and four Canadians were killed, and 50 others wounded. Further casualties occurred when the U.S. destroyer *Abner Read* struck an enemy mine in the harbor at Kiska and went to the bottom with the loss of 71 sailors and the wounding of 34 others.

Even with all the problems and mistakes, Americans, by the grace of God won the war and Alaska, per se, was spared what could have been considerable devastation had the imperial flag of Japan continued to fly over the islands. At last, all 70 Aleutian Islands were out of harm's way.

One other little known military fact is that America was preparing further nuclear holocaust on the Japanese homeland had not the atom bombs dropped on Hiroshima and Nagasaki brought surrender. Alaska was to become the selected site for further air missions with the devastating weapons. Among other places, Eilson Air Force Base would be a major takeoff area.

When the war ended, atom bombs were waiting. A few years later, on February 13, 1950, a frightening thing happened, kept secret from any press coverage. A B-36 plane took off from Alaska's Eielson field flying an atom bomb to Carswell Air Force Base in Texas. Flying southward off Princess Royal Island in British Columbia, the big bomber suddenly lost three of its six engines forcing the ditching of the plane and its deadly bomb. The 12 man crew parachuted to the isle, and the plane reputedly crashed at sea where the bomb detonated in an isolated area far from any center of population. The 10,000 pound "Fat Man" bomb was similar to the one that killed thousands at Nagasaki. As far as is known the bomb itself was not responsible for the loss of any humans, but probably played havoc with creatures under the sea. The military secretly dispatched a B-29 to the Canadian isle to rescue those that had parachuted to safety. Then ironically, the rescue plane crashed while landing at Great Falls Air Force Base in Montana, where eight lives were lost. Because of the regretful overall tragedy, a B-36, a B-29, an atom bomb, and several lives were snuffed out. As bad as it was, however, it could have been much, much worse.

Should another world conflict ever occur, the Aleutian's rockbound isles will become ever more important for air bases, submarine bases, communications, and supply. And so we end our epistle on a high note, for Alaska has become something special in the heartbeat of America.

Aerial view of the U.S. Army Port of Whittier, ice-free the year round, used primarily as a military cargo port since the early days of World War II. Naval reservist John D. Eicher, then a Lieutenant Commander, was assigned to the port in September 1950 as Naval Control of Shipping officer, and Commanding Officer of the Military Sea Transportation Service at Whittier, during the Korean War. Eicher, who spent the entire World War II period as an officer on the battleship Pennsylvania, *beginning with Pearl Harbor was promoted to the rank of captain in the Naval Reserve in 1959, upon his retirement from the service.*

Bibliography

Allen, Edward Webber. *The Vanishing Frenchman*. Rutland, Vermont and Tokyo, Japan: Charles K. Tuttle, 1959.

Andrews, Ralph W. and Harry Kirwin. *This Was Seafaring*. Seattle, Washington: Superior Publishing Co., 1955.

Andrews, Ralph W. and A.K. Larssen. *Fish and Ships*. Superior Publishing Co.: Seattle, Washington, 1959.

Bellah, James Warner. "West of the Mississippi." In *American Panorama*. Garden City, New York: Doubleday & Co., Inc., 1960.

Calkins, R.H. *High Tide*. Seattle, Washington: Marine Digest Publishing Co., 1952.

Faber, Jim. *Steamer's Wake*. Seattle, Washington: Enetai Press, 1986.

Fullo, Darren B. *Sea-Land In Alaska, An Illustrated History*. Seattle, Washington: Sea-Land Service Inc., 1995.

Gibbs, James A. *Disaster Log of Ships*. Seattle, Washington: Superior Publishing Co, 1971.

_____. *Pacific Square-riggers*. Seattle, Washington: Superior Publishing Co.,1969; Atglen, Pennsylvania: Schiffer Publishing Ltd., 1987.

_____. *Peril at Sea*. Atglen, Pennsylvania: Schiffer Publishing Ltd., 1986.

_____. *Shipwrecks of the Pacific Coast*. Portland, Oregon: Binford & Mort, 1957.

Kaplan, H.R. and Lt. James F. Hunt, USCG. *This Is The Coast Guard*. Cambridge, Maryland: Cornell Maritime Press, 1972.

London, Jack. *The Sea-Wolf*. New York City, New York: Gosset & Dunlap, 1904 .

Lubbock, Basil. *The Downeasters*. Glasgow, Scotland: Brown, Ferguson Ltd., 1929 and 1971.

Newell, Gordon. *H.W. McCurdy's Marine History of the Pacific Northwest*. Seattle, Washington: Superior Publishing Co., 1966.

Office of Statewide Programs. *Aids To Navigation In Alaska History*. Alaska Division of Parks, Dept. of Natural Resources, 1974.

Service, Robert W. *Ballads of a Cheechako*. New York, New York: Barse and Hopkins, 1909.

_____. *The Spell of the Yukon*. New York, New York: Barse and Hopkins.

Tornfelt, Evert E., and Michael Burwell. *Shipwrecks of the Alaska Shelf and Shore*. Anchorage, Alaska: U.S. Department of Interior, OCS Region, 1992.

Wright, E. W. *Lewis and Dryden's Marine History of the Pacific Northwest*. Portland, Oregon: Lewis and Dryden Publishing Co., 1895.

U.S. Light Lists (Pacific Coast). U.S. Government Printing Office, various years.

U.S. List of Merchant Vessels. U.S. Government Printing Office, various years.

Zeusler, Admiral Frederick A. *Explorer's Journal*. 1960

PERIODICALS AND NEWSPAPERS CONSULTED

Alaska Magazine
Cruise Travel Magazine
Ketchikan Daily News
Marine Digest
New Alaskan
National Geographic
The Alaska Bear

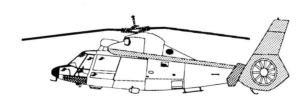